Juran on Leadership for Quality

An Executive Handbook

J. M. Juran

D1470776

THE FREE PRESS

New York London Toronto Sydney Tokyo Singapore

FREE PRESS
A Division of Simon & Schuster, Inc.
1230 Avenue of the Americas
New York, NY 10020

Copyright © 1989 by Juran Institute, Inc.

FREE PRESS and colophon are trademarks
of Simon & Schuster, Inc.

Designed by
Manufactured in the United States of America

10 9 8 7 6 5 4 3 2 1

Library of Congress Cataloging-In-Publication Data

Juran, J.M. (Joseph M.)
    Juran on leadership for quality: an executive handbook / J.M.
Juran.
    p. cm.
    Bibliography: p.
    Includes index.
    ISBN 0-7432-5577-1
    1. Quality control—Handbooks, manuals, etc. 2. Quality
assurance—Handbooks, manuals, etc.   I. Title.
TS156.J79   1989
658.5'62—dc19   88-21306
                                                          CIP

For information regarding the special discounts for bulk purchases, please contact Simon & Schuster Special Sales at 1-800-456-6798 or business@simonandschuster.com

Contents

Preface

This book has its origins in the early 1950s, during my first visit to Japan. I had been invited by the Japanese Federation of Economic Associations (Keidanren) and the Japanese Union of Scientists and Engineers to come to Japan for two months, study their approach to quality, provide a critique, and conduct training courses in managing for quality. The invitation included a request that I conduct special seminars for heads of companies.

The Japanese organized two such special seminars, each of two day's duration. Each was attended by about seventy presidents of leading Japanese companies—the industrial leadership of Japan.

Over the next two and a half decades the demand for such seminars was quite limited. I did conduct some in various European countries as well as during some repeat visits to Japan. There was also some demand, mainly in the United States, from individual companies—cases in which the upper management cleared a day to have a seminar on managing for quality.

The demand quickened during the late 1970s to an extent such that I prepared a formal set of notes and structured a formal seminar on the subject. The result of this work was a book titled *Upper Management and Quality,* first offered in early 1978. Experience soon showed up some inadequacies in the notes. To remedy these deficiencies, I continually revised this book from 1979 to 1983. These revisions met with progressively better reception.

During the 1980s, there emerged an explosive growth in demand for quality-management seminars. During the seven-year interval from 1981 to 1987 we at Juran Institute sponsored many open seminars, which were attended by thousands of managers, worldwide. Even greater was the growth of in-house seminars conducted for specific companies at their locations. There were over three hundred such in-house seminars worldwide, attended by over ten thousand managers. The sponsoring companies included multinational giants whose most senior executives cleared the time to attend and to participate in discussing the subject of managing for quality.

After ten years of continual revisions, it is my hope that the present treatment of the subject will show itself to be more enduring than its predecessors, but this remains to be seen. We are dealing here with a subject that has been undergoing rapid and drastic change as a result of competition in the marketplace as well as of the vulnerability of industrialized societies that have redesigned life styles in ways that depend heavily on the quality of goods and services.

An important source of the concepts, case materials, and other inputs to these editions has been the feedback we have received from the managers who have participated in the seminars. We have secured these inputs from discussions at the seminars, consulting experiences with client organizations, papers presented at our annual conferences on quality improvement (IMPRO), and still other forms of feedback. All those managers out there—they who face the realities—have been generous in sharing their experiences, and we are most grateful to them for their openness and forthrightness.

My purpose in this book is to (1) provide companies with the strategies needed to attain and hold quality leadership, (2) define the roles of upper managers in leading their companies to that goal, and (3) set out the means to be used by upper managers to supply that leadership.

Before going further, let us define some basic terms.

As used here, the word *company* includes any organized entity that produces products (goods or services), whether for sale or not, whether for profit or not.

As used here, the term *upper managers* (also *upper management*) always includes the corporate officers. In large companies it is common practice to create "divisions" that are given considerable autonomy with respect to specific sectors of the company's business. In such cases *upper managers* includes the division general managers and their staffs. In very large organizations some individual facilities may also be very large (e.g., an office or a factory). In any such case the local manager and his or her staff are upper managers to those employed at the facility.

Acknowledgments

Important contributions to this book have been made by the many managers and specialists whose experience and ideas are the prime source of progress in management. The critiques from participants in our seminars have been most helpful, and are reflected in this book.

Dr. Lennart Sandholm (of Bjorklund & Sandholm, Sweden) has been especially helpful through his active collaboration in the design and conduct of many seminars and courses on managing for quality.

Within Juran Institute, Dr. F. M. Gryna, Jr., has for many years participated in the design and leadership of various seminars, including the one on which this book is based. More recently, Dr. A. Blanton Godfrey joined Juran Institute as chairman and chief executive officer, and has become active in leadership of the quality-management seminar.

The manuscript of this book has been critiqued by Drs. Gryna and Godfrey; also by Frank M. Tedesco, Robert E. Hoogstoel, Dr. Al C. Endres, Dr. John W. Enell, Dr. William W. Barnard, Thomas P. Huizenga, and John F. Early, all of Juran Institute. These critiques have contributed importantly to the finished work.

The book was produced under the general direction of G. Howland Blackiston, with the editorial assistance of Marilyn M. Schmid, Linda T. Ellis, and Laura A. Sutherland.

Wilton, Connecticut   J. M. JURAN
                                                                    1988

] *vii* [

Quality: A Continuing Revolution

The purpose of this chapter is to provide a "lessons-learned" perspective on making quality happen.

The chapter shows that although human beings have always wished for high quality, they have over the centuries faced massive and changing forces requiring ever-changing strategies to reach their quality goals. It also shows that the current decades are uncommonly turbulent, requiring an unprecedented degree of managerial sophistication in choosing the needed strategies.

For supporting detail, the chapter traces out

1. How managing for quality has been undergoing continuing change over the centuries

2. Why quality has recently risen so much in importance

3. The origins of the quality crisis faced by so many companies

4. The responses of company managers

UNCHANGING DESIRES AND CHANGING FORCES

We start with the premise that *all* managers want their company to produce products of high quality and to do so at low cost. They want their company at the least to be competitive, and preferably to be the industry quality leader. These same managers also have personal goals that are affected by the results achieved with respect to quality: the results achieved by the company determine the image of the company managers.

These wishes of managers have not changed throughout recorded history. What has changed throughout recorded history are the strategies used to manage for quality. Such changes in strategy have been specifically designed to respond to specific political, social, and economic upheavals.

Recently such upheavals have reached convulsive levels. It is these convulsions that are causing upper managers to raise such critical questions as the following:

What role does quality play in the success of my company?

How can I evaluate my company's status with respect to quality?

How shall we, as a company, manage for quality in the face of the new challenges?

What must we, as a company, do that is different from what we have been doing?

What road shall we follow to go from where we are to where we want to be?

What should I, as a manager, do that is different from what I have been doing?

Such questions demand forthright answers. Our mission in this book is to supply those answers.

EARLY STRATEGIES OF MANAGING FOR QUALITY

We can gain perspective by looking back at the road traveled to date—at the early processes of managing for quality.

Human needs for quality have existed since the dawn of history. However, the means for meeting those needs—the processes of managing for quality—have undergone extensive and continuing change (Juran 1977).

Prior to the twentieth century, managing for quality was based on some ancient principles:

1. *Product inspection by consumers,* which is still widely used in today's village market places.

2. *The craftsmanship concept,* in which buyers rely on the skill and reputation of trained, experienced craftsmen. Some crafts-

men develop reputations that extend far beyond their village boundaries: they are viewed as living national treasures.

As commerce expanded beyond village boundaries, and with the growth of technology, additional concepts and tools were invented to assist in managing for quality:

1. Specifications by sample
2. Quality warranties in sales contracts

In large towns the craftsmen organized themselves into monopolistic guilds. These guilds were generally strict in their enforcement of product quality. Their strategies included

1. Mandated specifications for input materials, processes, and finished goods
2. Audits of the performance of guild members
3. Export controls on finished goods

The early American approach to managing for quality followed the practice prevailing in those European countries that had colonized the North American continent. Apprentices learned a trade, qualified to become craftsmen, and in due course might become masters of independent shops.

The Industrial Revolution, which originated in Europe, created the factory system, which soon outproduced the small independent shops and made them largely obsolete. The craftsmen became factory workers, and the masters became factory foremen. Quality was managed as before, through the skills of the craftsmen, supplemented by departmental inspection or supervisory audits. The Industrial Revolution also accelerated the growth of additional strategies, including

1. Written specifications for materials, processes, finished goods, and tests
2. Measurement, and the associated measuring instruments and test laboratories
3. Standardization in many forms

When the Industrial Revolution was exported from Europe to America, the colonists again followed European practice.

THE TAYLOR SYSTEM AND ITS IMPACT

Late in the nineteenth century the United States broke sharply with European tradition by adopting the Taylor system of "scientific management" (Juran 1973). Central to the Taylor system was the concept of separating planning from execution. This separation made possible a considerable rise in productivity. It also dealt a crippling blow to the concept of craftsmanship. In addition, the new emphasis on productivity had a negative effect on quality. To restore the balance, the factory managers adopted a new strategy: a central inspection department, headed by a chief inspector. The various departmental inspectors were then transferred to the new inspection department over the bitter opposition of the production supervisors.

The extreme dimensions of this strategy of inspection can be seen from the situation prevailing in the Hawthorne Works of Western Electric Company during the late 1920s. Hawthorne was at that time virtually the only manufacturing plant in the Bell System. At the peak (about 1928) it employed forty thousand people, of whom fifty-two hundred were in the inspection department.

Note that during this progression of events the priority given to quality declined significantly. In addition, the responsibility for leading the quality function became vague and confused. In the days of the craft shops, the master (then also the chief executive) participated personally in the process of managing for quality. What emerged was a concept in which upper management became detached from the process of managing for quality.

THE GROWTH OF VOLUME
AND COMPLEXITY

The twentieth century has brought an explosive growth of goods and services, both in volume and complexity. Vast industries have emerged to produce, market, and maintain such consumer goods as automobiles, household appliances, and entertainment devices. These goods are ever more complex and hence more demanding with respect to quality. Goods for industrial purposes (e.g., manufacturing facilities) are no less demanding.

Service industries have also undergone explosive growth in volume and complexity. The complexity is evident in the huge systems that provide energy, communication, transportation, and information processing. These systems likewise are ever more demanding as to quality, especially with respect to continuity of service, which is based on the reliability parameter.

Most of the strategies that have emerged to deal with these forces of volume and complexity can be grouped under two generic names for specialties:

1. *Quality engineering.* This specialty traces its origin to the application of statistical methods for control of quality in manufacture. Much of the pioneering theoretical work was done in the 1920s by the quality-assurance department of the Bell Telephone Laboratories.

The staff members included Shewhart, Dodge, and Edwards. Much of the pioneering application took place (also in the 1920s) within the Hawthorne Works of the Western Electric Company. The staff members included this author, who had joined the Hawthorne Works in 1924.

At the time, this pioneering work had little impact on industry or, for that matter, on the Bell System. What survived to become influential in later decades was Shewhart's control chart. By the 1980s it was in wide use as a major element of what was commonly called statistical process control.

2. *Reliability engineering.* This specialty emerged largely during the 1950s, as a response to "complex systems." It has spawned a considerable literature relating to reliability modeling and formulas, and data banks for quantifying reliability. It includes concepts for improving reliability during product design by, for example, quantifying factors of safety, reducing the number of components, and attaining quality at levels of parts per million.

GROWTH OF THE QUALITY DEPARTMENT

These new specialties needed a place on the organization chart. Companies met this need by creating broad-based departments variously called quality control, quality assurance, and so forth. These departments were headed by a quality manager and housed the quality-oriented activities: inspection and test, quality engineering, and reliability engineering.

The central activity of these quality-oriented departments remained that of inspection and test, that is, separating good product from bad. The prime benefit of this activity was to reduce the risk that defective products would be shipped to customers. However, there were serious detriments: This centralized activity of the quality department helped to foster a widespread belief that achievement of quality was solely the responsibility of the quality department. In turn, this belief hampered efforts at eliminating the causes of defective products; the responsibilities were confused. As a result, failure-prone products and incapable processes remained in force and continued to generate high costs of poor quality.

What emerged de facto was a concept of managing for quality somewhat as follows: Each functional department carried out its assigned function and then delivered the result to the next functional department in the sequence of events. At the end, the quality department separated the good product from the bad. For defective product that escaped to the customer, redress was to be provided through customer service based on warranties.

By the standards of later decades this concept of prime reliance on inspection and test was unsound. However, it was not a handicap if competitors employed the same concept, and such was usually the case. Despite the deficiencies inherent in this concept of "detection," American goods came to be well regarded in terms of quality. In some product lines American companies became the leaders in quality. In many product lines American companies became the leaders in productivity. In addition, the American economy grew to superpower size.

WORLD WAR II AND ITS IMPACT

During World War II American industry was faced with the added burden of producing enormous quantities of military products. A part of the grand strategy during World War II was to shut off production of many civilian products, such as automobiles, household appliances, and entertainment products. A massive shortage of goods developed amid a huge buildup of purchasing power. It took the rest of that decade (the 1940s) for supply to catch up with demand. In the interim the manufacturing companies gave top priority to meeting delivery dates, so that quality of product went down. (Quality always goes down during shortages.) The habit of giving top priority to delivery dates then persisted long after the shortages were gone.

During World War II, there emerged (or reemerged) a new strategy: "statistical quality control" (SQC). The War Production Board, in an effort to improve the quality of manufacture of military goods, sponsored numerous training courses in the statistical techniques evolved by the Bell System during the 1920s. (Interestingly, Dr. W. E. Deming, who became widely publicized during the 1980s, was one of the lecturers at some of the War Production Board courses. He was also briefly employed at the Hawthorne Works during the 1920s, but not in quality-related activities.) Many of those who attended became enthusiastic, and collectively they organized the American Society for Quality Control (ASQC). In its early years ASQC was strongly oriented to SQC and thereby stimulated further enthusiasm.

As it turned out, most of the applications in the companies were tool oriented rather than results oriented. So long as government contracts paid for everything, the companies could not lose. In due course the government contracts came to an end, and the SQC programs were reexamined from the standpoint of cost effectiveness. Most of them failed the test, resulting in wholesale cutbacks.

THE JAPANESE QUALITY REVOLUTION AND ITS IMPACT

Following World War II the Japanese embarked on a course of reaching national goals by trade rather than by military means. The major manufacturers, who had been extensively involved in military production, were faced with converting to civilian products. A major obstacle to selling these products in international markets was a national reputation for shoddy goods created by export of poor quality goods prior to World War II.

To solve their quality problems the Japanese undertook to learn how other countries managed for quality. To this end the Japanese sent teams abroad to visit foreign companies and study their approach, and they translated selected foreign literature into Japanese. They also invited foreign lecturers to come to Japan and conduct training courses for managers.

From these and other inputs the Japanese devised some unprecedented strategies for creating a revolution in quality. Several of those strategies were decisive:

1. The upper managers personally took charge of leading the revolution.

2. All levels and functions underwent training in managing for quality.

3. Quality improvement was undertaken at a continuing, revolutionary pace.

4. The work force was enlisted in quality improvement through the QC-circle concept.

In the early post-war period the affected American companies logically considered Janapese competition to be in price rather than in quality. Their response was to shift the manufacture of labor-intensive products to low-labor-cost areas, often offshore.

As the years unfolded, price competition declined while quality competition increased (Juran 1981).

During the 1960s and 1970s numerous Japanese manufacturers greatly increased their share of the American market. A major reason was superior quality. Numerous industries were affected,

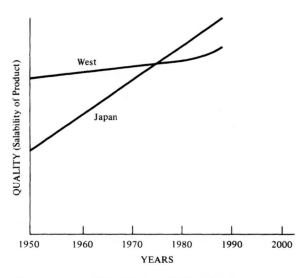

FIGURE 1-1 Japanese and Western quality: A contrast

for example, consumer electronics, automobiles, steel, and machine tools. Some researchers quantified the quality differences (Juran 1979; Garvin 1983).

The American companies generally failed to notice the trends. They adhered to the belief that Japanese competition was primarily price competition rather than quality competition. Some observers sounded warning signals: "The Japanese are headed for world quality leadership and will attain it in the next two decades because no one else is moving there at the same pace" (Juran 1967). The alarm was sounded at the Conference of the European Organization for Quality Control in Stockholm. The date was June 1966.

The most obvious effect of the Japanese quality revolution was their massive export of goods. The impact on the United States was considerable, especially in certain sensitive areas: The affected manufacturing companies were damaged by the resulting loss of sales. The work force and their unions were damaged by the resulting "export of jobs." The national economy was damaged by the resulting unfavorable trade balance.

LIFE BEHIND THE QUALITY DIKES

A further significant post-war phenomenon was the rise of product quality to a position of prominence in the public mind. This growth in prominence was the result of the convergence of multiple trends:

Growing concern about damage to the environment

Action by the courts to impose strict liability

Fear of major disasters and near disasters

Pressure from consumer organizations for better quality and more responsive redress

Growing public awareness of the role of quality in international competition (e.g., in trade and weapons)

Collectively these trends are a consequence of mankind's adoption of technology and industrialization. Industrialization confers many benefits on society, but it also makes society dependent on the continuing performance and good behavior of a huge array of technological goods and services. This is the phenomenon of "life behind the quality dikes"—a form of securing benefits but living dangerously. Like the Dutch who have reclaimed so much land from the sea, we secure the benefits of technology. However, we need protective dikes in the form of good quality to shield society against service interruptions and to guard against disasters.

RESPONSES TO THE IMPACTS

American companies' responses to life behind the quality dikes had a good deal of commonality about them. The strategies they adopted included

1. The creation of high-level committees to establish policies, goals, and action plans with respect to product safety, environmental damage, and consumer complaints

2. The establishment of specific programs to be carried out by the various functions (e.g., product design, manufacture, advertising, and legal)

3. Audits to assure that the policies and goals were met

In contrast, the responses to the Japanese quality revolution took many directions. Some of these directions consisted of strategies that had no relation to improving American competitiveness in quality. Rather, these were efforts to block imports through restrictive legislation and quotas, criminal prosecutions, civil lawsuits, and appeals to "buy American."

However, most upper managers recognized that the soundest response to a competitive challenge was to become more competitive. Not being trained or experienced in managing for quality, these same upper managers sought advice from the experts, internal and external. It turned out that the various experts proposed numerous strategies, including motivation for the work force, QC circles, statistical process control, and "awareness" for managers and supervisors. Still other strategies included computation of the cost of quality, project-by-project improvement, complete manuals of procedure, revision of organization structure, incentives for quality, automated inspection and test, and robotics.

Everyone of these (and other) directions has some merit under appropriate conditions. The upper managers were then faced with selecting one or more of the available strategies as the basis for a plan of action. They were experienced managers, but not in managing for quality. Generally they opted for "action now"—that is, do something plausible promptly rather than endure delay.

The results were generally less than satisfactory. In some cases the strategies selected (e.g., statistical process control and project-by-project improvement) were effective for specific fundamental quality needs, with resulting significant gains. More usually the strategies chosen had little relation to the companies' fundamental quality problems.

LESSONS LEARNED

The changing forces and the associated responsive strategies can be tabulated as in Figure 1-2. Figure 1-2 clearly demonstrates the following facts:

CONDITONS, FORCES	STRATEGIES ADOPTED IN MANAGING FOR QUALITY
Food gathering	"Incoming" inspection by consumers
Division of labor: food suppliers	Inspection by consumers in village marketplaces
Early manufactures; rise of village craftsmen	Reliance on skill and reputation of craftsmen
Expansion of commerce beyond village boundaries	Specification by sample; export controls by inspection; warranties
The guilds	Specifications: materials, processes, products; export controls; audits
The Industrial Revolution	Written specifications; measurement, instruments, test laboratories; extension of inspection; standardization
The Taylor system	Central inspection departments
Growth of volume and complexity	Quality assurance departments; quality engineering; reliability engineering
World War II	Training in statistical quality control
Life behind the quality dikes	Special organization and processes to protect society; audits
The Japanese revolution in quality (Japanese strategies)	Upper managers personally in charge
	Training in managing for quality extended to all functions
	Quality improvement at a continuing revolutionary pace
	QC circles
The Japanese revolution in quality (U.S. response)	Efforts to restrict imports
	Numerous strategies undergoing test

FIGURE 1-2 Changing forces and responsive strategies

1. "Changing forces" has been a continuing phenomenon.

2. Meeting the goal of quality leadership has required continuing change in strategy and, therefore, in expertise in managing change.

3. Generally managers have been quite sensible in their choice of strategies as applied to the then–existing conditions. However, as conditions kept changing, some of the prevailing strategies became increasingly out-of-date.

The experiences of all those companies have also provided a body of lessons learned: which strategies produced useful results, and why; which strategies failed, and why. Some of these lessons apply so widely that they will become a vital input to future grand strategy.

It has become evident that quality competitiveness for the years ahead requires a new basic approach. Merely adding new methods or tools to the traditional approach is not enough. The new basic approach is centered around the concept of *enlarging the strategic business plan to include quality goals*. The processes for meeting these quality goals then parallel the processes long used for meeting traditional goals such as for sales, product development, and profit.

This new basic approach is the subject of the remainder of this book. As we shall see, to make such an approach effective, upper managers must personally provide leadership in managing for quality to a degree that is unprecedented in most American companies. So fundamental a change should be preceded by a clear understanding of how to think about quality. To that end, the next chapter is devoted to how to think about quality.

HIGH POINTS OF CHAPTER 1

The purpose of this chapter is to provide a "lessons learned" perspective on making quality happen.

Human needs for quality have existed since the dawn of history.

Over the centuries the strategies of managing for quality have undergone continuing change in response to a continuing procession of changing political, social, and economic forces.

During this progression of events, upper management became detached from the process of managing for quality.

The Japanese revolution in quality was based on the creation of unprecedented strategies:

Upper management in charge

Training for all functions, at all levels

Quality improvement at a continuing, revolutionary pace

Work-force participation through QC circles

The phenomenon of life behind the quality dikes requires that we provide good quality to shield society against service interruptions and to guard against disasters.

Quality competitiveness for the years ahead requires a new basic approach.

How to Think About Quality

The purpose of this chapter is to provide upper managers with an understandable framework on which to build a coherent, unified approach to managing for quality. This framework is already familiar to upper managers, since it parallels what has long been done in managing for finance. Starting with this framework, it becomes feasible for upper managers to establish quality goals and to lead their organizations to those established quality goals through the unity provided by common concepts, strategies, processes, training, and motivation.

OBSTACLES TO UNITY

To achieve such unity requires overcoming various obstacles, which can be categorized as follows:

1. *Obvious obstacles arising from differences in viewpoint among the members of the management team.* These differences are usually stated openly and are substantive in nature. Experienced managers, through conventional analysis and discussion, are usually able to narrow these differences and to arrive at a consensus.

2. *Hidden obstacles arising from differences in premises, concepts, and even in the meanings of key words.* These differences are seldom stated openly, since the parties are usually not even aware that the differences exist. These same differences can and do confuse the analyses, discussions, and even the resulting agreements, that is, the parties come away from meetings with different views on what agreement was reached.

For example, the subject under discussion is, Does higher quality cost more or does higher quality cost less? There is a difference of opinion, or so it seems. However, the difference is due to the fact that the word *quality* has more than one meaning. Some of the managers are thinking that a "higher quality" deluxe hotel costs more than a "lower quality" budget hotel. Other managers are thinking that product from a "higher quality" process with yields of 98 percent will cost less than product from a "lower quality" process with yields of 80 percent. All managers are drawing logical conclusions from their respective premises. However, they are not aware that their premises differ and that this is traceable to the meaning of a word—that the same word *quality*, pronounced and spelled identically, has more than one meaning.

Such differences in premises, concepts, and word meanings are widespread. In consequence an entire chapter is devoted just to clear away some of the major obstacles to unity of managerial thinking. In addition, throughout all chapters we shall define the key words as we come to them. These same definitions will also be listed alphabetically in the glossary.

THE MEANING OF QUALITY

Reaching agreement on what is meant by *quality* is not simple. (The dictionary lists about a dozen definitions.) For managers, no short definition is really precise, but one such definition has received wide acceptance: quality is *fitness for use.*

This definition provides a short, comprehensive label, but it does not provide the depth needed by managers to choose courses of action. On closer examination we discover that fitness for use branches out in two rather different directions, as shown in Figure 2–1.

Figure 2–1 helps to explain why so many meetings to discuss managing for quality have ended in confusion. Some managers literally did not know what others were talking about because the same word—*quality*—has a dual meaning. Such confusion should not go on. Upper managers should assure that the company's manuals and training materials include clear definitions of the word *quality* and of the subsidiary terminology. (See the next section.)

SUBSIDIARY DEFINITIONS

The definitions of the word *quality* include certain key words that themselves require definition.

PRODUCT FEATURES THAT MEET CUSTOMER NEEDS	FREEDOM FROM DEFICIENCIES
Higher quality enables companies to:	Higher quality enables companies to:
Increase customer satisfaction	Reduce error rates
Make products salable	Reduce rework, waste
Meet competition	Reduce field failures, warranty charges
Increase market share	Reduce customer dissatisfaction
Provide sales income	Reduce inspection, test
Secure premium prices	Shorten time to put new products
The major effect is on sales	on the market
Usually, higher quality costs more	Increase yields, capacity
	Improve delivery performance
	Major effect is on costs
	Usually, higher quality costs less

FIGURE 2-1　Definitions of quality

Product

Product is the output of any process. Product consists mainly of goods, "software," and services.

Goods are physical things, such as pencils and color television sets.

"Software" has more than one meaning. A major meaning is instruction programs for computers. Another major meaning is information generally: reports, plans, instructions, advice, and commands.

Service is work performed for someone else. Entire industries are established to provide services in such forms as central energy, transportation, communication, and entertainment. Service also includes work performed for someone else *within* companies, that is, payroll preparation, recruitment of new employees, and plant maintenance. Such services are often called support services.

Product Features

A product feature is a property that is possessed by a product and that is intended to meet certain customers' needs and thereby provide customer satisfaction. Product features may be technological in nature—for example, the fuel consumption of a vehicle, the dimensions of a mechanical component, the viscosity of a chemical, or the uniformity of the voltage of an electric power supply. Product features may also take other forms—for example, promptness of delivery, ease of maintenance, and courtesy of service.

Customer

A customer is anyone who receives or is affected by the product or process. Customers may be external or internal.

External customers are affected by the product but are not members of the company that produces the product. External customers include clients who buy the product, government regulatory bodies, and the public (which may be affected by unsafe products or damage to the environment).

Internal customers are affected by the product and are also members of the company that produces the product. They are often called customers despite the fact that they are not customers in the dictionary sense; that is, they are not clients.

Product Satisfaction and Customer Satisfaction

Product satisfaction is a result achieved when product features respond to customer needs. It is generally synonymous with customer satisfaction. Product satisfaction is a stimulus to product salability. The major impact is on sales income.

Deficiencies

A product deficiency is a product failure that results in *product dissatisfaction.* Product deficiencies take such forms as power outages, failures to meet delivery dates, inoperable goods, blemished appearance, and nonconformance to specification. The major impact is on the costs incurred to redo prior work and to respond to customer complaints.

Product Satisfaction and Product Dissatisfaction Are Not Opposites

Product satisfaction has its origin in product features and is why clients buy the product. Product dissatisfaction has its origin in nonconformances and is why customers complain. There are many products that give little or no dissatisfaction; the products do what the supplier said they would do. Yet the products are not salable because some competing product provides greater product satisfaction.

The early forms of automated telephone exchanges employed electromagnetic analog switching methods. During the 1980s there was a major shift to digital switching methods, owing to their superior product features. As a result, analog switching systems, even if absolutely free from product deficiencies, were no longer salable.

EACH COMPANY NEEDS UNITY OF LANGUAGE

Some of the above definitions (and other definitions to come) may well be different from the definitions upon which some companies base their understanding of quality. Such companies will of course decide for themselves what definitions to adopt. However, in the interest of precise communication the definitions should be uniform throughout the organization. An essential tool for such unity is the *glossary*. The glossary also plays an essential role in the process of translating customer needs into supplier's language. (See chapter 4, the section Translation.)

MEASURES OF QUALITY

Each of the two forms of quality is measured in its own way.

Freedom from Deficiencies

The usual measure is not in terms of freedom from deficiencies but rather in terms of extent of deficiencies, such as error rate or fraction defective. This measure can be generalized by the expression:

$$\text{Quality} = \frac{\text{frequency of deficiencies}}{\text{opportunities for deficiencies}}$$

The numerator (frequency of deficiencies) takes such forms as number of defects, number of errors, number of field failures, hours of rework, and cost of poor quality.

The denominator (opportunity for deficiencies) takes such forms as number of units produced, total hours worked, number of units sold, and sales income.

Product Features

In this form of quality there is no universal unit of measure. Instead, the starting point is to find out from customers how they evaluate quality, that is, which product features they consider to be the key to meeting their needs.

A supplier of "express" transportation services measured quality primarily based on percent of cargo space utilized. He lost share of market because the clients measured quality primarily based on promptness of delivery.

A manufacturer of stainless steel was a supplier to a machine shop whose clients included the National Aeronautics and Space Administration (NASA). The steel met specifications, but the supplier lost share of market anyway because a competitor packaged the steel with greater cleanliness.

Product features are usually measured in terms of *variables*; e.g., delivery time is measured in days (or hours, minutes, and so forth); and annealing temperature is measured in degrees. In contrast, deficiencies are usually measured in terms of *attributes*; for example, a promise is kept or not, and a diameter is within specification or not.

HOW TO MANAGE FOR QUALITY: THE FINANCIAL ANALOGY

At the upper-management level the most important part of how to think about quality is the managerial processes to be used. To understand these processes upper managers have found it helpful to resort to analogy: to look first at how they conduct financial management. That answer is obvious. Financial management is carried out by use of three managerial processes:

1. *Financial planning.* This planning is centered on preparation of the annual financial budget. In turn, this preparation involves a companywide process that starts by defining the deeds to be done in the year ahead. These deeds are then translated into money equivalents. Such translation permits summary and analysis to determine the financial consequences of doing all those deeds. After revisions, the final result sets the financial goals for the company and its various divisions and departments.

2. *Financial control.* This well-known process is used to aid managers in reaching the established financial goals. The process consists of evaluating actual financial performance; comparing

this with financial goals; and taking action on the difference—the accountant's "variance." There are numerous subprocesses for financial control, such as cost control, expense control, and inventory control.

3. *Financial improvement.* This process takes many forms: cost reduction projects; purchase of new facilities to improve productivity; speeding up the invoicing process; development of new products to increase sales; and acquisition of other companies.

THE JURAN TRILOGY

Managing for quality is done by use of the same three managerial processes of planning, control, and improvement. Now the names change to

Quality planning
Quality control
Quality improvement

We shall refer to these three processes as the Juran Trilogy.[1] The conceptual approaches are identical with those used to manage for finance. However, the procedural steps are special, and the tools used are also special.

QUALITY PLANNING. This is the activity of developing the products and processes required to meet customers' needs. It involves a series of universal steps, essentially as follows:

1. Determine who the customers are.
2. Determine the needs of the customers.
3. Develop product features that respond to customers' needs.
4. Develop processes that are able to produce those product features.
5. Transfer the resulting plans to the operating forces.

We shall look at this process in some detail in chapter 4, "Quality Planning."

---

[1]The Juran Trilogy ® is a registered trademark of Juran Institute, Inc.

QUALITY CONTROL. This process consists of the following steps:

1. Evaluate actual quality performance.
2. Compare actual performance to quality goals.
3. Act on the differences.

We shall have a close look at this process in chapter 5, "Quality Control."

QUALITY IMPROVEMENT. This process is the means of raising quality performance to unprecedented levels ("breakthrough"). The methodology consists of a series of universal steps:

1. Establish the infrastructure needed to secure annual quality improvement.
2. Identify the specific needs for improvement—the improvement *projects*.
3. For each project establish a project team with clear responsibility for bringing the project to a successful conclusion.
4. Provide the resources, motivation, and training needed by the teams to

    Diagnose the causes

    Stimulate establishment of a remedy

    Establish controls to hold the gains.

We shall look more closely at this process in chapter 3, "Quality Improvement."

Three Universal Sequences

Notice that each of these three processes has been generalized into a universal sequence of steps. These same three universal sequences have been discovered and rediscovered, over and over again, by practicing managers. Figure 2–2 shows these sequences in abbreviated form.

The Juran Trilogy® Diagram

The three processes of the quality trilogy are interrelated. Figure 2–3, the Juran Trilogy diagram, shows this interrelationship.

The Juran Trilogy diagram is a graph with time on the horizontal axis and cost of poor quality (quality deficiencies) on the verti-

Managing for Quality

QUALITY PLANNING	QUALITY CONTROL	QUALITY IMPROVEMENT
Determine who the customers are	Evaluate actual product performance	Establish the infrastructure
Determine the needs of the customers	Compare actual performance to product goals	Identify the improvement projects
Develop product features that respond to customers' needs	Act on the difference	Establish project teams
Develop processes able to produce the product features		Provide the teams with resources; training, and motivation to:
Transfer the plans to the operating forces		Diagnose the causes
		Stimulate remedies
		Establish controls to hold the gains

FIGURE 2-2   The three universal processes of managing for quality

cal axis. The initial activity is quality planning. The planners determine who are the customers and what are their needs. The planners then develop product and process designs that are able to respond to those needs. Finally, the planners turn the plans over to the operating forces.

The job of the operating forces is to run the processes and produce the products. As operations proceed it soon emerges that the process is unable to produce 100 percent good work. Figure 2-3 shows that 20 percent of the work must be redone as a result of quality deficiencies. This waste then becomes chronic because *the operating process was planned that way.*

Under conventional responsibility patterns, the operating forces are unable to get rid of that planned chronic waste. What they do instead is to carry out *quality control*—to prevent things from getting worse. Control includes putting out the fires, such as that sporadic spike.

The chart also shows that in due course the chronic waste is driven down to a level far below the level that was planned originally. That gain is achieved by the third process in the trilogy: quality improvement. In effect, it is realized that the chronic waste is also an opportunity for improvement. So steps are taken to seize that opportunity.

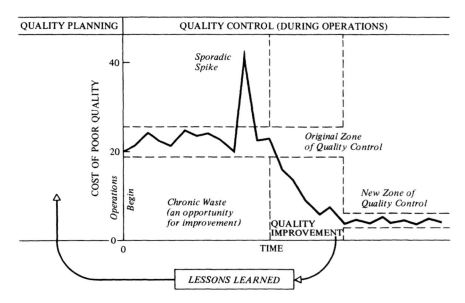

FIGURE 2-3   The Juran Trilogy diagram

The Juran Trilogy Diagram and
Product Deficiencies

The trilogy diagram (Figure 2-3) relates to *product deficiencies*. The vertical scale therefore exhibits such units of measure as cost of poor quality, error rate, percent defective, and service call rate. On this same scale perfection is at zero. What goes up is *bad*.

The result of reducing product deficiencies is to reduce the cost of poor quality, meet more delivery promises, and reduce customer dissatisfaction.

The Trilogy Diagram and Product Features

When the trilogy diagram is applied to product features, the vertical scale changes. Now the scale exhibits units of measure for such features as rated hours of life, millions of instructions per second, load-carrying capacity, and mean time between failures. For these features, what goes up is *good*.

For certain other product features, what goes up is bad—for example, waiting time in queues, power consumption, maintenance hours per 1000 operating hours, and time to restore service.

For ease in interpreting the diagrams we shall label the vertical scales as follows:

1. For *product features* we shall label the vertical scale "Product Salability." In such diagrams *what goes up is good*.

2. For *quality deficiencies* we shall label the vertical scale "Cost of Poor Quality." In such diagrams what goes up is bad.

SURVEY ON THE JURAN TRILOGY

Each of the processes of the trilogy is essential to managing for quality. However, companies vary in their effectiveness in applying these processes. As a result companies vary in their priorities for the future—that is, which process requires the earliest attention, and which process can be placed "on hold."

In view of this variation among companies, participants in quality management seminars have been surveyed to secure their perceptions. Figure 2–4 shows the kind of form used in such surveys.

Results of the Survey

The survey on the trilogy has been conducted among many upper managers in America and Europe. As of November 1987, data were available from over twenty-one hundred such managers. The data are as follows:

	PERFORMANCE RATINGS (%)		
	GOOD	PASSING	NOT PASSING
Quality planning	9	35	56
Quality control	26	54	20
Quality improvement	8	36	56

These proportions have not varied a great deal from seminar to seminar, whether in-house or open, whether in America or in Europe.

THE TOPICS THAT FOLLOW

This book is devoted to the mission of attaining and holding quality leadership. The three processes of the trilogy are all essential to

(Do not sign your name)

For those three basic processes through which we manage quality:
    Quality planning
    Quality control
    Quality improvement
how do you judge the performance of your company?

	PERFORMANCE RATING		
	Good	Passing	Not Passing
Quality planning	———	———	———
Quality control	———	———	———
Quality improvement	———	———	———

FIGURE 2-4 Survey on the trilogy

carrying out that mission. In view of the consistent findings of the survey, the next three chapters will be devoted to a discussion of quality improvement, quality planning, and quality control, respectively and in that order. Following these topics, we shall take up the application of these three processes to the major levels of activity:

Strategic quality management

Operational quality management

The work force and quality

Finally, we shall look at the motivational and training activities needed to support the mission.

Why in That Order?

The survey results show that in terms of need for revision, both quality planning and quality improvement should precede quality control. In terms of chronology, quality planning should precede quality improvement. However, the author has put quality improvement first. The principal reasons are as follows:

1. Investment in quality improvement provides an earlier and more measurable return than investment in either quality planning or quality control.

2. Quality-improvement projects usually arouse greater enthusiasm and stimulate a closer spirit of teamwork than projects in quality planning or quality control.

3. The quality-improvement projects collectively provide an essential input—lessons learned—to the quality-planning process.

HIGH POINTS OF CHAPTER 2

A hidden obstacle to unity in managing for quality is differences in premises, concepts, and even in the meaning of the key words.

Quality is fitness for use.

This basic definition branches into

1. Quality consists of those product features that meet customer needs

2. Quality consists of freedom from deficiencies

Product features provide customer satisfaction; the major effect is on sales income.

Product deficiencies create customer dissatisfaction; the major effect is on costs.

Product is the output of any process.

Product includes goods and services.

A customer is anyone who is affected by the product or process.

Customers may be external or internal.

Product satisfaction and product dissatisfaction are not opposites.

Measures of deficiencies are usually expressed in terms of a fraction:

$$\text{Quality} = \frac{\text{frequency of deficiencies}}{\text{opportunity for deficiencies}}$$

Evaluation of product features starts by asking customers how they evaluate quality.

Managing for quality is carried out by a trilogy of three managerial processes: quality planning, quality control, and quality improvement.

Each of the processes of the trilogy is carried out by a universal sequence of steps.

TASKS FOR UPPER MANAGERS

Assure that the company's manuals and training materials include clear definitions of the word *quality* and of the subsidiary terminology.

Quality Improvement

The purpose of this chapter is to

1. Explain the nature of quality improvement and its relation to quality leadership

2. Show how to establish quality improvement as a continuing process that goes on year after year

3. Set out the roles of upper management in making this happen

WHAT IS IMPROVEMENT?

As used here, *improvement* means the organized creation of beneficial change; the attainment of unprecedented levels of performance. A synonym is *breakthrough*.

Figure 3–1, the trilogy diagram (reproduced here from Figure 2–3), shows graphically the nature of quality improvement and its relation to quality planning and quality control.

One segment of the graph is shown below as Figure 3–2. It dramatizes the effect of quality improvement on operating results. Many final reports of successful improvement projects include just such graphs to dramatize the results achieved by the project team.

Quality Improvement: Its Relation to Fire Fighting

Quality improvement is very different from "fire fighting." In the trilogy diagram, (Figure 3–1), the removal of that sporadic spike is often called fire fighting. It merely restores performance to the prior chronic level, which was also the prior standard. In that

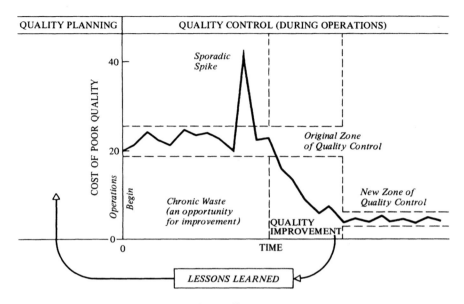

FIGURE 3–1   The Juran Trilogy diagram

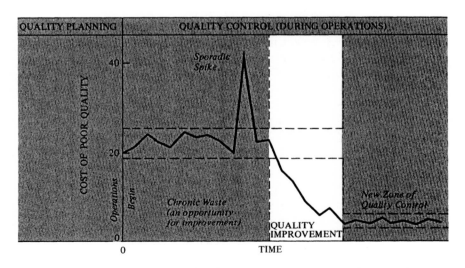

FIGURE 3–2   Effect of quality improvement on operating results

same trilogy diagram, the subsequent quality improvement takes the performance to unprecedented levels—closer to perfection than ever before.

QUALITY IMPROVEMENT AND QUALITY LEADERSHIP

Most companies engage in quality improvement every year. The improvements take such forms as

1. New product development to replace old models
2. Adoption of new technology (for example, computers to replace manual information systems)
3. Revision of processes to reduce error rates

Opposed to this improvement rate is a rate of deterioration resulting from such events as competitors bringing new, superior products to market; and the company's new products and processes being found to contain quality deficiencies, which then reduce product performance and create new chronic wastes. The result is a net rate of improvement that can be represented by the slope of the line in the model(Figure 3–3). The higher the net rate of improvement, the steeper the slope.

Suppose that we consider Figure 3–3 to represent the performance of company A. It is the industry quality leader. It is in a state of continuing quality improvement. It is profitable. On the face of it, company A can look ahead to a bright future.

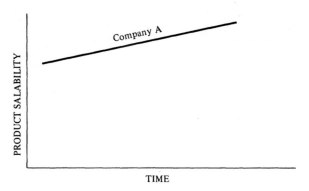

FIGURE 3–3   Rate of improvement, Company A

Now let us add some additional information.

Figure 3–4 shows that company B, a competitor, is not the quality leader. However, company B is improving at a faster rate. The present leader, company A, faces a clear threat of loss of quality leadership. The lesson is clear: the most decisive factor in the competition for quality leadership is the *rate* of quality improvement.

The contrasting rates in Figure 3–4 go far to explain why in so many product lines Japanese goods have attained quality leadership. The primary reason is that the Japanese rate of quality improvement has for decades been going on at a revolutionary pace compared with the evolutionary pace of the West. An estimate of the timing of this contrast as applied to the automobile industry is shown in Figure 3–5 (reproduced here from Figure 1–1).

THE RATES OF QUALITY IMPROVEMENT

Quality improvement is needed for both kinds of quality: product features and freedom from deficiencies.

To maintain and increase sales income, companies must continually evolve new product features and new processes to produce those features. Customer needs are a moving target.

To keep costs competitive, companies must continually reduce the level of product and process deficiencies. Competitive costs are also a moving target.

In the United States, improvement in these two forms of quality has progressed at very different rates. The difference is due in large part to the difference in organizational structure.

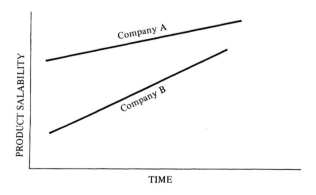

FIGURE 3–4   Two competing rates of improvement

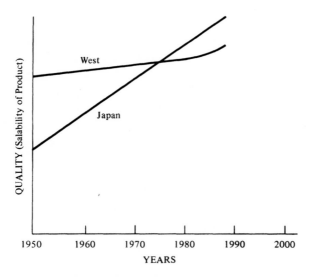

FIGURE 3–5   Japanese and Western quality: A contrast

Organization for Evolving New Product and Process Features

Many American companies maintain a special organizational structure to evolve new models of goods and services (plus associated new processes), year after year. This special organization structure usually includes

1. A new-products (and new-processes) committee that maintains a business surveillance over new developments

2. A structured procedure for shepherding the new developments through the various functional departments

3. Full-time product and process development departments that carry out the essential technological work

Note that the continued existence of this structure favors continued quality improvement: Product development is established as an official part of the company's business plan. There is clear responsibility for carrying out the essential technological work. Resources are provided—that is, the development departments are provided with personnel, laboratories, and other essentials.

Note also that the presence of this special organizational structure, although necessary, is not sufficient to assure a good rate of improvement of quality features. Many companies that do have organized structures for new-product development nevertheless are not strong competitors in product features: the cycle time for getting to market is lengthy; the new models include poor performance features; new chronic deficiencies are created. These weaknesses are usually traceable to weaknesses in their quality-planning process. We shall have a close look at that process in the next chapter, "Quality Planning."

Organization for Reducing Quality Deficiencies

In most American companies the rate of improvement with respect to quality deficiencies has been distinctly lower than the corresponding rate for products and processes. The difference is largely traceable to the absence of an organizational structure for making such improvements; reduction of quality deficiencies has not been an official part of the company's business plan, and responsibility for carrying out the work of such quality improvement has been vague. The resulting inadequacy in rate of quality improvement is bound to continue until steps are taken to provide the needed structured approach. The necessary steps are discussed in the following section.

THE ORIGINS OF QUALITY IMPROVEMENT

Some of the quality improvements that take place are a direct result of upper-management initiative and leadership. The chief example is new product development as a means of generating sales in the future. The upper managers personally participate in the business decisions relative to such new product development.

Much of the remaining quality improvement takes place at the initiative of the lower levels of organization. To a large degree this results in quality improvement being on a voluntary basis. Any such voluntary activity has difficulty competing against the mandated responsibilities of the operating managers—to meet their schedules, budgets, specifications, and other mandated standards. These mandated responsibilities are reinforced by the prevailing reward systems, which are largely based on evaluation of performance against mandated standards.

The Limitations

The foregoing sources of quality improvement fail to deal with certain major, crying needs. These needs consist of chronic deficiencies in products and processes due to inadequacies in prior planning. Some of these deficiencies are of an *intra*departmental nature; the symptoms, causes, and remedies are all within the scope of one departmental manager. However, the major wastes are *inter*departmental in nature. The symptoms show up in department X, but there is no agreement on what are the causes, and hence no agreement on what remedial action should be taken. Neither does there exist any organizational mechanism that can help the department managers deal with those interdepartmental problems.

The Emerging Consensus

These major wastes are huge. In the United States, probably about a third of what is done consists of redoing what was done previously, because of quality deficiencies. The emerging consensus is that these wastes should not continue on and on. Action should be taken to get rid of them. This action should not be on a voluntary basis; it should somehow be mandated. Since the bulk of the wastes are interdepartmental in nature, a special organizational structure should be provided to assist the managers in tackling problems that are beyond the scope of individual departments.

The remainder of this chapter is devoted to the quality-improvement process: (1) how to guide the company into a continuing, steep rate of quality improvement, and (2) the roles played by upper managers in that process.

QUALITY IMPROVEMENT: THE BASIC CONCEPTS

The quality improvement process rests on a base of certain fundamental concepts. These concepts are then linked together into a structured process: a repetitive-use process for making quality improvements. The elements of that process and their interrelation are shown in Figure 3–6.

Mobilizing for Quality Improvement

Establish quality council
Statement of responsibilities
Improvement policies, goals

ESTABLISH INFRASTRUCTURE	PROJECTS COLLECTIVELY	PROJECTS INDIVIDUALLY
Subcouncils	Strategic improvement goals	Nomination
Director of quality		Screening
Quality-improvement managers	Deployment	Selection
	Projects	Mission statements
Sponsors, champions	Resources	Project teams
Facilitators	Progress review	Life cycle of a project: diagnosis; remedy; cloning
Structured improvement process	Recognition	
	Rewards	
Training: methods; tools		

FIGURE 3–6   Quality improvement: The interrelation of elements

The message of Figure 3–6 is that going into annual quality improvement involves considerable change and restructuring. The details of Figure 3–6 constitute a process for managing that change.

For most companies and managers, annual quality improvement is not only a new responsibility; it is also a radical change in style of management—a change in culture. Therefore it is important to grasp the basic concepts before getting into the improvement process itself.

All Improvement Takes Place Project by Project

All quality improvement takes place project by project and in no other way. The critical word here is "project." We define a project as a problem scheduled for solution—a specific mission to be carried out. However, a better definition is provided by example. We shall therefore look at three real-life examples.

Florida Power and Light Company, a public utility, was enduring customer dissatisfaction because of a chronic condition of incorrect invoices—about sixty thousand per year. A quality improvement team was assigned to improve the quality of the invoicing process. The result was to bring the number of incorrect invoices down to about five thousand per year, with associated improvement in customer relations, and with a cost reduction in excess of a million dollars per year (American Productivity Center, Case Study 39, September 1984).

Becton Dickinson and Company, a health-products maker, undertook to improve customer service on "special" customer orders: orders for products that differed somewhat from the standard catalog items. A quality-improvement team found that a relative few customers and product types dominated the demand for special orders. The remedy was to add a modest number of special product types to the standard product line. The results were dramatic: the number of special orders per year declined from seven hundred to two hundred. The time required to fill special orders had averaged three months. The remedy permitted 85 percent of the orders to be filled in two days. The costs were reduced by $55,000 per year (Engle and Ball 1986).

Bethlehem Steel Corporation undertook to reduce "conveyor spillage" during a factory process. Again the results were dramatic: an annual cost reduction of about $400,000 per annum as well as a one-time saving of $500,000. The story is well narrated in the *Bethlehem Review,* the company's journal (*Bethlehem Review* 1982).

BETHLEHEM REVIEW

Juran Training's Paying Off

Because of its applicability to a wide range of Bethlehem plants, we followed the conveyor spillage subgroup—subgroup C-1—through its learning and problem solving sessions.

The group came from a cross section of plant production and service departments. Each person brought a special insight to the possible solution. That range of insight, that diversity of specialization is a keystone in Juran's approach to quality improvement and problem-solving—the more varied the input, the better the solution.

Important in the selection of the problem of conveyor spillage and belt carryover (the material that sticks to the surface of the belt on its return trip) were the dollars wasted—approaching half a million dollars. The costs come from lost material, the never ending clean up, and from damage to equipment on which the carry-over fell.

After establishing the dollar scope of the problem, the subgroup made trips through the plant to spot primary spillage points to find out what caused it. They looked closely at transfer points and at the design of transfer chutes.

They also ran tests of various types of belt wipers—many of their own design as well as commercially available wipers. Tests were run on a small conveyor in the craft training center—a conveyor used to train millwrights how to splice conveyor belting. The small, six-foot-long conveyor was also perfect as a place to test the effects of belt surface conditions, dryness of both belt and material conveyed as contributors to carryover.

Subgroup members checked with their counterparts at other Bethlehem operations as to transfer-point chute design and belt-wiping methods. After tests, some designs were abandoned; the more promising were modified and more tests were run.

Remember, a lot of the material moved on the several miles of conveyors at the plant is very fine and tends to stick to the belt's surface. The function of the wiper is to remove these fine materials before the belt makes its return trip.

When the Juran pilot training program was concluded the end of June, group C-1 submitted its report to Fred Daggett, plant general manager. He liked what he saw for three reasons: 1) there was a large saving in costs, 2) a long-standing housekeeping problem had been alleviated, and 3) the Juran approach to problem solving had worked and worked well.

Among other recommendations, the group suggests that transfer point M20-21 in the coke plant be modified. (It's the plant's worst spill and carryover spot.) An air-wipe system will be installed, backed up by a polyurethane wiper. The catch chute there will be modified so that all the fine material previously carried over by the belt will fall in a to-be-constructed bin.

Conveyor carryover elimination, the group estimates, can save the plant nearly $400,000 a year in lost material, cleanup costs, and damage to equipment onto which the material previously fell on its "empty" return trip.

That's a big saving in itself. But an even greater saving was discovered by C-1 members.

In years past, conveyor spillage and carryover material (coke plant cleanup) was periodically swept up as a housekeeping matter, shoveled into trucks, and hauled to the plant's waste dump. As the group studied their spillage and carry-over problem, their attention turned to the 10,000-ton accumulation of coal and coke breeze (or "braize" as coke-oven people call it) piled on the waste dump.

Chemical and physical tests run by the group on clean, uncontaminated carryover, proved it could be used as an ignition fuel in the plant's sintering operation when properly blended with other purchased fuel. Why not the 10,000 tons of breeze on the waste dump?

Sure enough it too, could be used as sinter plant feed if properly screened and sized and contaminants removed. This could be done at little expense—$2,000 for the screen and $2 a ton for labor—and with existing equipment.

So, what was a 10,000-ton eyesore and headache becomes an asset worth $45 per ton. The 10,000-ton stockpile of breeze on the waste dump could be consumed in the sinter plant, over a three-year period, as a portion of the ignition fuel—nearly a half million dollar find of buried treasure.

When we zeroed in on C-1's Juran learning experience, we felt the group's "problem" had applicability to many other Bethlehem operations. It was not, we realized, a "quality" problem in the strict sense of the word, but as we said earlier the Juran process is applicable to other than quality problems. It's a problem solving technique suitable for any problem area. It is simply an orderly process for problem solving. We certainly had no early indication that C-1's solutions would approach the million dollar level over three years.

Universally Applicable

Note that the foregoing examples demonstrate that quality improvement has universal application to

Service industries as well as manufacturing industries

Business processes as well as manufacturing processes

Support operations as well as production operations

"Software" as well as hardware

The feedback from companies that have gone into quality improvement on a significant scale support this concept of universality (see IMPRO).

The Backlog of Projects Is Big

A large backlog of projects is evident from an emerging data base. More and more companies are publishing papers describing their quality improvements, including the gains made. (See IMPRO 1983 et seq for examples.) These published results indicate that for companies in the sales range of $1 billion (milliard) per year, the average quality-improvement project has yielded about $100,000 of cost reduction (Juran 1985).

That same $1 billion company is likely to have a cost of poor quality in the range of 30 percent of sales, or about $300 million. At the rate of about $100,000 per project, there are three thousand quality improvement projects waiting to be tackled. Such a backlog will keep many teams busy for many years to come.

The Return on Investment Is High

Quality improvement does not come free. Each improvement project requires an investment in two forms:

1. A diagnosis to discover the causes of poor quality
2. A remedy to eliminate the causes

The emerging data base indicates that for projects at the $100,000 level, the investment in diagnosis and remedy combined runs to about $15,000. The resulting return on investment is among the highest available to managers. It has caused some managers to quip, "The best business to be in is quality improvement."

This return on investment offers some interesting contrasts to other forms of improving company profitability. A successful company in the sales range of $1 billion might well have dimensions somewhat as follows:

Sales	$1 billion
Investment	$500 million
Net income	$100 million
Cost of poor quality	$300 million

If such a company set out to cut the cost of poor quality by a third over a five-year span, it would need to complete about one thousand improvement projects (at about $100,000 each). It would need to invest about $15,000 per project, or about $15 million.

In contrast, if the company set out to accomplish an equivalent improvement in profit by growth in sales, the investment needed would be over ten times as high. This contrast is the basis for a gathering awareness among managers that *the return on investment in quality improvement is among the highest available to managers.*

Upper managers are well advised to secure, within their own companies, the estimates needed to compare (a) the potential return on investment in improvement with (b) the potential return from other opportunities for investment. This can be done by study of the quality-improvement projects recently completed. The methodology is as follows:

1. Identify the quality-improvement projects completed within the last year or two.
2. Estimate (a) what was gained and (b) what was the associated investment for each such project.
3. Determine the composite return on investment.

Quality Improvement Is Not Capital Intensive

The great majority of published quality-improvement projects tell of remedies achieved by "fine tuning" the process rather than by investing in a new process. As a rule of thumb, any process that is already producing over 80 percent good work can, by fine tuning, be brought up to the high 90's without capital investment. This same avoidance of capital investment is a major reason why quality improvement has so high a return on investment.

Impact of Quality Improvement on Productivity, Cost, and Delivery

The belief that "higher quality costs more" has had a long history and remains very much alive. As applied to quality in the sense of freedom from deficiencies, this belief has no relation to reality. Earlier we looked at three pertinent case examples: the invoices, the service-on-special-orders, and the conveyor-spillage case. The famous example of the color television set (Juran 1979) quantifies some of the impacts.

The Matsushita Company had purchased an American factory (Quasar). Matsushita then invested in various changes to improve quality: product designs that were less prone to field failures; manufacturing processes that were more precise and less prone to human error, and supplier-relations programs to improve the quality of purchased components. These changes not only improved quality; they also improved productivity and reduced costs, as shown by the following "before-and-after" data:

	1974	1977
Fall-off rate, i.e., defects (on assembled sets) requiring repair	150 per 100 sets	4 per 100 sets
Number of repair and inspection personnel	120	15
Cost of service calls	$22 million	$4 million

The ultimate users benefited greatly: the field failure rate had been cut by over 80 percent. The manufacturer also benefited through lower costs, higher productivity, more reliable deliveries, and greater salability.

Obviously if the quality improvement had consisted of going from a seventeen-inch screen to a twenty-four-inch screen, higher quality would have cost more. However, such a change would be an improvement in product features, in which case higher quality often does cost more.

QUALITY IMPROVEMENT DOES NOT COME FREE

The attraction of quality improvement is undeniable. Nevertheless, there is a cold reality that has been unwelcome to many upper managers: quality improvement does not come free. Such is the significance of that estimated $15,000 investment to make an improvement worth $100,000.

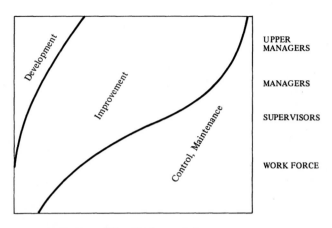

FIGURE 3-7   The Itoh model

A further cold reality is the new burden placed on the entire managerial hierarchy—managers, supervisors, and professional specialists. To go full scale into annual quality improvement adds about 10 percent to the work load of the entire management team, including the upper managers. In this connection it is interesting to look at the Itoh model of the allocation of time to the processes of (1) strategic planning, (2) improvement, and (3) control, as this varies with level in the hierarchy (Figure 3-7).

MOBILIZING FOR QUALITY IMPROVEMENT

A question raised by some upper managers is, "Why do we need to mobilize? Why don't we just do it?" One answer is to look back at those three improvement projects: the incorrect invoices, the poor service on special orders, and the conveyor spillage. Each of those had been a problem for years. Each could have been solved years before. Why were they not solved years before? The reasons are multiple, and include the following:

1. The problems had not been placed on an authoritative agenda and scheduled for solution.

2. There was no clear responsibility assigned to solve the problems.

3. It was not realized that a team was required.

For a lone project or just several projects there is little need for "mobilizing." However, the situation faced by companies is often very different, in the following ways:

1. The backlog of projects waiting to be tackled is very large. This is obvious from (a) the estimated size of the cost of poor quality and (b) the contrast (Japan versus the West) shown in Figure 1-1.

2. Such a backlog requires years to work off. Actually there is no end to it because competitive pressures are never ending.

3. To go to a revolutionary pace of quality improvement is unprecedented in scale.

4. It has been no one's responsibility to choose projects to be tackled, assign responsibility, and follow progress.

5. The prevailing reward system is oriented toward meeting operating goals, not toward making improvements.

So we do need to mobilize. We need to design a structure that will enable us to carry out unprecedented numbers of improvement projects at an unprecedented pace. That structure must come to grips with the essential specifics, such as identifying which projects to tackle and assigning clear responsibility.

Companies that have successfully completed many quality-improvement projects have all made use of a structured approach along the lines set out in Figure 3-6. This structure involves two levels of activity:

1. Establishing the infrastructure needed to deal with the projects *collectively*

2. Carrying out the projects *individually*

THE QUALITY COUNCIL

The first step in mobilizing for the projects collectively is to establish a quality council (also called quality improvement council, quality committee, and so forth). The basic responsibility of this council is to launch, coordinate, and "institutionalize" annual quality improvement. If no such council is in existence, *the upper managers should create one.*

Such councils have been established in many companies. Their experience provides some useful guidelines.

Membership

Council membership is typically drawn from the ranks of senior managers. The stakes are too high to establish the council solely at middle-management levels. Often the senior management committee is also the quality council.

In large companies it is common to establish councils at the divisional level as well as at the corporate level. In very large companies, some individual facilities may be so large as to warrant establishing a local quality council. When multiple councils are established they are usually linked together, that is, members of high-level councils serve as chairpersons of lower-level councils. Figure 3–8 shows schematically how quality councils are linked together.

It is a mistake to organize these councils solely in the lower levels of management. Such organization effectively limits any subse-

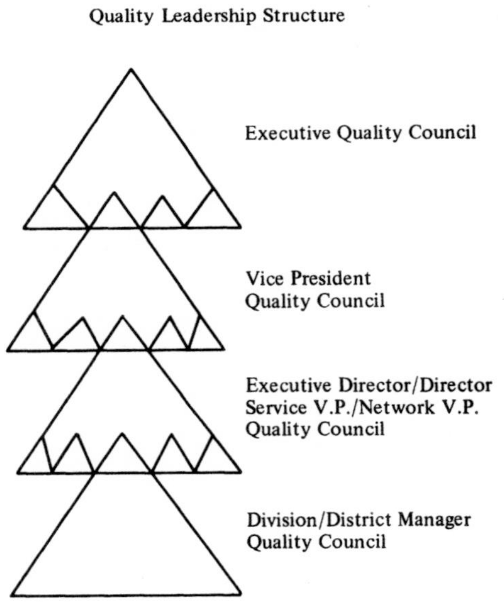

Quality Leadership Structure

Executive Quality Council

Vice President
Quality Council

Executive Director/Director
Service V.P./Network V.P.
Quality Council

Division/District Manager
Quality Council

FIGURE 3–8   How quality councils are linked together

SOURCE: AT&T Network Operations Group

quent quality-improvement projects to the "useful many," not to the "vital few" that can produce the greatest results. In addition, such organization solely at lower levels sends a message to all: quality improvement is not high on upper management's agenda. To avoid this, upper managers should *personally become the leaders and members of the senior quality councils.*

Responsibilities of Quality Councils

One of the first actions of a quality council is to define and publish its responsibilities so that (a) the members have a meeting of the minds and (b) the rest of the organization is kept informed relative to upcoming events.

Many quality councils have published such statements of responsibility. The major common elements have included

1. Formulating the quality improvement policy—for example, priority of quality, need for annual quality improvement, and mandatory participation

2. Estimating the major dimensions—for example, quality compared with competitors, cost of poor quality, and length of the new product's launch cycle

3. Establishing the project-selection process

4. Establishing the team-selection process

5. Providing resources: training, time for working on projects, diagnostic support, and facilitator support

6. Assuring that project solutions are implemented

7. Establishing needed measures—for example, progress on quality improvement, performance versus competitors, and managers' performance

8. Providing for progress review and coordination

9. Providing for recognition

10. Revising the reward system

Upper managers should see to it that each quality council *prepares and publishes a statement of its responsibilities.* (The foregoing list includes some terminology that we have not yet defined— e.g., diagnostic support and facilitator support. Every one of such terms will be defined as we proceed.)

Anticipating the Questions

Announcement of a company's intention to go into annual quality improvement always stimulates questions from subordinate levels. The list that follows includes many of the questions frequently asked.

What is the purpose of this new activity?

Why does the company need it?

How does this new activity relate to other ongoing company efforts to make improvements?

What priority does it have relative to those other efforts?

How does this new activity relate to other quality-oriented activities?

What jobs will be affected, and how?

Will those affected have an opportunity to participate in the planning?

What specific steps will be taken, and in what sequence?

How will results be measured?

To whom can we go to get answers?

Quality councils are well advised to anticipate the troublesome questions and, to the extent feasible, provide answers at the time of announcing the intention to go into annual quality improvement. Some senior managers have gone as far as creating a videotape to enable a wide audience to hear the identical message from a source of undoubted authority.

Role of the Quality Department

Many quality councils have found it useful to secure the assistance of the quality department to

1. Provide much of the information needed by the council for planning how to introduce quality improvement

2. Draft proposals and procedures

3. Carry out essential details such as screening nominations for projects

4. Develop training materials

5. Propose new measures for quality

6. Prepare reports on progress

It is also usual, but not invariable, for the quality manager to serve as secretary of the quality council.

THE PROJECT SELECTION PROCESS

This process is an essential part of the company's structured approach to quality improvement. It consists of a series of steps:

1. Project nomination

2. Project selection

3. Project mission statements

4. Publication

PROJECT NOMINATION

Nominations should be solicited from all areas of the company and, in addition, from cognizant outside sources. This concept of such a broad base of nominations is comparatively new.

Until the 1980s managers generally associated quality and quality improvement with factories, manufactured goods, and production processes. All that has been undergoing a drastic, irreversible change. An emerging label for the change is "Big Q, not Little Q."

Big Q and Little Q

The difference between "big Q" and "little Q" is summarized in Figure 3–9.

Relative to project nomination, the main impact of the concept of big Q is the large potential for improvement of business processes. This potential is evident from a look at some of the projects that have already been tackled:

1. Improving the precision of the sales forecast

2. Reducing the cycle time for bringing out new products

3. Increasing the success rate in bidding for business

4. Reducing the time required to fill customers' orders

5. Reducing the number of sales cancellations

TOPIC	CONTENT OF LITTLE Q	CONTENT OF BIG Q
Products	Manufactured goods	All products, goods and services, whether for sale or not
Processes	Processes directly related to manufacture of goods	All processes; manufacturing support, business, etc.
Customer	Clients who buy the products	All who are affected, external and internal
Industries	Manufacturing	All industries; manufacturing service, government, etc., whether for profit or not
Cost of poor quality	Costs associated with deficient manufactured goods	All costs that would disappear if everything were perfect

FIGURE 3–9   Contrast: Big Q and Little Q

6. Reducing the errors in invoices

7. Reducing the number of delinquent accounts

8. Reducing the time required to recruit new employees

9. Improving the on-time arrival rate (for airlines)

However, during the 1980s such projects were significantly outnumbered by projects related to factory goods and processes. Little Q was still very much in evidence.

Sources of Nominations

Some nominations can be derived from the formal data systems already in place. Examples of such systems include

1. Reports on customer dissatisfactions (for example, warranty charges, claims, complaints, and returns)

2. Evaluations of competitive quality

3. Sales-force reports

4. Service-call reports

5. Field-failure analyses

6. Accounting data on costs of poor quality

(Some of these data systems make specific provisions for analyzing the data in order to identify the problem areas.)

Even more dramatic are cases for which the traditional "cost-of-quality" studies make no provision in their accounting "categories." To illustrate:

Company X undertook a new product venture on which it incurred costs as follows:

	$ (MILLIONS)
Market research	0.5
Product design	6.0
Manufacture	36.0
Sales promotion	2.0
	44.5

The product proved to be unsalable. Competitor Y had meanwhile come to market first and had saturated the market with a product possessing features that responded satisfactorily to customer needs.

Note in this connection the risks involved in defining quality as "conformance" to something. The product of company X conformed to its specifications. The product also did what company X said it would do. The product also met the customers' needs. The product was unsalable for a quality reason unrelated to conformance: a competitor's product met customers' needs better and met them first.

There are many other sizable examples of cost of poor quality that have not been brought to light because of a focus on little Q:

1. Peer review of software development

2. Sales-force efforts consumed in helping customers secure redress for deficient products

3. Customer-service-department efforts associated with product deficiencies

4. Product design changes made for numerous avoidable reasons

MARKET RESEARCH AS A SOURCE OF PROJECT NOMINATIONS

It is all too easy to overlook the need for market research as a source of nominations for improvement projects. Customers who encounter product dissatisfactions are often vocal and insistent. In contrast, customers who encounter product features that are not competitive often quietly become noncustomers.

To conduct the needed research requires identifying the questions to which answers are needed. The nature of customers' needs and the methodology for discovering them are set out in chapter 4, in the sections Customers' Needs and Methods for Discovering Customers' Needs, respectively.

We can note here that securing nominations from the field may require creating new data sources through such means as purchasing data from users and installing of recording instruments.

In still other cases nominations are the result of new perceptions. An example is the spare-parts business. Spare-parts sales have traditionally been a source of profitable business. However, each such sale means that some customer has encountered a product failure. Increasingly, companies that have profited from the sale of spare parts are discovering that their customers look for suppliers whose products don't fail.

Cost of Poor Quality as an Aid to Project Nomination

As used here, *cost of poor quality* (COPQ) is the sum of all costs that would disappear if there were no quality problems. In all companies the prevailing cost accounting system quantifies some—a minority—of these costs. The majority are scattered throughout the various overheads. This incompleteness of the cost data has led some advocates to urge that the accounting system be expanded to quantify all the cost of poor quality. These advocates contend that the availability of such figures will stimulate quality improvement as well as provide the basis for a continuing scoreboard.

Many companies have in fact undertaken expansion of the accounting system to quantify the "quality costs." All too often these programs have run into maddening delay because of the time required to define the accounting categories, argue out the classifications, and set up the data system. (The very term "quality costs" is confusing whereas the term "cost of poor quality" is clear.) Still more delay has resulted from preoccupation with a level of accuracy not needed for managerial decision making.

The resulting figures did provide the companies with useful information for project nomination. However, very few of the companies had created the structure needed to choose projects and assign responsibility. Consequently, enlarging the accounting system seldom led to quality improvement.

In contrast there are many companies that have made extensive quality improvements without prior enlargement of the accounting system. They secured their project nominations from other sources, such as those described in the previous section Sources of Nominations.

The Nomination Machinery

Nominations must come from human employees. The data systems are impersonal: they make no nominations.

Quality councils receive nominations from several main sources:

Calling for nominations. The council invites all personnel to submit nominations, either through the chain of command or to a designated recipient, for example, the council secretariat.

Making the rounds. In this approach specialists (for example, quality engineers) are assigned to visit the various departments, talk with the key people, and secure their views and nominations.

The council members themselves. They become the focal point for extensive data analyses and proposals.

Whatever the method used, the upper managers should direct that nominations be addressed *to all products and processes, business as well as manufacture,* that is, big Q rather than little Q.

Nominations from the Work Force

The work force is potentially a useful source of nominations for projects. Workers have extensive residence in the workplace. With regard to some symptoms of problems, no one is better versed than the work force.

Formal solicitation of nominations from the work force also carries some risks. The work force may view such solicitation as a commitment to act on the nominations. Yet these nominations consist mainly of "useful-many" projects along with proposals of a human relations nature. It should be made clear that the workers' nominations must compete for priority with all other nominations. Failing this, the risk is that the work force will be deciding which projects the managers should tackle.

PROJECT SELECTION

The council (or a designated subcouncil) screens the nominations for the purpose of choosing the projects to be tackled. In doing so, companies have learned to establish two sets of criteria for project selection:

1. Criteria for choosing the first projects to be tackled by any of the project teams
2. Criteria for choosing projects thereafter

Criteria for the First Projects

During the beginning stages of project-by-project improvement, everyone is in a learning state. Projects are assigned to project teams who are in training; completing a project is a part of that training. Experience with such teams has evolved a broad criterion: *the first project should be a winner.* More specifically:

The project should deal with a *chronic* problem—one which has been awaiting solution for a long time.

The project should be *feasible.* There should be a good likelihood of bringing it to a successful conclusion within a few months. Our feedback from companies using the videocassette series— *Juran on Quality Improvement®*—show that the most frequent reason for failure of the first project is failure to meet this criterion of feasibility.

The project should be *significant.* The end result should be sufficiently useful to merit attention and recognition.

The results should be *measurable* in money as well as in technological terms.

Criteria for Projects Thereafter

These criteria aim to select projects that will do the company the most good:

Return on investment. This factor has great weight and is decisive, all other things being equal. Projects that do not lend themselves to computing return on investment must rely for their priority on managerial judgment.

The amount of potential improvement. One large project will take priority over several small ones.

Urgency. There may be a need to respond promptly to pressures associated with product safety, employee morale, and customer service.

Ease of technological solution. Projects for which the technology is well developed will take precedence over projects that require research to discover the needed technology.

Health of the product line. Projects involving thriving product lines will take precedence over projects involving obsolescent product lines.

Probable resistance to change. Projects that will meet a favorable reception take precedence over projects that may encounter strong resistance, for example, from the labor union or from a manager set in his ways.

Providing the Cost Figures

To meet the above criteria (especially that of return on investment) requires information on the costs being incurred due to poor quality. Since company accounting systems are incomplete with respect to such information, managers look for ways to supply what is missing. Their main efforts toward solution have been the following:

1. *By estimates.* This is the "quick and dirty" approach. It involves only a modest amount of effort. It can in a few days or weeks provide an evaluation of the approximate amount of cost of poor quality and where this is concentrated.

2. *By enlarging the accounting system.* This is much more elaborate. It requires a lot of work from various departments, especially accounting and quality. It also runs into a lot of calendar time, often two to three years.

Experience shows that the estimates are good enough. They provide information that is adequate for managerial decision making, and they do so with much less work and in far less time.

To illustrate, a potential project is estimated to have a cost of poor quality of $300,000. There is a debate as to the accuracy of the estimate. The contesting estimates range from $240,000 to $360,000—quite a wide range. Then someone makes an incisive observation: "It doesn't matter which estimate is right. Every one of those figures is too big. We should tackle that project."So the managerial decision is identical despite a wide range of estimate.

Elephant-sized and Bite-sized Projects

Some projects are "elephant-sized"; that is, they cover so broad an area of activity that they must be subdivided into multiple bite-sized projects. In such cases one project team can be assigned to "cut up the elephant." Other teams are then assigned to tackle the resulting bite-sized projects. Unless such subdivision takes place, the original team might take years trying to carry out the broad project.

In the case examples given earlier in this chapter, the invoice project in effect required several teams, each assigned to a specific segment of the invoicing process. In contrast, the cases of special orders and conveyor spillage were bite-sized from the outset.

The quality council faces up to this problem during preparation of the mission statements. For elephant-sized projects the mission should be drawn so as to assign the subdivision of the broad subject before assigning teams to the smaller pieces.

"Global" Projects

Some projects that may seem to be elephant-sized are in fact bite-sized. These are usually projects that have wide and repetitive application:

A project team develops computer software to find errors in spelling. Another team evolves an improved procedure for processing customer orders through the company. A third team works up a procedure for conducting design reviews.

What is common to such projects is that the end result permits repetitive application of the same process to a wide variety of tasks: many different misspelled words; many different customer orders; many different designs.

Reaching a Consensus

To start with a long list of nominations and end up with a short list of agreed-upon projects requires the help of some sort of methodology. Often this is done in two stages:

1. The nominations are screened by a subcouncil, by the council secretariat, or by some other designated entity. The screening process examines each nomination in relation to the criteria set out above. Use is also made of the Pareto principle for separating the "vital few" nominations from the "useful many." The end result of this stage is a "short list" of nominations, each of which is supported by the available information (compatibility with the criteria, cost estimates, and so forth).

2. The quality council makes the final determination of how many and which projects to tackle.

Special tools have been devised to help teams to arrive at a consensus. An example is "nominal group technique," described in chapter 10, "Training for Quality."

PROJECT MISSION STATEMENTS AND PUBLICATION

For each project selected, the council prepares a mission statement. This statement sets out the goal of the project. In the three projects discussed earlier, the bare-minimum mission statements would read somewhat as follows:

Reduce the rate of incorrect invoices going to clients.

Reduce the time required to give service to clients on special orders.

Reduce the amount of conveyor spillage.

As companies gain experience in the quality-improvement process such mission statements get fleshed out, including a degree of quantification.

The list of selected projects is officially published. Such publication confers legitimacy. The projects on that published list become a part of next year's business plan. (The remaining nominations didn't make it this year; they will have to wait their turn.)

THE PROJECT TEAM

For each selected project a team is designated. This team, usually six to eight persons, then has the responsibility of completing the project.

Why a Team?

The reason for assigning the project to a team is that the major quality problems are interdepartmental in nature. The symptoms may be evident in only one department, but there is no agreement on where the cause lies and hence no agreement on what should be the remedy. Experience has shown that the most effective organizational mechanisms for dealing with such interdepartmental problems are interdepartmental teams.

The Team Membership

The team is designated by the council after consultation with the departmental managers affected. The team selection process usually requires consideration of (1) which departments should be represented on the team, (2) what level in the hierarchy the team members should come from, and (3) which individuals in that level.

The departments to be represented usually consist of the following:

1. *The ailing departments.* They endure the effects of the symptoms.

2. *The suspect departments.* They are widely believed to harbor the causes. (They do not necessarily agree that they are suspect.)

3. *The remedial departments.* They will likely end up providing

the remedies. This is speculative, since in many cases the causes and remedies come as surprises.

4. *The diagnostic departments.* They are needed in projects that require extensive data collection and analysis.

Choice of level in the hierarchy depends on the subject matter of the project. Some projects relate strongly to the technological and procedural aspects of the products and processes. Such projects require team membership from the lower levels of the hierarchy. Other projects relate to broad business and managerial matters. For such projects the team members should have appropriate business and managerial experience.

Finally comes the choice of which individuals. This choice is negotiated with the respective department heads, giving due consideration to the prevailing work loads and competing priorities.

Legitimacy and Rights

Once the team is selected the names of the members are published in association with their project mission. Such publication assigns responsibility: the company looks to the team to carry out their project as a part of their overall job assignment. This same publication also provides legitimacy to the team and gives it certain rights, such as the right to

1. Hold meetings, deliberate, and publish minutes and reports

2. Request needed contributions from nonmembers

3. Request information and other assistance pertinent to the project

Teams of Upper Managers

Some projects by their nature require that the team include members from the ranks of upper management. Here are some examples of quality-improvement projects tackled by teams that included upper managers:

1. Preparing a statement of the company's quality policy

2. Shortening the time to put new products on the market

3. Improving the accuracy of the sales forecast

4. Reducing carryover of failure-prone features into new product models

5. Establishing a teamwork relationship with suppliers

6. Developing measures of quality needed for strategic quality management

7. Establishing the system of recognition and rewards for quality improvement

8. Improving the administrative activities associated with warranty costs

There are also additional, persuasive reasons urging that all upper managers personally serve on some project teams: Leadership by example is one reason. Personal participation on project teams also enables upper managers to understand what they are asking their subordinates to do; what kind of work is involved; how many hours per week are demanded; how many months it takes to complete a project; what kinds of resources are needed. Lack of upper-management understanding of such realities has contributed to the failure of some well-intentioned efforts to institute annual quality improvement.

Membership from the Work Force

Some companies have been testing out project teams whose membership includes work-force personnel. The reasons are mainly to

1. Increase worker participation and thereby improve human relations and job satisfaction

2. Secure specific worker contributions to the project, such as knowledge of symptoms and theories of causes

These are clearly worthwhile objectives. What is not fully tested is whether multifunctional project teams are the most effective way of reaching such objectives.

In the case of contributions to the project it is feasible to secure work-force inputs on an ad hoc basis, for example, by inviting the workers to specific meetings.

Relative to work-force participation there are various alternatives—for example, QC circles and suggestion systems. In this connection it is useful to understand in detail the contrast between

FEATURE	QC CIRCLES	PROJECT TEAMS
Primary mission	To improve human relations	To improve quality
Secondary mission	To improve quality	To improve participation
Scope of project	Within a single department	Multidepartmental
Size of project	One of the useful many	One of the vital few
Membership	From a single department	From multiple departments
Basis of membership	Voluntary	Mandatory
Hierarchical status of members	Typically in the work force	Typically managerial or professional
Continuity	Circle remains intact, project after project	Team is ad hoc, disbands after project is completed

FIGURE 3-10   Contrast: QC circles and project teams

multifunctional project teams (of managerial personnel) and QC circles. Figure 3-10 tabulates this contrast.

TEAM RESPONSIBILITIES

Team responsibilities are defined in

1. *The project mission statement.* This mission statement is prepared by the quality council, and is unique to each team.

2. *A charter that is alike for all teams.* The charter sets out the activities to be carried out by the team in order to accomplish its mission.

The Team Charter

The team charter is a form of impersonal supervision for each team. (The teams have no personal "boss.") The activities set out in the charter can be summarized as follows:

Analyze the symptoms.

Theorize as to the causes.

Test the theories.

Establish the cause(s).

Stimulate a remedy.

Test the remedy under operating conditions.

Establish controls to hold the gains.

The foregoing list of activities is the universal sequence of events through which quality improvement takes place, over and over again. The validity of this sequence has been demonstrated in thousands of quality-improvement projects completed with the aid of the videocassette series Juran on Quality Improvement. Many of these projects have been described at the annual IMPRO conferences.

This universal sequence of activities will now be elaborated. The sequence is more readily understood if the activities are grouped into two "journeys," diagnostic and remedial.

The Diagnostic Journey

The diagnostic journey starts with the outward symptoms of a quality problem and ends with the determination of the cause or causes. This journey includes some activities that are common to all improvement projects:

Understanding the symptoms. Symptoms are usually communicated in words—for example, incorrect invoices, late deliveries, conveyor spillage, "I don't feel well." Such expressions are open to differences in interpretation as a result of the multiple meanings of some words. In addition, such expressions seldom identify precisely what is outwardly wrong: in which respects are the invoices wrong; which tooth is aching. Understanding the symptoms requires digging in to discover the meanings behind the words. Often it is necessary to conduct an "autopsy" (see with one's own eyes) to learn precisely what the symptoms are.

Theorizing as to causes. All knowledge advances theory by theory—by affirming or denying the validity of theories. A good process for theorizing is brainstorming. People who are affected by the problem are convened and asked to propose theories as to causes. These theories are then organized into interrelated groups. Such organization simplifies understanding and becomes an aid in deciding which theories to choose for testing.

Testing the theories. Usually there are numerous theories. The project team then tests selected theories, making use of the many diagnostic tools that have been evolved. In due course the team establishes the real cause or causes of the symptoms. At that point the diagnostic journey is over, and the remedial journey begins.

For some projects the testing of theories requires data collection and analysis on a small scale. In such cases the project-team members themselves usually do the associated work.

Other projects require extensive data collection and analysis to test the theories. In such cases it is usual for the project team to delegate or "subcontract" the work to "diagnosticians"—persons who have the time, skills, and objectivity needed to carry out data collection and analysis. Despite such delegation the project team remains responsible for the successful completion of the project. For further elaboration, see the section Organization for Diagnosis and Remedy, which follows in this chapter.

The Remedial Journey

The remedial journey starts with the known cause or causes and ends with an effective remedy in place. The associated activities of the project team include the following:

Stimulating the establishment of a remedy. In most companies the project team does not have the responsibility to establish a remedy. For reasons of jurisdiction and professional skills this responsibility is placed on the cognizant functional department. However, the project team does have the responsibility to follow up and stimulate until the remedy has been established.

Testing the remedy under operating conditions. In most companies the project teams retain the responsibility to assure that the remedy really works, and does so under operating conditions. The project team also has the responsibility to assure that the remedy is optimal, that is, that "the cure is not worse than the disease."

Establishing controls to hold the gains. Some remedies are irreversible because of the inherent technological change. Other changes are reversible. For such reversible changes the project team has the responsibility to assure that appropriate controls are established—procedures, reports, audits, and so forth—that will assure the holding of the gains.

Ready, Fire, Aim

A frequent failing among untrained teams is to apply a remedy before the cause is known. This can come about in various ways:

1. An influential or insistent team member "knows" the cause and pressures the team to apply a remedy for that cause.

2. The team is briefed on the technology by the acknowledged expert. The expert has a firm opinion about what is the cause of the symptom and the team does not question the expert's opinion.

3. A consultant (internal or external) urges that the team apply a remedy for which he or she is an expert. The team applies the remedy without knowing what the disease is.

In such cases the remedy is applied but the problem remains. The results are loss of time and effort as well as dissension among the team members.

ORGANIZATION FOR DIAGNOSIS AND REMEDY

To complete its mission the project team enlists the aid of numerous company functions. Figure 3–11 on the facing page shows how all these functions collectively help the project team carry out its mission.

In Figure 3–11 the various organizations and functions are as follows:

1. *The project team.* It has the official responsibility to carry out the assigned project mission.

2. *Ad hoc resources.* These include all who are in a position to help the project. They are on call to provide information about symptoms, theories as to causes, and expertise in specific areas of know-how.

3. *The diagnostic function.* This is any entity that carries out the job of data collection and analysis. This function may be performed by the project team or it may be assigned to specialists.

	Project Team	Ad hoc Resources	Diagnostic Function	Remedial Function	Operating Department
Diagnostic Journey					
Establish plan of approach	X				
Study symptons	X	X			
Theorize as to causes	X	X			X
Collect and analyze data to test theories			X		
Establish cause(s)	X				
Remedial Journey					
Stimulate remedy	X				
Provide remedy				X	
Test remedy under operating conditions	X			X	X
Establish controls to hold the gains	X				X
Report results	X				

FIGURE 3–11   Organization for diagnosis and remedy

4. *The remedial function.* This is any organization that provides a remedy for the cause.

5. *The operating department.* This is any organization or group in which the remedy is installed.

TEAM ORGANIZATION

The team has no boss in the personal sense. It is supervised impersonally by the mission statement and by the charter.

The Structure

The team does have some structured organization, as follows:

1. A *chairperson,* appointed by the council, who shares the responsibilities with all members. Only the administrative responsibilities are unshared.

2. A *secretary* who drafts the agendas, minutes, reports, and so forth, for approval by the team.

Facilitators

Most companies make use of "facilitators" to assist project teams, mainly those teams that are working on their first project. Facilitators are usually supervisors or specialists who have undergone special training for this purpose. In most cases their role as facilitator is a part-time assignment, over and above their "regular" job.

The usual roles of facilitators consist of a selection from the following:

Explain the company's intentions. The facilitator has usually attended briefing sessions at which there has been explanation of what the company is trying to accomplish. Much of this briefing is of interest to the project teams.

Assist in team building. In this role the facilitator helps the team members to learn to act as a team—that is, to intercommunicate, contribute theories, challenge the theories of others, share experiences, and propose lines of investigation. Where the concept of using teams is relatively new to a company, this role may require working directly with some individuals, stimulating those who are unsure about how to contribute and restraining those who become overenthusiastic.

Assist in training. The facilitator has usually gone through the training course on quality improvement and has likely guided other teams through their first project. Such experiences enable the facilitator to play a teaching role—to provide previews of what will be coming up and lead the discussion relative to the content of the training materials.

Relate experiences from other projects. The facilitator has multiple sources from which to provide such experiences:

1. Project teams previously served

2. Meetings of facilitators at which they share the experiences of their respective project teams

3. Final reports of project teams, as published in-house

4. Projects reported in the literature

Assist in redirecting the project. The facilitator usually has a detached view that can help him or her to sense when the team is getting bogged down. This may take place as the team gets into the project and finds itself getting deeper and deeper into a swamp. It may also take place at the very outset: it may be discovered that the project mission is too broad, too vaguely defined, or not doable. The facilitator, being in a detached status relative to the project, can usually sense such situations earlier than the team members and can help guide them to a redirection of the project.

Assist the project team chairperson. The facilitator is *not* a member of the project team and generally should avoid getting into the substance of the project. However, the facilitator can be helpful to the team chairperson by

1. *Stimulating attendance.* Most nonattendance is due to the conflicting demands made on each member's time. The remedy often must come from the member's boss.

2. *Improving human relations.* Some teams will include members who have not been on good terms with each other, or who develop a degree of conflict during the progress of the project. Action to direct the energies of such members into constructive channels should normally take place outside of the team meetings.

In some cases the chairperson is part of the problem. In such cases the facilitator may be the person in the best position to help out.

Report progress to the councils. In this role the facilitator is a part of the process of reporting on the progress of the projects collectively. Each project team issues minutes of its meetings. In due course each project team also issues its final report. However, reports on the projects collectively must be worked up in other ways. The facilitators are often a part of this reporting process.

Note that most of the above roles of facilitators are needed only during start-up. As project teams and team members acquire training and experience in carrying out quality-improvement projects, the need for facilitator support declines sharply.

Sponsors, or Champions

The teams are not attached to the chain of command on the organization chart. This can be a handicap in the event the team encounters an impasse. For this reason some companies assign council members or other upper managers to be sponsors, or champions, for specific projects. These sponsors provide the teams with direct access to a high level in the hierarchy.

QUALITY-IMPROVEMENT MANAGERS

Some companies go beyond the use of facilitators to help the quality-improvement teams. They create a category of specialist called quality-improvement managers (or a similar title). Following intensive training in the quality-improvement process, they are assigned full time to the quality-improvement activity. Their responsibilities vary but usually include

1. Assisting in project nomination and screening
2. Conducting training in the quality-improvement process
3. Coordinating the activities of project teams and facilitators
4. Providing consulting and support service
5. Assisting in the preparation of summarized reports for upper managers

Note that as in the case of the facilitators, some of the activities are needed only during the start-up phases of annual quality improvement.

THE LIFE CYCLE OF A PROJECT

Following selection by the council, the project is defined in a mission statement and is assigned to a project team. The team then meets, usually once a week for an hour or so. During each meeting the team reviews the progress made since the previous meeting, agrees on the actions to be taken prior to the next meeting, and assigns responsibility for those actions.

Gradually the team works its way through the steps in its charter. The diagnostic journey establishes the causes. The remedial journey provides the remedies and establishes the controls to hold the gains.

During all this time the team issues periodic progress reports as well as minutes of its meetings. These reports are distributed to team members and also to nonmembers who have a need to know. Such reports form the basis for progress review by upper managers.

The final report contains, as a minimum, a summary of the results achieved, along with a narrative of the activities that led to the results. However, as companies acquire experience in making quality improvements, the teams learn to look for ways in which their project has provided "lessons learned" that can be applied elsewhere in the company.

Cloning

There are many situations in which the remedy for a completed project can be applied to similar problems elsewhere. In regionally organized companies, a solution to a problem in region A may be applicable to similar problems in regions B, C, and D. In the case of manufactured goods, a solution to a problem in product model K may be applicable to models L, M, and N.

As companies acquire experience in the quality-improvement process, they make the project teams responsible for bringing such potential cloning to the attention of the quality councils and the pertinent line managers.

Replanning

For many chronic quality problems, the remedy consists of replanning some aspect of the process or product in question. That remedy may in turn become an input to revision of the planning process so as to avoid creation of new chronic problems during future planning.

We shall have a closer look at this potential for revising the planning process in the section Lessons Learned in chapter 4, "Quality Planning."

RECOGNITION

The term *recognition* is used here in the sense of public acknowledgment of successes that are related to quality improvement. Success consists primarily of results traceable to completed improvement projects. Auxiliary successes consist of such things as taking training courses and submitting nominations for projects.

When companies address the problem of recognition, they usually do a superb job. They enlist the collective ingenuity of those who have special skills in communication (human relations, marketing, advertising) as well as the line managers. The numerous forms of recognition reflect this ingenuity:

1. Certificates, plaques, and the like, are awarded for serving as a facilitator, completing training courses, or serving on project teams.

2. Project teams present their final report in the office of the ranking local manager.

3. Project summaries are published in the company news media, along with team pictures. Many companies have created special news supplements or special newsletters devoted to quality improvement.

4. Dinners are held to honor project teams.

5. Prizes are awarded to teams judged to have completed the "best" projects during some designated time period.

Published accounts of successful projects serve not only to provide recognition; they also serve as case materials for training purposes, and as powerful stimulators to all.

Communication

The communication associated with recognition can add greatly to the clarity and credibility of management's message. Human interest stories deal with the people behind the projects, their families, and their work environment. Well related accounts of successful projects supply a ring of reality to the earlier management advocacy and to the promises made in the training materials.

REWARDS FOR QUALITY AND QUALITY IMPROVEMENT

As used here, the term *rewards* refers to those salary increases, bonuses, promotions, and so forth that are more or less keyed to job performance. Our present focus is on those rewards that are keyed to performance on quality and on quality improvement.

Of course, job performance covers performance on numerous parameters: productivity, on-time delivery, and costs, as well as quality. In view of this, upper managers have generally concluded that quality-oriented rewards should be woven into the overall reward system.

Quality-oriented performances logically divide between

1. The long standing responsibility of meeting quality goals
2. The new responsibility of improving quality

Evaluation of Performance in Meeting Quality Standards

Job performance has long included meeting quality standards. The effect of the new emphasis on quality has been to raise the weight given to the quality parameter in the overall performance evaluation.

Automobile manufacturers have for years evaluated the performance of their dealers with respect to various parameters, including quality of service to automobile buyers. During the 1980s, the manufacturers demanded better quality of service. A strategy employed by one of the manufacturers was to increase the weight given to quality of service to a total of 50 percent; that is, quality of service received as much weight as all other parameters combined.

Evaluation of Performance in Making Quality Improvements

For most operations, quality improvement is a new parameter. This new parameter must be woven into the performance evaluation system for all levels of the hierarchy. Failure to do so sends a strong signal to the operating managers: quality improvement has low priority.

The newness of the quality-improvement parameter has required development of ways to evaluate performance—new "metrics" are needed. Some of these new ways are already in use; others are still undergoing development. Those already in use relative to projects collectively include

1. The number of improvement projects started, in progress, completed, and aborted
2. The value of completed projects, in terms of improvement in

product performance, salability, reduction in costs, and return on investment

3. The percentage of managers active on improvement projects

A further problem in evaluation relates to the performance of individual team members—how to evaluate each individual's contribution to a team project. As of the late 1980s, there was no consensus on how to do this. Until new ways are evolved, this evaluation must be left to supervisory judgment. For a case example, see McGrath 1986.

PROGRESS REVIEW

Upper managers, including the quality council, have two major interests in the progress being made on quality improvement:

1. *Progress on the key projects individually.* Certain projects are of high-level importance to an extent that commands the personal interest of upper managers. The project teams' progress reports help these upper managers to keep informed about the progress being made.

2. *Progress on all projects collectively.* Here the upper managers need summaries in such forms as are set out in the preceding section.

Such summarized information is not readily evident from the individual progress reports. It takes added work to analyze these reports and to prepare the summaries needed by upper managers. As companies acquire experience in quality improvement, they tend to design standardized reporting formats in ways that simplify preparation of the summaries needed by upper managers.

Usually this added work is assigned to the secretary of the quality-improvement council. This secretary (who often is also the director of quality) enlists the aid of the facilitators, the team chairpersons, and other such sources to help organize the information system. It is also usual to enlist the help of the finance department to validate the estimates used to evaluate cost reductions and return on investment.

Upper managers should *personally participate in the review of progress on improvement.* To this end upper managers should assign clear responsibility for establishing the organizational machinery needed to provide progress reports on key projects and on the projects collectively.

THE TIMETABLE

Typically it takes several years to establish quality improvement as a continuing, integral part of a company's business plan. This interval is disappointing to many managers. Yet such has been the experience of companies who have succeeded. (Most companies have spent the several years but failed to reach the goal.)

This interval of several years is made up of the following components or steps:

1. *Study of alternatives, and decision to go down the road of annual quality improvement.* This step usually consumes a minimum of six months.

2. *Selection of a test site and conduct of a pilot test* (training, pilot projects, and so forth). This step takes about a year.

3. *Evaluation of test site results, revision of approach, and the decision to scale up.* This step takes about six months.

4. *Scaling up across the company; merging into the business plan.* This step runs one to two years.

Carrying out all these steps within even a few years of calendar time has turned out to be challenging. It has required careful scheduling of the organizational moves, training, and still other elements of a complex change in culture.

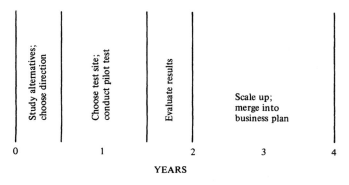

FIGURE 3-12   The timetable for installing annual quality improvement

THE ROLES OF UPPER MANAGEMENT

The picture of a company reaping big rewards through quality improvement is incomplete unless it includes some realities that have been unwelcome to most upper managers. Chief among these realities is the fact that the upper managers must participate personally and extensively in the effort. It is not enough to establish policies, create awareness, and then leave all else to subordinates. That has been tried, over and over again, with disappointing results. In contrast, the gratifying experiences have helped to identify the specifics—the criteria for what constitutes participation by upper managers. (Some of these have already been touched on. They are included here for completeness.)

Serve on the Quality Council

This is fundamental to upper managers' participation. It also serves as an indicator of priorities to the rest of the organization.

Establish Quality Goals

Goals are specific targets to be met. Each goal should be quantified and should have a target date for completion.

At upper management levels the quality goals are usually in the "macro" category, such as

1. Launching the new product model X at a quality level that is competitive with the three principal competitors

2. Reducing the number of incorrect invoices by 80 percent over the next three years

3. Reducing field failures by a factor of ten over the next ten years

4. Reducing design changes by a factor of ten over the next five years

5. Reducing software bugs at system test by a factor of ten in five years

6. Reducing the cost of poor quality by Y million over the next three years

Obviously such goals are "wish lists" until they are deployed to lower levels. These levels identify the specific projects to be carried out to meet the macrogoals. These same levels also identify the resources required to carry out the projects.

Lacking goals approved by upper management, the improvement projects have great difficulty competing against the traditional operating goals.

Provide Resources

On the face of it, quality improvement should be well supported by resources, since it yields so high a return on investment. The actual record is quite different.

Upper managers have generally provided resources for training personnel in awareness and in statistical tools. In contrast, most upper managers have not provided the resources needed to set up the infrastructure (councils, project teams, a process for improvement, etc.). Even where the project concept is accepted, the upper managers have generally failed to make provision for the time needed by the teams to bring the projects to a conclusion.

The time needed for quality improvement deserves some emphasis. To go full scale into quality improvement adds about 10 percent to the work load of the management team, including the upper managers. This time is consumed by such activities as attending team and council meetings, doing the homework, reviewing progress, and providing recognition. Of all the needs for resources, this one has the greatest personal impact on the team members.

Review Progress

Progress reviews become a regular, scheduled activity for upper managers. The methodology for this has been set out previously in the section Progress Review.

Give Recognition

The personal participation of upper managers is also required in award ceremonies and in the media activities that are an important adjunct of companywide quality improvement.

Revise the Reward System

Traditional reward systems have provided rewards for meeting quality standards but not for quality improvement. The reward system must be opened up to give significant weight to performance on quality improvement.

Serve on Project Teams

The reasons behind this form of leadership were set out earlier, in the section Teams of Upper Managers.

Face Up to Employee Apprehensions

A major purpose of quality improvement is to reduce the amount of work that is now being redone as a result of poor quality. Such potential reduction in rework is logically a source of apprehension for those now engaged in doing the targeted rework. Their obvious question is: What will happen to me if this work is eliminated? To a degree this same apprehension extends to other persons and entities: the supervisors of the affected areas; the colleagues of the affected workers, the labor union, and the community.

As seen by many employees, the company in one sense is asking them to participate in helping to eliminate jobs—their own jobs or those of colleagues. This potential conflict of interests becomes a reality unless the upper managers establish an action plan that provides an acceptable degree of assurance. The alternatives within such an action plan are well known:

1. Use the vacancies created by attrition (resignations, retirements, and so forth) as a source of jobs for those affected.

2. Retrain those affected to qualify for other jobs.

3. Reassign affected employees to other areas that do have job openings.

4. Offer early retirement as a means of creating job openings.

5. Identify job openings in other companies in the same community.

6. Provide lump-sum termination assistance if all else fails.

In some companies the upper managers have not waited for the apprehension to build up to an unacceptable level. Instead they have prepared and published a policy statement that aims to assure the employees that (a) the company understands the apprehensions and (b) is prepared to deal constructively with job displacements. The following is an example of such a statement:

> The purpose of the Quality Improvement Process is to create and maintain a healthy, growing, and profitable company with stable employment. While quality improvement activities may eliminate work, no employee will lose employment as a direct result of his involvement in Quality Improvement Process efforts.

THE ILLUSION OF DELEGATION

Efforts to Delegate

During the 1980s many upper managers undertook to secure quality improvement by

1. Establishing broad quality "goals" in such forms as "Quality has top priority" and "Do it right the first time"
2. Delegating the execution to the rest of the organization

This approach often included training in "awareness" and was usually accompanied by well-staged spectacles, slogans, and banners all designed to impress on subordinates that quality was now to be a top-priority goal.

The results generally fell far short of expectations. The upper managers who sponsored these approaches became collectively disillusioned. Some became bitter: their organization had failed them.

The upper managers who launched these approaches were experienced managers. They felt that what they were proposing was logical and feasible. They had established the goals, or so it seemed. They had delegated the execution. After all, ability to delegate is one of the essential skills of a manager. It was then up to the rest of the organization. Yet that organization failed to carry out its assignment.

Contrasts in Delegation

The reasons behind this collective disillusionment become clear when we contrast two very different delegations: (1) the traditional work loads within any organization, and (2) those recent

ELEMENTS OF DELEGATION	DELEGATION OF TRADITIONAL WORK LOAD	TYPICAL RECENT EFFORTS TO DELEGATE QUALITY IMPROVEMENT
Goals	Clear: schedules, budgets, specifications, etc.	Vague: Quality has top priority; do it right the first time
Responsibility	Clear: specific as to departments, individuals	Vague, general
Resources	Provided as part of the business planning	Not provided; not a part of business planning
Training	Oriented to job performance	Oriented to quality awareness
Measures of performance	In place: reports on performance versus goals	Not provided
Reviews of performance versus goals	Regularly scheduled; personal reviews by upper managers	Not provided
Rewards	Keyed to performance against goals	Not provided

FIGURE 3-13   Contrast in delegation

well-intentioned efforts to delegate quality improvement. Figure 3–13 shows how the author explained this contrast to a disillusioned upper manager, the CEO of his company.

Figure 3–13 shows that the traditional work-load delegation is clear, highly structured, and enforced by a system of measures and rewards. In contrast, typical recent delegations of quality improvement have been vague, unstructured and devoid of enforcement. It was unrealistic to expect that from the perspective of busy subordinates, something so vague could compete successfully against the traditional work load.

The middle column of Figure 3–13 is in effect a listing of those features of delegation that are decisive in securing priority of action from subordinates:

Clear goals take priority over vague goals.

Goals for which resources are provided take priority over goals for which resources are not provided.

Performances that are reviewed by upper managers take priority over performanes that are not so reviewed.

Here Comes Another One

For a really significant change to take place it is vital that upper managers be widely *perceived* as participating. The reason for this is the "here-comes-another-one" syndrome.

In most companies not a year goes by without a "drive" of some sort—a drive to improve productivity, human relations, costs. These drives are launched with advocacy and ceremony. The upper managers make the principal speeches at the launching. Often the drive includes beneficial education and training.

But usually there follows a series of negatives: added burdens are placed on the subordinates; upper management participation is no longer in evidence; the results do not live up to the predictions of the advocates; the drive does not persist—it shrivels up and is swept off center stage by the next drive.

In many companies, this pattern has persisted, drive after drive. In such companies it is quite logical for subordinates to draw the cynical conclusion, "Here comes another one."

The upper managers may sincerely state that this new effort to gain quality leadership is "different." It is intended to go on and on. No fooling. None of this will be persuasive to subordinates who have gone through a few cycles of such statements of intent followed by uninspiring results. What *will* be persuasive is unprecedented deeds carried out by upper managers—the very kinds of deeds previously set out in the section The Roles of Upper Management.

MOTIVATION FOR QUALITY IMPROVEMENT

To institutionalize annual quality improvement is a profound change in culture, requiring a correspondingly profound change in the systems of recognition and rewards. Lacking such a responsive change, the priorities of the operating managers will not change. Such was the experience of the 1980s.

In chapter 9, "Motivation for Quality," we shall examine the nature of the changes needed in the systems of recognition and rewards. Meanwhile, we can at this point notice a very practical aspect of the need to revise the system of motivation.

The effects of a successful quality-improvement project show up in the form of improved results—for example, greater salability and lower costs. However, these improved results do not necessarily show up in the performance measures of the project-team members. In a sense, most or all of the project-team members have spent their time and effort to improve someone else's performance! Accordingly, other means must be devised to provide recognition and rewards.

TRAINING FOR QUALITY IMPROVEMENT

To establish annual quality improvement requires extensive training of the entire management team in the quality-improvement process and its methods and tools. We shall examine all of this in chapter 10, "Training for Quality."

HIGH POINTS OF CHAPTER 3

As used here, "improvement" means the organized creation of beneficial change, the attainment of unprecedented levels of performance.

The most decisive factor in the competition for quality leadership is the rate of quality improvement.

The low rate of improvement relative to product deficiencies is largely traceable to the absence of an organizational structure for making such improvements.

The major wastes are interdepartmental in nature.

These major wastes are huge. In the United States, probably about a third of what is done consists of redoing what was done previously, because of quality deficiencies.

Quality improvement should not be on a voluntary basis; it should somehow be mandated.

All quality improvement takes place project by project and in no other way.

The return on investment in quality improvement is among the highest available to managers.

Quality improvement is not capital intensive.

Quality improvement does not come free.

To go full scale into annual quality improv
percent to the work load of the entire man؟
ing the upper mnagers.

The first step in mobilizing for projects (
lish a quality council.

Quality councils are well advised to ant؟
questions and, to the extent feasible, proviue a.._
of announcing the intention to go into annual quality improve
ment.

The first project should be a winner.

All knowledge advances theory by theory—by affirming or denying the validity of theories.

Failure to include quality improvement in the performance-
evaluation system sends a strong signal to the operating managers: quality improvement has low priority.

Typically it has taken several years to establish quality improvement as a continuing, integral part of a company's business plan.

It is not enough to establish policies, create awareness, and then
leave all else to subordinates.

To convince subordinates that quality improvement is intended
to go on and on requires that unprecedented deeds be carried out
by upper managers.

TASKS FOR UPPER MANAGERS

Upper managers are well advised to secure, within their own companies, the estimates needed to compare (a) the potential return
on investment in improvement with (b) the potential return from
other opportunities for investment.

If no quality council is in existence, the upper managers should
create one.

Upper managers should personally become the leaders and
members of the senior quality-improvement councils.

Upper managers should see to it that each quality council prepares and publishes a statement of its responsibilities.

Upper managers should direct that nominations for projects be

sed to all products and processes, business as well as manu-
ure—that is, big Q rather than little Q.

Upper managers should personally participate in the review of progress on improvement, and they should

Establish quality goals

Provide resources

Review progress

Give recognition

Revise the reward system

Serve on project teams

Face up to employee apprehensions

Quality Planning

This chapter presents to upper managers a universal approach for launching new products and processes in ways that will

1. Meet customers' needs
2. Minimize product dissatisfaction
3. Avoid costly deficiencies (costly redoing of prior work)
4. Optimize company performance
5. Provide participation for those who are affected

As in previous chapters, "products" is not limited to salable goods and services; it includes the outputs of business processes as well. Similarly, "customers" is not limited to clients; it extends to all who are affected by a company's products and processes.

DIVISION OF THE SUBJECT

This chapter focuses on the universal planning process—the steps that must be taken to determine customer needs and to respond to those needs. The application of this universal planning process to specific levels and functions within the organizational hierarchy is dealt with in later chapters, as follows:

LEVELS IN THE HIERARCHY	CHAPTER IN WHICH APPLICATION IS DEALT WITH
Upper management	6. "Strategic Quality Management"
Middle levels	7. "Operational Quality Management"
Work-force level	8. "The Work Force and Quality"

These same chapters will also deal with the organizational infrastructure needed to apply the universal quality-planning process.

QUALITY PLANNING:
DEFINITIONS AND RELATIONSHIPS

.erminology relating to quality planning has not been stan-
'dized. In view of this we shall define the key words and terms
.s we go along. Each of these definitions sets out what is meant
by a particular word or term as it is used in this book.

What Is Quality Management?

Quality management is the totality of ways through which we
achieve quality. Quality management includes all three processes
of the quality trilogy: quality planning, quality control, and quality
improvement.

What Is Quality Planning?

Quality planning is the activity of (a) determining customer needs
and (b) developing the products and processes required to meet
those needs.

In using this definition, note that quality planning is required
for numerous products—not only the goods and services that are
sold to clients but also many internal products, such as purchase
orders, invoices, and reports. Quality planning is also required for
numerous processes, many of which are internal business processes—for example, recruitment of new employees, preparing
sales forecasts, and producing invoices.

The Alligator Hatchery

There is an interrelation between quality planning and quality improvement. It is well described by the plight of the fabled manager
who was up to his waist in alligators. Under that analogy each live
alligator is a potential quality improvement project. Each completed improvement project is a dead alligator.

If our fabled manager succeeded in exterminating all alligators
then quality improvement would be complete—for the moment.
However, the manager would not be finished with alligators. The
reason is that *the planning process has not changed.*

In effect, the quality planning process is a dual hatchery. A benign hatchery produces new, useful quality plans. A malignant
hatchery produces new alligators. Quality improvement can take

care of the existing alligators, one by one. However, to stop the production of new alligators requires shutting down that malignant hatchery.

THE DAMAGE DONE AND UPPER MANAGEMENT RELUCTANCE

The damage due to deficient quality planning has been, and is, considerable. An important part of that damage is inadequate competitiveness in the market place, so that sales income is reduced. Another important part of the damage is the resulting chronic cost of poor quality. About a third of the work in the United States economy consists of redoing what was done previously.

Collectively, the damage done to sales and costs adds up to a problem of upper-management magnitude. This damage should not go on, but it will go on so long as that malignant hatchery remains in operation. Moreover, that hatchery has deep roots in the company. It has been running for such a long time that nothing short of leadership by the upper managers can shut it down.

For upper managers to provide this leadership requires that they

1. Understand how quality planning is being done
2. Understand how quality planning should be done
3. Provide the needed infrastructure and resources

Many upper managers are not enthusiastic about devoting the time needed to take such actions. It would be much simpler if they could somehow set broad goals to improve quality planning and then delegate—that is, stimulate their subordinates to meet the goals. That approach has been tried. It has failed because the prevailing ways of quality planning are so completely woven into the existing fabric of company activities. The leadership for change *must come from the upper managers.*

WHO HAS BEEN DOING QUALITY PLANNING?

Most quality planning is done by experienced amateurs: people who have never been trained in the concepts, methods, skills, and tools of planning for quality. These experienced amateurs include the upper managers.

Why Use Experienced Amateurs?

We use experienced amateurs because we assign responsibility for planning mostly on a functional basis. For example, the responsibility for the design of a purchase order (a product) and of a purchasing procedure (a process) is typically assigned to the purchasing manager. That manager then has the problem of planning for multiple parameters: technology, cost, schedule, and productivity, as well as quality. Those assigned to do the planning are likely to be expert in the purchasing function but seldom expert in how to plan for quality.

To make matters more complex our most important processes are multifunctional. The work performed in department A is then "handed off" to department B, and so on. These handoffs become numerous in such major processes as sales forecasting, new product launching, manufacture, and billing.

Even in "simple" intradepartmental cases, there is much quality planning by experienced amateurs. The department supervisor is usually a master of the technology—for example, word processing or plastic molding. However, the supervisor is seldom a master in quality planning.

In many cases, responsibility for quality planning is assigned to nonsupervisors. Obvious examples are the craft workers. They likewise are masters of their craft but are often only experienced amateurs in quality planning.

This situation is usually at its worst at the highest levels of the company, since strategic quality management has usually been nonexistent.

Use of Quality Professionals

In many manufacturing companies wide use has been made of quality planning by "quality professionals"—that is, quality engineers and reliability engineers. In such companies the organizational structure usually provides for these professionals to assist the line engineers and managers, who retain the overall planning responsibility. However, this arrangement has its own array of limitations, such as debates over jurisdiction and personality differences. The emerging consensus is that the planners (the experienced amateurs) should themselves become proficient in using the methods and tools of modern quality planning. This emerging consensus requires a massive cultural change: a major revision of the thought and behavior patterns of those experienced amateurs. In turn, such a change requires extensive training in methods and tools as well as the motivation to use them. Here again, leadership must come from the upper managers.

Use of Inspection and Checking

The deficiencies in quality planning have stimulated wide use of inspection and checking to detect and correct errors. In one sense this concept has value. Undetected errors are much more costly to remedy at later stages. However, this detection process does little to prevent the errors from happening in the first place. In fact, inspection and check can easily become a way of life, and help to perpetuate the deficiencies in quality planning. The method is competitive only if competitors do the same thing.

MULTIPLE LEVELS OF QUALITY PLANNING

In the foregoing discussion of quality planning by experienced amateurs there emerged four levels of quality planning:

1. *The worker level.* We shall examine quality planning at this level in chapter 8, "The Work Force and Quality."

2. *The departmental level.* We shall look at this in chapter 7, "Operational Quality Management."

3. *The multifunctional level.* This level is concerned with broad processes, such as new-product development, recruitment, purchasing, and billing. Such processes thread their way through multiple company functions. Chapter 4 is mainly concerned with planning such processes and their products (e.g., salable goods and services, recruits, purchase contracts, and invoices).

4. *The corporate or divisional level.* This will be discussed in chapter 6, "Strategic Quality Management."

The Processor Team

Activities at these four levels are carried out by various entities: the work force, supervisors, managers, project teams, the division, and the company. Each such entity carries out a form of processing. We shall use the term *processor team* as a generic name for any entity that carries out a process. (Processor teams often include membership from outside the company.) Our glossary entry is therefore as follows: a processor team is any organizational unit (of one or more persons) that carries out a prescribed process.

THE TRIPLE ROLE

Every processor team conducts a process and produces a product. To do so the processor team carries out three quality-related roles, which are depicted in Figure 4–1—the TRIPROL diagram.[1] The diagram shows the interrelation among three roles:

Customer. The processor team acquires various kinds of inputs that are used in carrying out the process. The processor team is a customer of those who provide the inputs.

Processor. The processor team carries out various managerial and technological activities to produce its products.

Supplier. The processor team supplies its products to its customers.

To illustrate, the company is a processor team. In its role as a *customer,* it receives such inputs as

1. Information concerning client needs, competitive products, and government regulations
2. Money from sales and investors
3. Purchased goods and services
4. Feedback from customers

In its role as a *processor,* the company converts these and other inputs into products such as sales contracts, purchase orders, salable goods and services, invoices, and reports of many kinds.

In its role as *supplier,* the company provides clients with goods,

[1]TRIPROL™ is a trademark of Juran Institute, Inc.

OUR ROLE

Customer	Processor	Supplier

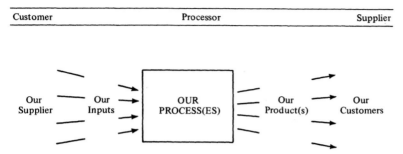

FIGURE 4–1 The TRIPROL diagram

services, and invoices, and provides suppliers with purchase orders, payments, and feedback. Information is provided to all.

The concept of the triple role is simple enough. However, the application can become quite complex as a result of the presence of large numbers of suppliers, inputs, processes, products, and customers. The greater the complexity, the greater the need for an orderly structured approach to quality planning. The backbone of this structure is the quality-planning road map.

THE QUALITY-PLANNING ROAD MAP

Despite the existence of multiple organizational levels, and despite the many varieties of goods, services, and operating processes, the quality-planning process can be generalized into one coherent, universal series of input-output steps. Collectively these steps make up the quality planning road map (Figure 4–2).

In narrative form the steps on the quality-planning road map are as follows:

1. Identify who the customers are.

2. Determine the needs of those customers.

3. Translate those needs into our language.

4. Develop product features that can optimally respond to those needs.

5. Develop a process that is optimally able to produce the product features.

6. Transfer the process to the operating forces.

] *87* [

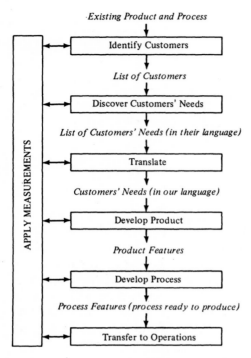

FIGURE 4-2   The quality-planning road map

This sequence is stitched together by several commonalities:

1. The interlocking input-output chain, in which the output for any step becomes the input for the next step

2. The triple-role concept, under which every activity plays the triple role of customer, processor, and supplier

3. The establishment of common units of measure and means for evaluating quality

It may seem surprising that one such road map is so universal: that it can provide directions for planning a very wide range of products and processes. Yet such is the case. Many practicing managers have invented and reinvented similar road maps. Many company procedures include similar road maps for specific products or processes. The road map has been field tested, extensively.

This same road map becomes our guide for the rest of this chapter.

WHO ARE THE CUSTOMERS?

The first step in quality planning is to identify who the customers are. Figure 4–3 shows the input-output diagram for this first step on the road map. To add a bit of detail:

The *input* is the subject matter of the planning—the product (or process) under consideration.

The *process* consists of the activities conducted to discover who is affected by the product.

The *output* is a list of those who are affected—the customers.

INPUT
Existing Product
and Process
PROCESS
Identify Customers
OUTPUT
List of Customers

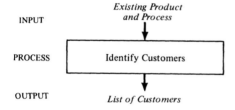

FIGURE 4–3 Input-output diagram for identifying customers

The Flow Diagram

The flow diagram (Figure 4–4) is a planning tool widely used to help identify the customers.

The flow diagram depicts the various steps in a process and their

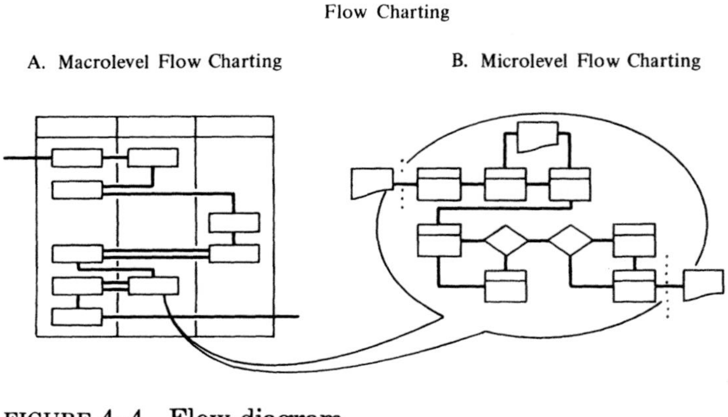

Flow Charting
A. Macrolevel Flow Charting
B. Microlevel Flow Charting

FIGURE 4–4 Flow diagram
Source: AT&T Network Operations Group

interrelation. When such flow diagrams are prepared by teams of managers, they usually derive multiple benefits, as follows:

Provides understanding of the whole. Each team member is fully knowledgeable about his or her segment of the process but not fully knowledgeable about the complete process. The flow diagram supplies the missing knowledge to an unprecedented degree.

Identifies customers previously neglected. A surprising finding by some test teams has been that much planning is done without first identifying all the important customers. It has been widely assumed that "everyone knows" who the customers are. But it turns out that without the discipline of preparing the flow diagram some essential customers are neglected or even overlooked.

The most widespread areas of neglect have consisted of internal customers. However, when teams specifically address the question, Who are the customers? they identify more clearly the external customers as well. For example, a government tax collecting agency found that its customers included the taxpayers, the Treasury Department, the Congress, the administration, the practitioners (accountants and lawyers who prepare the tax returns), the law courts, the public, and the media.

Identifies opportunities for improvement. Most flow diagrams exhibit subprocesses or "loops," which are a form of redoing what was done previously. Each such loop is then regarded as a suspect chronic deficiency that should not be carried over into the new or revised plan.

CLASSIFICATION OF CUSTOMERS

Any major process affects numerous customers. Often the number is so great that it is necessary to prioritize—to allocate the available resources in accordance with the significance of the impacts. Consequently a further step in identifying the customers is to classify the customers according to the size of the impacts. The most common such classification is by use of the Pareto principle (Juran 1975). Under that principle we classify customers into two basic categories:

1. A relative few ("vital few"), each of whom is of great importance to us.

2. A relatively large number of customers, each of whom is only of modest importance to us (the "useful many")

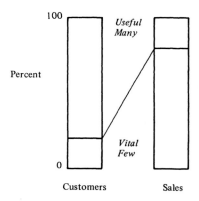

FIGURE 4-5 Pareto analysis of customers and sales volume

Figure 4-5 shows this relationship graphically.

For example, hotel rooms are booked by two types of clients:

1. Travelers who arrive one by one at random

2. Planners of meetings and conventions who book blocks of rooms far in advance

The planners of meetings and conventions constitute the vital-few customers. These planners receive special attention from the hotel. The travelers are the useful many, and they receive standardized attention.

Vital Few Customers

The vital few customers are usually easy to recognize. Obvious examples include large buyers of a company's products, senior managers, whether internal or external, and those who represent powerful forces with which we must reach an accommodation (e.g., government regulators, labor union officials, and influential members of the media).

Key Interfaces

Companies and their clients interface in multiple ways. The most familiar examples are seen in service companies. A hotel guest may have occasion to interface with many hotel employees, such as doorman, reception clerk, bellman, telephone operator, housekeeper, dining-room waiter, and cashier. Among such multiple contacts some may be *key interfaces*. To illustrate:

BUSINESS	EXAMPLE OF KEY INTERFACE
Banking	Bank teller and depositor
Restaurant	Waiter and diner
Hotel	Reception clerk and guest
Retailing	Salesperson and shopper
Telephone	Operator and subscriber

Part of the answer to the question, Who are the customers? consists of identifying the key interfaces.

A Customer Is a Cast of Characters

When the customer is an organization it is likely that the customer is also a cast of characters.

Those who sell supplies to hospitals soon learn that their customers include the hospital administrator, the purchasing director, the quality director, various heads of specialized departments (e.g., pharmacy, X-ray, histology, and cardiology), and various professionals (e.g., physicians, surgeons, and nurses). All have needs, and all have some degree of influence on what is to be bought, and from whom.

Obviously, the "cast-of-characters" concept also applies to internal organizations.

Internal Customers

Internal customers include the managers of the affected departments. Their influence on quality is considerable.

Internal customers also include the work force. Individually, they are among the useful many. Collectively, they are one of the vital few.

Consumers

Consumers are a vital category of useful-many customers. Their limited technological literacy forces them to rely heavily on fallible, biased human sensing in making their decisions about which products to buy. They discover the technological adequacy of the product later, through subsequent usage. The results of that usage are then influential regarding repeat purchases.

Suppliers face these realities in various ways:

1. Accept some consumer perceptions, bias and all, and then design products and practices to respond to those consumer perceptions.

2. Try to change consumer perceptions by such methods as providing demonstrations or opportunities for trial use of products.

3. Publish technological data and propaganda to stimulate changes in perceptions.

Classification Based on Use

A second system of classifying customers is based on what they do with a product:

Processors. They use a product as inputs to their process. They then perform additional processing after which they sell the resulting product to *their* customers. In consequence, the initial product affects multiple levels of customers.

Merchants. They buy a product for resale. As part of the resale they may perform some processing along with breaking bulk and repackaging. As with the processors, the initial product affects multiple levels of customers: the merchant, the merchant's clients, and so on through the distribution chain.

Ultimate users. They are the final destination of the product. In some product lines there is a market for used products, so that there are multiple tiers of ultimate users.

The public. Members of the public may be affected by a company even though they do not buy its products. The most obvious impacts relate to product safety or to damage to the environment. There are other impacts as well.

A ROLE FOR UPPER MANAGERS

The chapters that follow will make specific recommendations for action by upper managers with respect to applying structured quality planning at various levels. In this chapter, which deals with the generalized step-by-step planning process, there arise the following questions:

What role should upper managers play at each step of the planning process?

What role should upper managers play with respect to the quality planning process generally?

We have reached a point that requires a degree of direct involvement of upper managers with the overall quality-planning process and with specific steps in that process. One form of such involvement is through the auditing of the quality-planning process. Some of this auditing relates to the quality-planning process generally. (See the section Upper-management Auditing of the Quality-Planning Process.) Some of this auditing relates to specific elements of the quality-planning process. With respect to the step of identifying customers, upper managers should assure that the methods in use for identifying customers are able to *provide the quality planners with the essential customer base.*

Such auditing has direct application to the methods in use for identifying customers. In theory, it is possible to identify key customers (and other customers) without all the formality of flow diagrams and Pareto analyses. The planners can rely on mental images and memories, as many of them have been doing for years. However, the test results have demonstrated the superiority of the formalized approach.

ORGANIZING THE INFORMATION

An essential part of good quality planning is to use structure: to organize the information so that work is clearly defined and responsibility is clearly established. This structure begins with the list of customers. This list is entered into the left-hand column of a spreadsheet, as in Figure 4–6.

The customers may be grouped into logical categories. Vital-few customers and key interfaces are identified by standard symbols. The remaining columns will be filled in later, with information about customer needs.

CUSTOMERS' NEEDS

Discovery of customers' needs is the second step on the quality-planning road map. Figure 4–7 shows the input-output diagram.

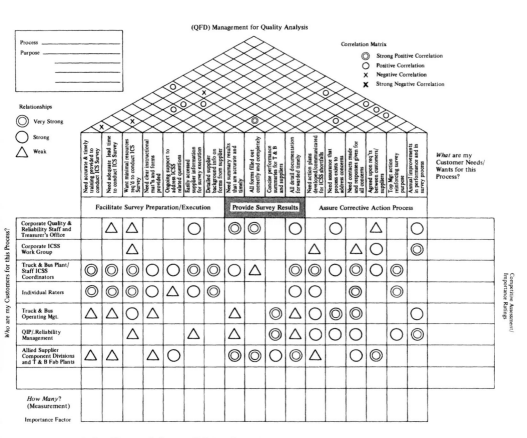

FIGURE 4–6   Spreadsheet: List of customers
Copyright 1988 General Motors Corporation. Reprinted with permission.

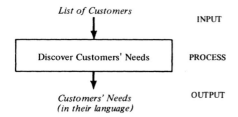

FIGURE 4–7   Input-output diagram for identifying customers' needs

Stated Needs and Real Needs

Human beings need such things as nourishment, shelter, and transportation. To meet these needs they may buy (or lease) food, dwellings, and bicycles. So at the very outset, suppliers should secure answers to such questions as,

What benefit are you hoping to get from this product?

What are the features that lead you to buy this product rather than a competing product?

Securing answers to such questions can be a lot of work.

During Ford Motor Company's development of the Tarus-Sable models, the company identified the key product features that were influential in consumers' decisions about which model of automobile to buy. The work of identifying these key product features (over four hundred of them) was an enormous undertaking (Veraldi 1985; Business Week 1986).

Perceived Needs

With growing affluence, customers' needs proliferate into areas that can be baffling to technologists. Identical goods and services command radically different prices, depending on the shops in which they are sold: budget, deluxe, or intermediate. Consumers can develop brand loyalties and mind-sets to an extent that makes the facts academic. An example is the Stew Leonard fish story.

Some customers refused to buy fish wrapped in transparent paper. To them wrapped fish was not fresh fish; the only fresh fish was unwrapped fish on ice. Leonard then added a fish bar with ice in it. The sale of wrapped fish did not decline, but total fish sales doubled.

Cultural Needs

Cultural needs abound. Among internal customers they relate to such needs as job security, self-respect, respect of others, continuity of behavior patterns, and still other elements of what are broadly called cultural values. Although such needs are real, they are seldom stated openly. Instead they are stated in disguised form. For example, a proposed new process threatens to eliminate the need for some human expertise; the expertise will be built into the technology. The present human experts will resist introduction of the new process. Their reasons will be on plausible grounds—the effect on costs, on other customer needs, etc. The one reason they will not give is, "This change will reduce my status."

Needs Traceable to Unintended Use

Many quality failures arise because the customer uses the product in a manner different from that intended by the supplier. This practice takes many forms. Untrained workers are assigned to processes requiring trained workers. The truck is overloaded; the tires are underinflated; the oil is never changed. Documents are misfiled.

Planners should dig in and learn what will be the actual use (and misuse) and what are the associated costs. Acquiring such information obviously requires close teamwork between supplier and customer.

Lessons for Quality Planners

Clearly quality planning will be deficient if the knowledge of customers' needs is deficient. The quality planners must accept the reality that in a competitive society the customers have the last word. The customers' needs may be unstated; they may seem "unreal." Yet the customers' needs must be discovered, and they must be acted on. (See Muroi (1987) for a Japanese case example of identifying customer needs and then using the resulting information for quality planning.)

METHODS FOR DISCOVERING CUSTOMERS' NEEDS

There are several principal methods in use.

Be a Customer

In some cases it is feasible for the planners to use the product and so acquire first-hand experience as a customer.

In other cases work may be organized to reduce the number of "handoffs." A process that employs twenty clerical steps may be redesigned so that one person does all the steps. That person becomes his or her own customer, over and over again. In like manner, an assembly line may be abolished, so that one worker assembles the complete unit. Similarly, craftsmen who make a complete product from basic materials are their own customers, over and over again.

Alternatively, the role of customer may be carried out through training. For example, some hotel chains require prospective hotel managers to work successively in the various hotel departments: dining room, housekeeping, finance, reception. Similar rotational practices are followed by some members of other chains, for example, banks and supermarkets. In certain Japanese manufacturing companies the product designers undergo training that includes participation as follows:

In the factory they spend time at various production stations so that they *make* the kinds of product they will be designing.

In retail stores they *sell* the kinds of products they will be designing.

In service shops they *repair* the kinds of products they will be designing.

Communicate with Customers

This is the most widely used form of discovering customers' needs. It is adaptable to a great many types of supplier-customer relationships.

A good deal of this communication takes place at the initiative of customers. In the case of external customers it takes such forms as complaints, returns, and claims (including lawsuits). Each of these product *dissatisfactions* requires individual redress. Collectively they can also be a threat to the marketability of a product.

A maker of household appliances was competitive with respect to product features, price, and delivery dates. However, it was not competitive with respect to field failures and warranty costs, and this became a major source of customer complaints. Within several years the company (B) lost all its leadership in market share as shown in the following table:

| | | COMPANIES WHO WERE LEADERS | | |
| | | IN MARKET SHARE DURING: | | |
PRODUCT MODEL	BASE YEAR	BASE YEAR PLUS ONE	BASE YEAR PLUS TWO	BASE YEAR PLUS THREE
High price	A	C	C	C
Middle price	B	B	C	C
Low price	C	C	C	C
Special	B	B	B	C

The foregoing table became influential in stimulating the upper managers of company B to take action to improve product reliability.

Internal customers also take the initiative to communicate cases of product dissatisfaction. These are usually stimulated by excess costs and delays that are traceable to poor quality received from supplier departments. Each such case demands redress. Collectively they can add up to a shockingly high cost of poor quality. They are also a threat to morale—to the ability of company personnel to work together as a team.

Companies also need communication on product *satisfaction*—why customers buy the product. Information about product satisfaction seldom comes through customers' initiatives. Instead, companies must take the initiative to conduct the necessary market research.

Communication with customers is not limited to verbal methods, oral or written. Some of the most revealing communication is derived from the study of behavior.

Marriott Hotels observed that guests were ignoring complimentary bath crystals. So the company dropped them in favor of another free feature—cable television—which was far better received.

Market Research

To discover the quality needs of customers we make use of the tools of market research. As a minimum we need answers to the following questions:

Which product features are of major importance to you?

With respect to these key features, how does our product compare to that of our competitors?

What is the significance of these quality differences to you, in money or in other ways that might be important to you?

Beyond these basic questions we need to establish an atmosphere that permits a free flow of open-ended, supplemental questions as well.

Market research should also be extended to former clients and to nonclients. The "exit interview" can be used to secure information from departing clients. In the case of nonclients, the basic purpose is to discover why they are someone else's clients.

In the case of products sold to processors it is often necessary to communicate with *their* customers, since the impact of the products passes through. A similar need may exist with respect to merchants and their customers.

If the customer is a cast of characters the principal players are not necessarily those who sign the purchase contracts. For example, some companies who sell supplies to hospitals find it useful to establish communication with physicians and nurses through creation of professional councils.

Each of the vital-few customers should be contacted in depth. Such contacts normally require careful prior preparation—for example, identifying the questions to which answers are needed, soliciting customers' nominations for agenda topics, and sending the agenda out in advance.

The useful-many customers are too numerous to contact individually in depth. Instead, other methods are used, such as contacting a *sample* of the useful-many in depth, and using questionnaires or similar means of mass contact.

The useful many includes the work force. Successful communication here requires overcoming certain inherent biases that may be present:

An atmosphere of blame. If present, it always inhibits the free flow of communication.

The supervisor-subordinate relationship. The fact that the boss asks the question tends to influence the answer the subordinate gives.

Conflict in loyalties. Workers may be wary of communicating information that might create problems for their colleagues or for the union.

Overcoming such biases requires the use of special tools and precautions in data collection and analysis.

Simulate Customers' Use

A third way to identify the needs of customers is to simulate customers' use. Numerous product-quality comparison tests are conducted by trained specialists under controlled laboratory conditions, rather than by a consumer panel under conditions of actual use.

Simulation has certain advantages over study during actual use. During simulation we are able to exclude unwanted variables. Such exclusion enables us to determine with greater precision the effect of specific quality features on overall fitness for use. In addition, simulation is less costly than market research under actual field conditions.

Simulation also has limitations. Laboratory conditions do not fully represent operating conditions: they are "an imitation of the real thing." (That is the literal meaning of simulation.)

Customers' Needs Are a Moving Target

Customers' needs do not remain static. There is no such thing as a permanent list of customers' needs.

We are beset by powerful forces that keep coming over the horizon and are ever changing directions: new technology, market competition, social upheavals, international conflicts. These changing forces create new customers' needs or change the priority given to existing ones.

In the early 1970s an international cartel was able to raise the price of crude oil nearly tenfold. As a result, the need for "low fuel consumption" rose remarkably in the scale of priorities. In turn, this cascaded down to raise the priority of such customers' needs as fuel efficiency of engines, weight of motor vehicles, and weight of components.

SYSTEMATIC ORGANIZATION OF NEEDS

The needs of customers are so numerous that planners have evolved systematic approaches to deal with such large numbers. One of these systems organizes customers' needs into a logical interrelated pyramid of needs: primary, secondary, tertiary, and so on.

The automobile is a widely understood example. The primary customer need is transportation. The secondary needs consist of such things as safety, comfort, economy, spaciousness, durability, and appearance (not necessarily in that order). One of these secondary needs—economy—gives rise to tertiary customer needs such as low purchase price, low financing cost, low operating and maintenance cost, and high resale value.

In turn, the tertiary need of low operating and maintenance cost breaks down into further needs such as warranty coverage, fuel efficiency, dependability, and adequate service. These breakdowns continue until each need becomes definable in technological terms.

Despite the fact that customer needs can become very numerous, each requires specific quality planning. Each requires a means of measurement, a goal , a product design, and a process design. To simplify life for the planner, and to assure that nothing is missed, the needs are arrayed in an orderly fashion.

The Spreadsheet

The most convenient form of orderly arrangement is the spreadsheet (matrix, quality table, etc.). In the spreadsheet, the customers' needs are listed in the left-hand column so that each horizontal row is devoted to a single need. Primary, secondary and tertiary needs (and so on) are distinguished by differences in the amount of indentation from the left-hand margin. Figure 4–8 lists some customer needs for automotive travel.

In Figure 4–8 only the left-hand columns of the spreadsheet have been filled in. The remaining (vertical) columns will be filled in as the quality planning progresses. The columns will show such information as product features, units of measure, and goals. The intersections of rows and columns are in due course filled in with coded designations to show priorities, planning decisions, and actions.

Note: Spreadsheets must be prepared for the needs of *internal*

Where we are on the spreadsheet:

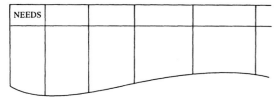

NEEDS				

NEEDS		
Primary	Secondary	Tertiary
Economy	Low purchase price	≈
	High trade-in value	∼
	Low financing cost	≈
	Low operating and maintenance cost	Warranty coverage
		Fuel efficiency
		Dependability
		Adequate service
	High resale value	≈
∼		

FIGURE 4–8   Spreadsheet: Customer needs

customers as well as external customers. Many quality-planning projects are concerned with internal processes and procedures whose impact is mainly on internal customers.

A ROLE FOR UPPER MANAGERS

Many upper managers involve themselves in the discovery of customer needs. They do so by methods such as

1. Visits with key customers

2. Review of reports on market researches, sales, customer service, product dissatisfactions, etc.

3. Attendance at industry conferences and shows

Upper managers who carry out such activities are able to provide the rest of the organization with insights and perspectives that might otherwise escape emphasis. In addition such activities reduce the likelihood of upper managers being stampeded by specific instances of product failures.

In contrast, few upper managers have involved themselves with the *methods* used to discover what the needs of customers are. These methods are the means for carrying out a vital part of the quality-planning process. It follows that upper managers should, as part of their auditing of the quality-planning process, assure that the methods used for determining customer needs *provide the inputs essential for subsequent product and process development.*

TRANSLATION

Customer needs may be stated in any of several languages:

1. The customer's language
2. The producer or supplier's ("our") language
3. A common language

When customer needs are stated in the customer's language, it becomes necessary to translate such needs into either our language or a common language. This necessity applies to internal customers as well as to external customers.

The translation takes the form of an input-output diagram (Figure 4–9).

Vague Terminology and Multiple Dialects

Translation within and between companies is plagued by the limitations of language. Identical words have multiple meanings. Descriptive words do not describe with technological precision. Various company functions employ local dialects that are often not understood by other functions. The concept of what is important varies widely from function to function.

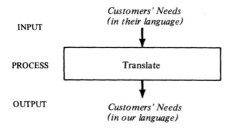

INPUT

PROCESS

OUTPUT

FIGURE 4-9   Input-output diagram for translation

A simple example is the multiple dialects within the company hierarchy. At the bottom is the common language of things; at the top is the common language of money. Those in the middle need to be bilingual. Figure 4-10 shows this hierarchy in graphic form.

To deal with all this confusion requires special processes and special tools.

Special Organization to Translate

In the case of external customers the volume of translation may require setting up a special organization to do the translation.

A common example is the order-editing (processing) department, which receives orders from clients. Some elements of these orders are in client language. Order editing translates these ele-

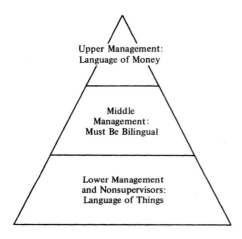

FIGURE 4-10   Common languages in the company

ments into the producer or supplier's language (e.g., product code numbers and acronyms). The translated version is then issued as an internal document within the company.

A second example is the technical-service department. The specialists in this department are knowledgeable about a company's products. Through their contacts with customers they learn of customer needs. This combined knowledge enables them to assist both companies to communicate, including assistance in translation.

The Glossary

This useful remedy requires agreeing on the precise meanings of key terms and then publishing the agreements. The publication takes the form of a glossary: a list of terms and their definitions (see the glossary to this book). The publication may be embellished by other forms of communication, such as sketches, photographs, and videotapes.

Standardization

As industries mature they adopt standardization for the mutual benefit of customers and suppliers. This standardization extends to language, products, and processes.

In the case of physical goods, standardization is very widely used. Without it a technological society would be a perpetual Tower of Babel.

All organizations make use of short designations for their products: code numbers, acronyms, words, and phrases. Such standardized nomenclature makes it easy to communicate with internal customers. If external customers adopt the nomenclature, the problem of multiple dialects disappears.

The airline flight guide publishes flight information for multiple airlines. This information is well standardized. Some clients learn how to read the flight guide. For such clients, communication with the airlines is greatly simplified. In effect, the client translates from his dialect into that of the airlines.

Measurement

Saying it in numbers is the most effective remedy for the language problem. We shall be encountering the application of measure-

ment throughout the remaining chapters. '
look specially at the nature of measureme
chapter 5, "Quality Control."

Application to Managerial '

A critical problem in translation is "produ..
ture. These include policies, objectives, plans, organ...
ture, orders (commands), advice, reviews, incentives, and audits.
The customers are mainly internal, across all functions and all levels. The problem is to assure that internal customers interpret these products in the ways intended by the internal suppliers. In turn, there is the problem of assuring that the responses are made in ways that minimize misunderstanding.

It helps to put these "products" into writing. The thought processes that precede writing are more thorough than those that precede oral communication. It also helps to hold face-to-face briefings, which provide opportunity for two-way exchange. And it is a big help if work has been done to establish glossaries, standardization, and measurement.

A Role for Upper Managers

Companies endure extensive costs and delays as a result of poor communication that originates in poor translation. (No one knows the size of "extensive.") These costs and delays go on year after year. The remedies (glossaries, standardization, and measurement) are known. However, the remedies evolve slowly because they share the common feature of "invest now for rewards later."

Glossaries, standardization, and measurement do not result from the conduct of day-to-day operations. Instead they are the result of specific projects set up to create them. (Typically, the vagueness goes on and on until such projects are created. In addition, such projects are inherently multidepartmental in nature.) Upper managers should accelerate this evolution by creating project teams whose missions are directed at *establishing the needed glossaries, standardization, and measurement.*

Fitting the Translations into the Spreadsheet

This can be done by entering the translations into the vertical column adjacent to the list of customer needs. (In some cases no

on the spreadsheet:

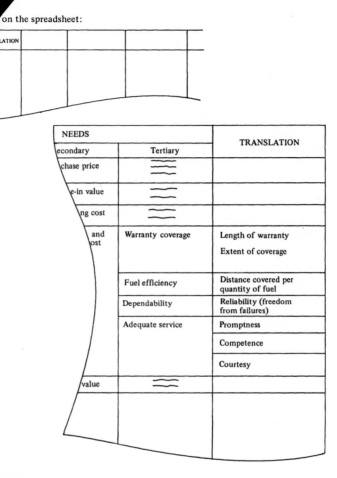

NEEDS		TRANSLATION
econdary	Tertiary	
chase price	≈≈	
e-in value	≈	
ng cost	≈	
and ost	Warranty coverage	Length of warranty Extent of coverage
	Fuel efficiency	Distance covered per quantity of fuel
	Dependability	Reliability (freedom from failures)
	Adequate service	Promptness
		Competence
		Courtesy
value	≈	

FIGURE 4–11 Spreadsheet: Customer needs

translation is needed; the customer needs are already stated in the producer's language.) Figure 4–11 shows the spreadsheet for the automobile needs updated to include the translation.

PRODUCT DEVELOPMENT

Translation of customer needs makes it possible to proceed with product development in accordance with the input-output diagram of Figure 4–12.

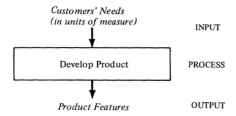

FIGURE 4–12   Input-output diagram for product development

Product Development Defined

Product development is the activity of determining the product features that respond to customer needs.

Note that in this book the word *product* is defined very broadly, so that the end result of product development can consist of such things as designs, reports, specifications, and computer programs. Also note that the definition of the term *product development* has not yet been standardized. The two most popular definitions can be seen by referring to the spiral of progress in quality, Figure 4–13.

In Figure 4–13 one turn of the spiral shows the usual progression of events for creating a (manufactured) product and putting it on the market. Some companies use the term *product develop-*

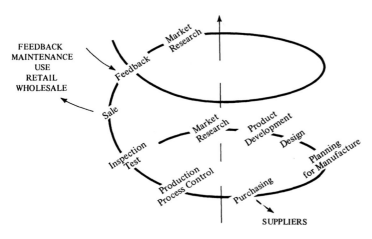

FIGURE 4–13   The spiral of progress in quality

ment to designate that segment of the spiral that is labeled "product development." Such is also the definition in this book. Other companies use the term to designate the entire progression of events—that is, an entire turn of the spiral. (AT&T calls this entire progression the "product realization process." Ford Motor Company calls it "concept to customer." We shall call it "one turn of the spiral.")

The Most Important Product

The term *product* covers a wide variety of end results. The most important product is the goods and services that bring in the company's income.

Note that within the spiral (Figure 4–13) there is a continuing series of deliveries of products from suppliers to customers:

PRODUCT	SUPPLIER	PRINCIPAL CUSTOMER
Information on needs	Client	Product development
Product designs	Product development	Process development
Process designs	Process development	Production
Goods, services	Production	Marketing
Goods, services	Marketing	Clients

Other Products

There are also many other products that go to external or internal customers. The following table lists some of these products, along with who the suppliers are and who the principal customers are.

PRODUCTS	SUPPLIERS	PRINCIPAL CUSTOMERS
Invoices	Finance	Clients
Purchase orders	Purchasing	Suppliers
Financial statements	Finance	Managers
Recruits	Personnel	All departments
Office Space	Office service	All office departments
Legal advice	Legal department	All departments

Product Features: The Criteria

Ideally every product feature should meet certain basic criteria:

1. *Meets the needs of our customers.* "Needs" here means all customers' needs: stated, perceived, real, and cultural.

2. *Meets our needs as a supplier,* including the needs of our internal customers.

3. *Meets competition.* The fact that a product meets customer needs does not assure that customers will buy it; a competitor's product may be better, or give better value. Hence, meeting competition is an important criterion for product developers.

4. *Minimizes the combined costs.* Customers and suppliers incur costs when they use or supply the product, and each tries to keep their respective costs to a minimum. However, the true optimum as viewed by society is to minimize the combined costs.

The Disciplines

The product development function makes use of multiple disciplines for determining product features. In the case of goods, the major response to customer needs is through *technology.* This response is carried out by product designers (engineers, physicists, chemists, etc.) who employ the laws of nature and associated technological tools (e.g., tables of properties of materials).

Technology, although necessary, is no longer sufficient. Growing competition and society's dependence on quality now require that the disciplines for determining product features include the quality-oriented disciplines. The more important of these include

1. Models and data systems for evaluating and predicting product reliability and maintainability

2. Process-capability studies for evaluating and predicting producibility

3. Experiments for discovering the optimum result attainable from multiple converging variables

4. Spreadsheets for assembling numerous interrelated data into condensed, easy-to-grasp forms

5. Methods for evaluating cost of poor quality

6. Methods for guarding against human error

7. Decision trees, flow diagrams, and still other aids to quality analysis and decision making

Limitations on Use

Although these methods and tools can aid quality planning during product development, their use has been limited. In the great majority of companies the product developers have lacked training in the use of such tools; the training was concentrated among the specialists in the quality department. Collaboration was limited as a result of jurisdictional and personal differences. The overall result has been that phenomenon of quality planning being done by experienced amateurs. The basic remedy for quality planning by amateurs is to train the amateurs to become professionals.

Such a conversion will not take place without the initiative and involvement of upper managers. Therefore upper managers should take steps to assure that product developers *become trained in the use of modern techniques of quality planning for product development.* (For a discussion of training in this area of quality planning, see chapter 10.)

PRODUCT DESIGN

An essential part of product development (i.e., providing the product features required to meet customer needs) is product design. As used here, *product design* is the activity of defining the product features required to meet customer needs.

Product design is a creative process based largely on technological or functional expertise. The designers are design engineers, systems analysts, and still other planners. The end results of product design are specifications, drawings, and procedures.

A good deal of product design is technological in nature and is thereby outside our scope. However, the technology interacts with the methods and tools of quality planning. For example, a new design normally requires a test plan to demonstrate that the product features do meet customer needs. Design of such a test plan then involves such elements as reproducibility of measurement, variation in materials, sampling variation, and statistical significance. Proper consideration of these elements, along with interpretation of the resulting data, is best done with the aid of quality-planning tools.

Optimizing Product Designs

There is full agreement that product features should meet the criteria previously set out for the "optimum":

1. Meet customers' needs and our needs.
2. Minimize the combined costs.

Arriving at this optimum is in part a problem in technology. During the design of goods numerous variables must be manipulated: environmental conditions, properties of materials, and configurations of components. These manipulations (often called trade-offs) were traditionally carried out by use of engineering judgment. Now this judgment can be aided by some powerful statistical tools that simplify finding the optimum.

The Urge to Suboptimize

The major obstacle to arriving at the optimum has been the urge to suboptimize. This urge is obvious in relationships between companies. In market-based societies, the dominant tradition has been for each company to look out for its own interests: to meet its own quality needs and to minimize its own costs.

The same urge is also present within companies. It is fostered by the prevailing systems of departmental goals and by the practice of conferring departmental monopolies with respect to decision making.

Internal Monopolies

Many internal departments are given specific jurisdiction over certain areas of decision making. This jurisdiction is enforced through a monopoly on the approval of the documents that can generate action. Various critical documents do not become official until they bear the approval of the departments recognized as having jurisdiction. For example:

DEPARTMENT	JURISDICTION
Product design	Approve specifications
Marketing	Sign sales contracts
Purchasing	Sign purchase contracts
Staff departments	Establish schedules; issue procedures manuals; interpret regulations

The decisions inherent in such documents can and do affect quality. Yet the associated jurisdictions are generally interpreted as having a degree of monopoly over the respective areas of decision making. Cases abound in which the monopoly departments, to meet their departmental goals, have created problems and crises for internal customers. The remedy for misuse of these monopolies is participation by those affected.

Participation

Participation involves a dialogue among suppliers, processors, and customers, whether external or internal. This dialogue typically takes place through design-review teams or through joint planning. The benefits of participation are formidable:

Early warning of upcoming problems. "If you plan it this way, here is the problem I will face."

Data to aid in finding the optimum. The various customers are frequently in a position to provide data in the form of costs that will be incurred, process capability of facilities, and so forth. Such data are of obvious help in optimizing overall performance.

Challenge to theories. Specialist departments are typically masters of their own specialty but seldom masters of the specialties of other departments. In the absence of participation by those other departments, the risk is that unproven theories or unwarranted beliefs will prevail. Participation by the customers provides an informed challenge.

Creating such participation requires creation of an atmosphere of mutual trust. In turn, this requires face-to-face meetings, mutual visits to see and understand operations, the sharing of experiences and feedback, and the exchanging of critiques and ideas.

All this communication and sharing must be done with sincerity. Any "secret" holding back is soon sensed and resented. The resulting mutual suspicion is an obstacle to the free flow of communication, and thereby to finding the optimum.

Creating participation also requires a stimulus, since the forces of suboptimization are usually in charge. In many companies the necessary stimulus will have to come from upper management, because the habit of suboptimization is so deeply rooted. Upper management should, during its auditing of quality planning, assure that the product-development process *includes effective safe-guards against suboptimization.*

Joint Planning

An extension of participation is joint planning. Such joint planning is already going on in many forms:

1. Some service companies prepare and publish information to help customers analyze their needs. A widespread example has been in the area of energy conservation.

2. Many manufacturing companies offer a service of "technical representatives" to visit with customers, analyze their needs, and provide consulting assistance.

3. The "just-in-time" concept of manufacture requires extensive joint planning between customer and supplier.

Joint planning has the maximum potential for arriving at the optimum. That optimum can involve profound changes.

A major activity in the postal service is sorting the mail based on destination. It was determined by joint studies that companies who send out large volumes of mail were in a position to presort such mail with less effort than the postal service, and with resulting speedier delivery. In turn, the postal service established a discounted price for presorted mail.

The literature already includes reports of joint product-improvement teams that included members from customer and supplier companies alike. (See, for example, Kegarise and Miller 1985; also Branco and Willoughby 1987.) Note, however, that creation of joint teams that cross company boundary lines involves so much effort and so much cultural resistance that nothing short of upper-management participation can provide the stimulus.

Carryover of Prior Product Designs

Designers often face a choice of whether to "carryover" existing designs, adapt existing designs, or create new designs.

For unchanging customer needs, carryover of existing designs may be the most efficient solution. Some of these designs have been in operation for years, and their performance has met customer needs as well as competition. In such cases carryover not only reduces design effort and the associated time interval; it also reduces the costs and time required to conduct model tests and field tests for the new design. Some companies offer rewards to designers who make such efficient use of proven existing designs—for example, "Thief of the Month."

Carryover of existing designs can also do a lot of damage. This is certainly the case if the existing designs are seriously failure prone.

The original dry copier was an enormous success in the market place: it outperformed all previous methods of copying documents. The copier was also failure prone—a serious annoyance to users. Nevertheless the supplier's successive product designs carried over many failure-prone features, model after model. In due course the competitors found ways around the patents and came up with designs that were significantly less failure prone. The effect on share of market was considerable, and required the original supplier to revise its practices.

Carryover of failure-prone features is a widespread form of cancer. It is not self-healing; designers prefer to spend their time creating the new, not cleaning up the old. Here is yet another fruitful area for upper-management auditing: upper managers should, as part of their auditing of quality planning, assure that the practice of carryover of prior designs *has adequate safeguards to prevent the carryover of failure-prone features.*

Proliferation: The Need for Structure

A major phenomenon in all technological societies is the growth of technological activity, in volume and complexity. This growth gives rise to a proliferation of customer needs, product features, and process features, along with their myriad interactions.

When products were simpler it was feasible for product developers to keep track of everything in their heads. Then as more and more complexity set in, the practices of the product developers diverged. Some continued to keep track of everything in their heads. Others resorted to structure. They invented such things as spreadsheets, countdowns, and checklists to back up human memory and guard against human error.

More recently, there has emerged a widespread suspicion that lack of structure is somehow related to some serious deficiencies in the product-development processes. Product development seems to be a slow, wasteful, and deficient process. There are numerous design changes, unforeseen internal crises, and field failures. A product may be "developed" several times before all is debugged. This suspicion has raised some questions that should be addressed by upper managers:

Does this proliferation require that product development be conducted using a structured approach to deal with all the complexity?

Should a structured approach be mandated by upper managers?

A Role for Upper Managers

In the past, upper managers kept out of such matters; they were content to "leave technology to the technologists." However, in cases of great complexity the effects of proliferation become widespread: they extend into business economics, multifunctional relationships, and human relationships. These are matters that go well beyond technology and hence should not be left solely to the technologists. Therefore upper managers should, as part of their auditing of the quality-planning process, assure that the product-development process *provides an adequate response to the effects of proliferation.*

To provide substance to this audit, the evaluation should:

1. Identify the extent to which earlier cycles of product development have included redoing of prior work, and where this redoing has been concentrated. (See the section The Santayana Review, later in this chapter.)

2. Determine the extent to which such major concentrations could have been avoided by a more structured approach to product development.

The Pros and Cons of Structure

During their audit the upper managers should also review the pros and cons of a structured approach, and the effect of these on the company's situation.

The cons. It is a lot of extra work to prepare the spreadsheets (and other elements) of the structured approach. Moreover, to prepare the spreadsheets requires extensive collaboration with external and internal customers, again adding to the work of product development and to the length of the cycle time. The instinctive reaction of most product developers is to avoid such structured approaches. Generally they feel that their training and experience has qualified them to carry out their function, and that all that structure largely adds cost and delay without adding value.

The pros. The benefits of a structured approach include the following:

1. It is an aid to human effectiveness, supplementing human memory and helping to guard against human error.

2. It is an aid to participation in quality planning; that is, completing the spreadsheets requires inputs from the affected departments.

(For case examples of product development employing various elements of structure, see Iwahashi 1986; also Fosse 1987.)

The "extra work and delay" during product development is a fact that is obvious to the product developers and that should be taken seriously by everyone else, including upper managers. The expectation of a much larger gain can be depicted by a model such as Figure 4–14.

Figure 4–14 has often been used to explain the difference in the approach to product development in the United States and in Japan. Note, however, that this model is not necessarily persuasive to product developers. To many of them the model is an unproved theory.

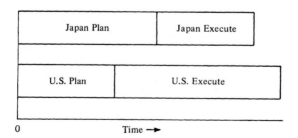

FIGURE 4–14 Brief planning and lengthy execution versus lengthy planning and brief execution

The Quality-Planning Spreadsheet

The spreadsheet (also matrix, quality table, etc.) is the primary tool used during a structured approach to quality planning.

Some Generic Spreadsheets

During the process of launching new products, use is made of three generic forms of spreadsheet, Figures 4–15, 4–16, and 4–17.

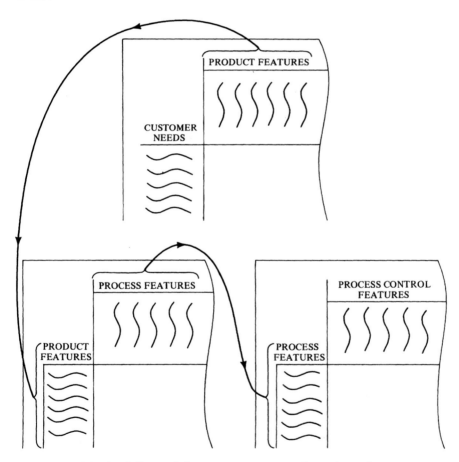

FIGURE 4–15 (*top*) Spreadsheet: customer needs and product features; FIGURE 4–16 (*bottom left*) Spreadsheet: Product features and process features; FIGURE 4–17 Spreadsheet: Process features and process control features

In the first of these spreadsheets the customer needs are listed in the horizontal rows. The vertical columns are then used to accumulate the product features required to meet those customer needs.

In the second generic spreadsheet the product features are moved into the horizontal rows. The vertical columns are then used to accumulate the process features required to produce the product features.

In the third generic spreadsheet the process features are moved into the horizontal rows. The vertical columns are then used to accumulate the process control features needed to keep the process at its planned level of operation.

Use of Standardized Symbols

Experience with spreadsheets has resulted in the creation of symbols to express relationships. (Some of these symbols are undergoing standardization.) Figure 4–18 shows a segment of the relationship of customer needs to product features (quality characteristics) for ink used in pens (Iwahashi 1986).

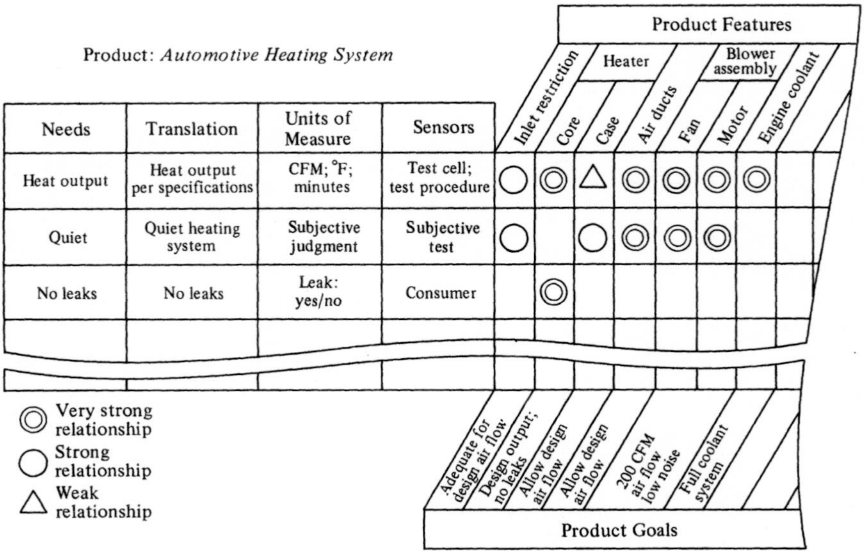

FIGURE 4–18 Example of spreadsheet showing standardized symbols

For complex products the totality of information (customer needs, product features, and processing features) becomes huge and extends over many spreadsheets. Planners and operations personnel are required to tune into and out of this array of information, over and over again. They are helped considerably if the spreadsheets and symbols have standardized formats.

Limitations of Spreadsheets

It is a fact that the spreadsheet assembles a great deal of information into condensed, convenient form, and is clearly an aid to a systematic approach. Through judicious use of symbols, a great deal of information can be compressed into a small space.

It is also easy to be carried away by the elegance and convenience of the spreadsheet. The spreadsheet *does not provide answers;* it is mostly a depository for answers. For example, a column in a spreadsheet can easily be headed up "salability." However, to evaluate salability can require extensive data collection and analysis.

Other Tools

The structured approach to quality planning for product development makes use of a wide assortment of tools beyond the spreadsheet. Some of these tools are specially designed to aid in defining tasks and responsibilities, such as the phase (or stage) system, and product subdivision or breakdown. Other tools are designed to conduct specific kinds of analysis, such as criticality analysis, competitive analysis, salability analysis, failure-mode and failure-effect analysis, and value analysis. A considerable literature is available respecting these tools, along with training courses under various sponsorships.

Chapter 10 includes a listing and some discussion of various quality-oriented tools.

QUANTIFICATION OF PRODUCT FEATURES: PRODUCT GOALS

At the outset of product development, customer needs are stated in *qualitative* terms. The resulting product features are expressed

CUSTOMER NEEDS (in qualitative terms)	RESULTING PRODUCT FEATURES (in quantitative terms)
Promptness	Delivery time
Reliability	Mean time between failures
Safety	Tensile strength
Roominess	Spatial dimensions
Purity	Parts per million of impurities

FIGURE 4-19 Qualitative customer needs and quantitative product features

in *quantitative* terms. To illustrate, Figure 4-19 lists some customer needs in qualitative terms (left-hand column).

The right-hand column shows some corresponding product features. Note that these product features are stated in quantitative terms. Such terms are needed to provide a basis for setting quantitative product goals—goals in terms of aimed-at values and tolerance limits. These goals then become the targets for the process developers and the operating forces.

To make matters more complicated, goals for many product features are established at two levels: (1) for product units individually and (2) for product units collectively.

To illustrate, a goal for promptness of service may be established at five minutes for any individual cycle of service. However, for the cycles collectively, the goal may be expressed as "85 percent of the clients shall be served within five minutes of entering the queue."

A similar practice is followed in the case of goods. A designer's specification for a mechanical component may define dimensions in terms of nominal values and tolerances. That definition then applies to each and every unit of product. However, the purchase orders, sampling tables, and so forth, may be designed to impose a limit on nonconforming units in terms of X parts per million.

The goals for product features of individual units are typically established by the product developers. The associated evaluations of quality are usually in terms of variables, that is, quantities on a scale of measurement. In contrast, the goals for the units collectively are typically established by the operating forces as a part of their system of control. The associated evaluation is usually in terms of attributes, that is, a count of nonconforming units relative to total units.

PROCESS DEVELOPMENT

This step on the quality-planning road map starts with the product-quality goals. It ends with a process capable of meeting the product goals under operating conditions. The input-output diagram is shown in Figure 4–20.

Definitions

A *process* is "a systematic series of actions directed to the achievement of a goal." As used here, the term includes all functions, nonmanufacturing as well as manufacturing. It also includes the human forces as well as the physical facilities.

As used here, *process development* is a generic term that includes the activities of product design review, choice of process, and process design, provision of facilities, and provision of software (methods, procedures, cautions). Our emphasis is on process design, which is defined as follows: the activity of defining the specific means to be used by the operating forces for meeting the product goals. This definition covers (a) the physical equipment to be provided; (b) the associated software (the brain and nervous system of the equipment); and (c) information on how to operate, control, and maintain the equipment.

Quality Planning by "Experienced Amateurs"

As in the case of product development, the quality-planning content of process development is carried out largely by "experienced amateurs"—for example, systems analysts and process engineers. An essential step toward improving process development is to provide these process developers with quality-oriented training. The

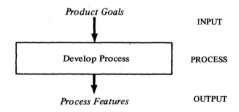

Product Goals — INPUT

Develop Process — PROCESS

Process Features — OUTPUT

FIGURE 4–20 Input-output diagram for process development

nature of that training is described in chapter 10, "Training for Quality."

PROCESS CAPABILITY

Planners are greatly aided by tools that help to predict the future:

Credit managers are aided by Dun and Bradstreet ratings on creditworthiness.

Engineers who design goods are aided by tables that set out the properties of materials and the failure rates of components.

The Concept

In the case of process development a major aid for prediction is "process capability": the inherent ability of a process to carry out its intended mission.

All processes have an inherent capability for performance. This capability can be evaluated through data collection and analysis. The resulting evaluation of capability becomes a valuable aid both during quality planning and during subsequent conduct of operations.

Process capability is an ancient and universal concept. It is applicable to manufacturing processes and business processes; to manufacturing industries and service industries; to processes run by the work force and processes run by upper managers. (Upper managers have long evaluated markets as to sales potential, and business units as to potential return on investment.)

Quantification

What is "new" is the trend to quantify process capability and to standardize the methods, tools, and terminology. This trend has recently been quite extensive in manufacturing processes. Such quantification enables manufacturing planners to judge in advance whether specific manufacturing processes are able to hold proposed engineering tolerances. This principle has been extended to supplier relations. Increasingly one of the criteria for contract awards is that the suppliers' processes possess process capabilities that are adequate to meet the engineering tolerances.

In the United States, one of the features of the movement known generally as "statistical process control" has been quantification of process capability. It is now widely accepted that companies that make use of such quantification of process capability during manufacturing planning will outperform companies that do not.

In manufacturing processes, quantification of process capability is based on evaluation of process variability. In quantified terms, process capability is equated to six standard deviations (six sigma) of process variability. Many specifications, contracts, and criteria now incorporate this definition of process capability.

Application of the process capability concept runs into a good deal of detail, most of which is beyond the scope of this book. One important element of detail is the need to distinguish between process *capability,* which is the inherent ability of the process, and process *performance,* which is the actual result achieved, and which often falls short of the inherent ability. The case example in the following section illustrates this difference.

Extension Beyond Manufacture

Quantification of process capability in nonmanufacturing processes is not yet at the level of standardization reached in manufacturing processes. Nevertheless the concept of process capability can help to plan for quality in nonmanufacturing processes. The potential is illustrated by the case of the insurance policy writers (Figure 4–21). Note that this case involves a service industry, a business process, human error, and the distinction between process capability and process performance.

The process consists of a "policy writer" armed with a keyboard. The inputs are mainly the customer's order, a blank policy form, the company manuals, and the training of the workers. The output is insurance contracts ready for signature.

During operations the policy writers fill in the blank policy forms with data from the various inputs. The policies then go to a checker who reviews them for errors. During a certain time period the checker reported eighty errors, as shown in Figure 4–21.

Policy Writer

Error Type	A	B	C	D	E	F	Total
1	0	0	1	0	2	1	4
2	1	0	0	0	1	0	2
3	0	(16)	1	0	2	0	(19)
4	0	0	0	0	1	0	1
5	2	1	3	1	4	2	(13)
6	0	0	0	0	3	0	3
27							
28							
28							
Totals	6	(20)	8	3	(36)	7	80

FIGURE 4–21   Matrix of errors by insurance policy writers

Those eighty errors when divided by six workers result in an average of 13.3 per worker. However, the workers varied widely in their error proneness. Four were well below the average—their errors numbered 6, 8, 3, and 7, respectively. Two (workers B and E) were well above the average—20 and 36, respectively. None was close to the average.

In the case of worker B, her total of 20 errors is inflated by 16 errors of a single error type. This was found to be due to her misunderstanding of a part of the procedure. Her performance is represented by 20 errors, but her inherent capability is represented by 4 errors.

In contrast, worker E made 36 errors, and made them in virtually all error categories. So the number 36 does reflect the error proneness of worker E on this type of work. This number was so high compared with the rest that it suggested worker E was misassigned to this type of work.

Still another significant phenomenon is the 13 errors of type 5. Every worker made one or more errors of this type. The total was significantly above the average for all error types. Analysis showed that the policy writers' interpretation of the instruction differed from that of the inspector. When this difference was cleared up the abnormality of error type 5 disappeared.

On the basis of capability (omitting worker E) the numbers of errors for the five policy writers become 4, 3, 5, 2, and 5, respectively. The average becomes 3.8, and each worker is close to the average. The number 3.8 would then represent our best estimate of the capability of the process.

Data Banks on Process Capability

The merits of the process-capability concept have led to the creation of data banks (also data base) on process capability. Such data banks are then used by planners in ways such as predicting results in advance of conducting operations, securing early warning of deficiencies, and choosing the best from the available alternatives.

Data banks on process capability are found in all company functions and in the outside world as well.

In the world of sports there are extensive records of the past performance of teams and individual athletes. These records are widely used to assign teams to various league classifications, determine handicaps and seedings for individuals, predict future performance, and establish pay scales.

Implications for Upper Managers

Upper managers are well advised to *become knowledgeable about the growing role of the process-capability concept.* In some cases there is no longer any choice: major customers mandate use of the concept and the methodology behind the concept. It has a growing role to play in all processes, including those carried out by upper managers.

PROCESS DESIGN

The end result of process design is a definition of the means to be used by the operating forces for meeting the product goals. To arrive at this definition the process designers require various inputs, especially knowledge of the product quality goals, of the operating conditions, and of the capability of alternative processes.

To avoid quality planning by "experienced amateurs" the process designers should also be trained in the skills and tools associated with the planning process. These include understanding of the anatomy of processes, of the concept of process capability, and of the nature and use of flow diagrams and spreadsheets. Of these skills and tools the most powerful is probably the concept of process capability.

Carryover of Existing Process Designs

The problem here is similar to that discussed previously with regard to carryover of prior product designs. In some cases there is much to be gained by carryover of a proven process. There is also the risk of carrying over an uninvited, unwelcome guest: a chronic quality problem that has never been solved.

In the early days of computer installations it was common practice to design the new data-processing systems to do electronically what had previously been done manually by clerks and paperwork. Often this approach carried over into the electronic data system the deficiencies of the prior manual system. The "manual mess" became locked into an "automated mess."

To defend against such uninvited guests, process designers should inform themselves about the process capability of the potential carryover.

Design to Reduce Human Error

All operating processes involve some degree of human participation. However, human performance is subject to various errors due to inadvertence, lack of technique, and bias. In some processes, including some critical processes, the limiting factor in securing high quality is the error proneness of the human participants.

Numerous tools are available to enable planners to reduce human error. See in this connection the section Human Sensing in chapter 5. (For further elaboration, see Juran 1988, page 96, and the associated discussion.)

Human error can also be reduced at managerial levels. An example is application of the redundancy concept by requiring that a jury of opinion check out critical estimates. In like manner, interdepartmental teams can be used to help arrive at optimal decisions.

ANATOMY OF PROCESSES

Most major processes consist of multiple operations (also called steps, tasks, unit processes, etc.). Examples of such operations are opening the mail and heat treating. Such operations are linked together in various ways, mainly by a combination of a procession (Figure 4–22) and an assembly tree (Figure 4–23).

An example of a sizable procession is the approach used by one large company for producing its credit cards.

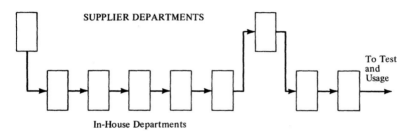

FIGURE 4–22   The procession

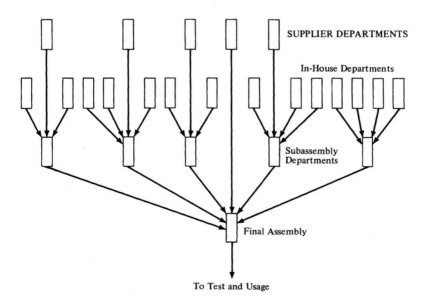

FIGURE 4–23   The assembly tree

] *129* [

The procession consists of twenty-two separate operations (steps), which take place within the domains of five different vice presidents. The process is slow; it takes several weeks to issue a credit card. The process is also error prone. For every one hundred applications that enter the process, only eighty-five emerge—the rest are lost somewhere. Some applicants receive multiple cards.

The credit-card case is an example of a "macroprocess" with no "owner." In such cases the problems are not normally soluble solely by refining the steps in the procession—the microprocesses. It is also necessary to review the basic planning—the anatomy of the process. Applied to the credit-card case, the critical questions would include,

Should such a process involve the hierarchies of five different vice presidents?

Can the number of steps be reduced dramatically?

An example of a successful reduction in the number of steps in a process is that of the telephone directories:

Every telephone company produces numerous telephone directories, one for each city served. In one telephone company the directories were prepared for publication using a procession of twenty-one clerical steps, each step being performed by a separate employee. (Some steps required more than one person's full time, so the total department consisted of thirty-three employees.) The reorganization gave each employee the job of preparing a complete telephone directory; that is, each person performed all the twenty-one clerical steps needed to do the job. The results of the change were stunning:

	BEFORE	AFTER
Annual turnover of employees	28	0
Absenteeism rate	2.8%	0.6%
Errors per 1000 lines	3.9	1.1

In our dialect, the anatomy of the process was changed from a procession to an autonomous unit.

CRITICAL PROCESSES

As used here, *critical processes* are those that present serious dangers to human life, health, and the environment, or that risk the loss of very large sums of money. Such processes must obviously be planned with ample margins of safety with respect to structural integrity, fail-safe provisions, redundancy, multiple alarms, and other safeguards of modern technology. Additional safeguards are provided by such methods as

A basic process design that provides the operating personnel with ample time to deal with crises

Training and qualifying examinations for the operating personnel

Rigorous structured maintenance procedures, enforced by audits

Systematic feedback and investigation of "critical incidents"

Beyond providing such safeguards for the process, the basic planning must also include *planning of the operating quality-control system.* This is quite different from what is done in less critical processes. There the planning of the control system is largely left to the operating forces.

The methodology for planning process controls is the same, irrespective of who does the planning. We shall look at this methodology in the next chapter.

OPTIMIZING PROCESS DESIGN

This subject has much in common with optimizing product design. (See the section Optimizing Product Design, earlier in this chapter.) The criteria are the same: to meet the needs of both supplier and customer, and to make the combined costs a minimum. The remedies are likewise the same: participation, design review, and joint planning. All are aimed at providing the planners with the same early warning: If you plan it this way, here will be the consequences in my area.

In process development a major area for internal optimization lies between the process developers and the operating forces. This area faces the same problems of internal monopolies as are present in the product-development area. The remedies are similar for both areas.

THE PROCESS DESIGN SPREADSHEET

For process design the spreadsheet takes the form shown in Figure 4–24.

In this spreadsheet the product features are listed in the horizontal rows. The vertical columns are used for entering the various process features needed to produce the product features and meet the product goals. The process features in the vertical columns consist of such things as processing equipment, instruments, and process conditions.

The intersections of rows and columns are then coded to identify the areas of impact—which process features are pertinent to which product features. The codes also indicate the nature and extent of the impact, for example, critical or noncritical. That coded information in the intersections then becomes an input to subsequent spreadsheets.

PRODUCT FEATURE	PRODUCT GOAL	PROCESS FEATURES				
		Parts Bin Arrangement	Wave Solder Conditions			
			SOLDER TEMP.	CONTACT TIME	ALLOY PURITY	. . .
Identity of components	100% correct part numbers inserted	* *				. . .
Component polarity	100% correct orientation	*				. . .
Continuity of solder joints	100% continuity		* *	* *	* *	. . .
. . .	. . .	. . .	. . .	. . .	. . .	

Key: * * Strong relationship
* Weak relationship

FIGURE 4–24 Spreadsheet: Product features and process features

PLANNING PROCESS CONTROLS

This topic is discussed in chapter 5, "Quality Control," beginning with the section Planning for Control.

MEASUREMENT FOR PROCESS DESIGN

Here the major measure is process capability: the inherent reproducibility of the process. This concept has universal application. In the case of manufacturing processes it has been widely applied and has undergone much standardization. It has also been applied on a selective basis to business processes, but in this area standardization has lagged. (For further discussion, see the section Process Capability, earlier in this chapter.)

TRANSFER TO OPERATIONS

Transfer to operations includes a transfer of responsibility from the planners to the operating managers. These managers understandably do not want to accept responsibility for results if the process cannot do its intended job—in our dialect, if the process lacks process capability or lacks controllability.

In some cases, proof of process capability can be provided by direct measurement of the process, as described in the section Process Capability. Where such direct measures are not feasible there are other ways. These include the following:

The dry run. This is a test of the process under operating conditions. The purpose is to test the process. Any resulting product is not sent on to customers.

A bank data-processing manager purchased computer software designed to replace manual processing of a complex data system. She tested the software by running the same input data through both systems—manual and computer—and then comparing the results.

The pilot test. This is a step intermediate between the planning phase and full-scale operations. The approach goes by various names:

A "test town" for trying out a new marketing plan

A "pilot lot" for testing out a manufacturing process

A "test department" for trying a new managerial concept, e.g., QC circles

The Acceptance test. This is a highly structured form of testing common in computer systems and applicable in other environments as well. Sets of initial conditions, inputs, relevant interventions, and operating conditions are prepared by a special team not directly involved in constructing the process being tested. These sets are intended to stress in relevant ways the important functionality and possible dimensions on which the process could fail. The test using these factors is then conducted either by a specific test group or by the operating forces. The creators of the process do not conduct the test.

Simulation. This takes such forms as prototype construction and testing, market surveys prior to sale, rehearsals, and mathematical models. Simulation is an imitation of the real thing, with many benefits and risks. The risks can be reduced if the operating personnel participate in the simulation planning and in the subsequent interpretation of results.

In some companies, transfer of the process from planning to operations is structured and formalized. An information package is prepared consisting of certain standardized essentials: goals to be met, facilities to be used, procedures to be followed, instructions, and cautions, along with supplements unique to the project. In addition, provision is made for briefing and training the operating forces in such areas as maintenance and dealing with crises. The package is accompanied by a formal letter of transfer of responsibility. In some of these companies this transfer takes place in a near ceremonial atmosphere. In other companies, formality is minimal.

LESSONS LEARNED

Early in this chapter we observed that the quality-planning process has been a dual hatchery that produced benign plans and also malignant alligators. The rest of the chapter then unfolded a quality-planning road map that if followed would produce benign plans without malignant alligators. To follow this road map the planners needed to make use of a structured approach and various tools. One of these tools—lessons learned—was not discussed in its own right; it was taken for granted. Now it is time to look specifically at lessons learned and at its close relative: retrospective analysis.

Lessons learned is a catchall phrase describing what all of us have learned from experience. In varying degrees, all living species store their experiences in their memory. Human beings go further. They extend their memories through records and libraries; through systems of beliefs, rituals, and taboos; through the design of their products and processes. Collectively, human use of the concept of lessons learned has been decisive in human dominance over all other animal species. So awesome a result suggests that the degree of use of lessons learned can also play a significant role in competition in the marketplace.

More specifically, lessons learned consists of conclusions drawn from history—from data on repetitive cycles of prior activity. An obvious example is the science of astronomy, which is based on numerous observations of prior cyclical movements of celestial bodies. Practical applications of this knowledge include the calendar and when to plant crops. This same concept of lessons learned from historical data has been widely used to improve quality of performance.

Years ago in the days of sailing ships a U.S. naval officer, Mathew Maury, was assigned to the Department of Metrology. That department was also the depository for the logs of naval voyages—hundreds of thousands of them. Each log recorded the conditions encountered by the vessel during its voyage: current speeds and depths, water depths and temperatures, wind directions and strengths. Maury compiled and entered this information into standardized graphic format on the navigation charts. For example, wind direction was shown by an arrow pointing downwind; the length of the arrow designated wind strength.

One of the first ships to use Maury's charts was the WHDC *Wright,* on a voyage from Baltimore to Rio. The previous record for the trip was 55 days. The *Wright* made it in 38 days. In 1851 the *Flying Cloud* sailed from New York to San Francisco in 89 days. The previous record was 119 days.

In our terminology Maury studied history. He reviewed the records of many prior voyages. He extracted from those records certain information that was pertinent to the planning of future voyages. He then organized this information into a form that was readily digestible by the operating personnel.

Industry abounds in opportunities of the sort seized upon by Mathew Maury. Sometimes, as in Maury's case, the historical records are already in existence. What is missing is analysis.

Many sports teams make a video record of each game they play. These records are often reviewed after the game. Such reviews obviously help to explain what happened during specific games, and this feedback is useful. What is seldom done is to review the games collectively in order to discover the vital few repetitive strengths and weaknesses of the macroplaying process.

There has been no convenient, agreed-upon term to be used as a label for this process of deriving lessons learned from retrospective analysis—conclusions drawn from data on repetitive cycles of prior activity. The author proposes to call this process the Santayana review.[2]

THE SANTAYANA REVIEW

The Santayana review is selectively applied in our industries. The most extensive application is to high-frequency cycles of activity. In contrast, it is underapplied to low-frequency cycles. A few examples will make this clear.

Application to High-Frequency Cycles

In this chapter we looked at several cases involving high-frequency cycles. They included the following:

[2]Explanatory note by the author: This is the second time I have ventured to name an analytical process after a historical figure. In the late 1940s I identified the principle of the "vital few and trivial many" with the Italian engineer and economist Vilfredo Pareto. This principle has since become a basic tool of managerial analysis, and the term "Pareto principle" has become deeply rooted in managerial literature.

The philosopher George Santayana once observed that "Those who cannot remember the past are condemned to repeat it." That is a terse and accurate explanation of the operation of the alligator hatchery.

Errors in invoices. Every year the electric power utility produced millions of invoices. About sixty thousand were in error each year. By tracking a sample of the errors, the company identified the major causes. Remedial action then reduced the errors to about five thousand per year.

Mass manufacture. In some manufacturing companies, goods are produced in volumes of millions of units per year. By measuring samples, it is possible to evaluate process capability. This evaluation then becomes a valuable input to quality planning.

Applications of the Santayana review to such high-frequency cases are numerous. The data are available in large numbers; it is even necessary to use sampling to avoid drowning in data. Many such applications are made without the need for upper-management intervention.

Application to Intermediate-Frequency Cycles

As used here, *intermediate frequency* is an order of magnitude of tens or hundreds of cycles per year—a few per month or week. Case examples in this chapter have included the following:

Rating of creditworthiness. A data bank (Dun and Bradstreet) secures information on many companies relative to creditworthiness. This information includes prior cycles of credit extended, along with the associated performance on paying debts. The resulting reports are widely used in financial planning.

Quality rating of suppliers. Many manufacturing companies maintain data systems on the quality of products received during prior cycles of purchase from outside suppliers. The resulting summaries are then used as planning inputs to future purchasing decisions.

Applications of the Santayana review to cases of intermediate frequency have been comparatively few in number. Yet the opportunities abound. To illustrate:

Bidding for business. Many companies must secure their sales through competitive bidding. In some industries the proportion of successful bids can run as low as 10 percent. It is quite feasible to analyze prior cycles of bids (successful as well as unsuccessful) in order to improve the proportion of successful bids.

Recruitment of employees. Some companies have successfully reduced the time to recruit new employees. They did so by first analyzing prior cycles of recruitment to learn which steps in the process were the most time-consuming.

The limited use of the Santayana review for intermediate frequency is traceable to some realities of the Santayana review:

1. It is a lot of work now, for benefits to come later, and with no known way of computing return on investment.

2. There is no clear responsibility for doing such work.

Usually these obstacles preclude compilation of lessons learned on any macroscale, unless the upper managers intervene. However, these obstacles do not preclude creation of compilations on a microscale. These abound in the form of local departmental and individuals' "squirrel's nests."

To organize Santayana reviews for macroprocesses requires multidepartmental project teams and a project-by-project approach such as is described in chapter 3.

Application to Low-Frequency Cycles

As used here, *low frequency* refers to a range of several cycles per year down to one cycle in several years. Examples on an annual schedule include the sales forecast and the budget. Examples on an irregular schedule include new product launches, major construction projects, and acquisitions.

Use of the Santayana review for such activities has been rare. Each such cycle is a sizable event; some are massive. A review of multiple cycles becomes a correspondingly sizable undertaking.

A case example is the historical reviews conducted by a team of historians in British Petroleum:

> The team conducts reviews of large business undertakings, such as joint ventures, acquisitions, and major construction projects. The reviews are concerned with matters of business strategy rather than with conformance to functional goals. Each review consumes months of time and requires about forty interviews to supply what is not in the documented history. The summarized conclusions and recommendations are presented to managers at the highest levels (Gulliver 1987).

A widespread activity that desperately needs application of the Santayana review is the launching of new products. Such launchings are carried out through a macroprocess. Each product launched has a degree of uniqueness, but the macroprocess is quite similar from one cycle to another. Such being the case, it is entirely feasible to apply the Santayana review.

Much of the time required for product development is a form of waste: redoing what was done previously, and extra work imposed on customers as a result of prior deficiencies. The extent of these delays can be estimated from a study of prior cycles. Such a study can identify which activities within the product-development cycle have caused the bulk of the delays, and how much delay they have caused.

Similarly, the cost of product development is high because so much is wasted. All that rework and all those crises cost money. The bulk of this cost of poor quality does *not* take place within the product-development department. An example is seen in a new-product project that incurred expenses as follows:

	$ MILLION
Market research	0.5
Product development	6.0
Manufacturing processes	36.0
Marketing planning	2.0
Total	44.5

All this was lost because a competitor had captured the market two years earlier with an adequate product.

Note that the bulk of the loss—80 percent—took place *outside* of the product-development department.

An Opportunity for Breakthrough

Companies have been slow to apply the Santayana review as a means for major undertakings. There is a serious need for such application in the product launch cycle—a turn of the spiral. Despite the opportunities for breakthrough, very few companies have reviewed this cycle in depth to establish the cause-and-effect relationships. The reasons are, again,

1. It is a lot of work.
2. It is no one's responsibility.

This impasse should be broken, and only the upper managers can break it. Upper managers should take steps to *establish the organizational machinery needed to apply the Santayana review to selected critical macroprocesses.*

The necessary organization consists of

1. A multifunctional team of managers to guide the review. Their job is to

   Define the mission

   Identify the questions to which answers are needed

   Review progress

   Apply the findings

2. A historian assigned to review the history of prior cycles and to provide the needed answers.

Forms of Lessons Learned

Lessons learned are compiled into various forms for use by human planners and decision makers. The following are among the more usual forms:

The data bank. This is a collection of numerous essential inputs specially organized to facilitate retrieval.

The check list. This is an aid to human memory—a reminder of what to do and what not to do.

The countdown. This is a list of deeds to be done, in a predetermined manner.

Merits of Lessons Learned

Once available, the foregoing (and other) forms of lessons learned exhibit some useful, built-in features:

1. They make available to any user the collective experience and memories of numerous individuals, organized in ways that permit ready retrieval.

2. They are of a repetitive nature: they can be used over and over again for an indefinite number of planning cycles.

3. They are impersonal: they avoid the problems created when one person gives orders to another person.

UPPER MANAGEMENT AUDITING OF THE QUALITY-PLANNING PROCESS

This chapter has set out a number of specific areas of the quality-planning process that merit upper management auditing. Beyond such specifics, there is a need to audit the overall approach to quality planning. Conduct of such audits requires adequate preparation—an adequate factual base for decision making.

The Factual Base

The most helpful factual base is derived from a review of prior planning projects—a review quite similar to the Santayana review. To secure such a review, upper management should designate a team to analyze some prior projects of quality planning for macroprocesses. Such analysis should concentrate on providing answers to results-oriented questions such as,

How well were customers' needs met?

How lengthy was the cycle time?

How extensive was the redoing of prior work?

The analysis should also examine the quality-planning process used to secure these results. Here the need is to provide answers to questions such as,

What specific features of the quality-planning process seemed to have been associated with well-planned projects?

What specific obstacles were encountered by the planners?

What can be done to help the planners (e.g., superior data base and training)?

A further goal of the upper-management audit should be to contribute to an ever-growing body of knowledge on how to plan for quality. This body of knowledge will include lessons learned with respect to critical procedural steps—for example, participation by customers, and essential planning tools. In due course such a body of knowledge is formalized into a guide to quality planning and into case material for training in how to plan for quality.

HIGH POINTS OF CHAPTER 4

To stop the production of new alligators requires shutting down the malignant hatchery.

Nothing short of leadership by the upper managers can shut down the alligator hatchery.

Most quality planning is done by experienced amateurs—people who have never been trained in the concepts, methods, skills, and tools of planning for quality.

The emerging consensus is that the planners (the experienced amateurs) should themselves become proficient in using the methods and tools of modern quality planning.

The backbone of a structured approach to quality planning is the quality-planning road map.

A customer is a cast of characters.

We have reached a point that requires a degree of direct involvement of upper managers with the overall quality-planning process and with specific steps in that process.

The customers' needs may be unstated; they may seem "unreal." Yet they must be discovered and acted on.

As a minimum we need answers to the following questions:

Which product features are of major importance to you?

With respect to these key features, how does our product compare to that of our competitors?

What is the significance of these quality differences to you, in money or in other ways that might be important to you?

Market research should also be extended to former clients and to nonclients.

Customers' needs are a moving target.

The basic remedy for quality planning by amateurs is to train the amateurs to become professionals.

The major obstacle to arriving at the optimum has been the urge to suboptimize.

The spreadsheet does not provide answers; it is primarily a depository for answers.

In the case of process development, a major aid for prediction is process capability: the inherent ability of a process to carry out its intended mission.

Human use of the concept of lessons learned has been decisive in human dominance over all other animal species.

The launching of new products desperately needs application of the Santayana review.

TASKS FOR UPPER MANAGERS

The leadership for change in quality planning must come from the upper managers.

The leadership for training planners must also come from the upper managers.

Upper managers should assure that the methods in use for identifying customers are able to provide the quality planners with the essential customer base.

Upper managers should assure that the methods used for determining customer needs provide the inputs essential for subsequent product and process development.

Upper managers should create project teams whose missions are directed toward establishing the needed glossaries, standardization, and measurement.

Upper managers should assure that product developers become trained in the use of modern methods of quality planning for product development.

Upper management should assure that the product-development process includes effective safeguards against suboptimization.

Upper managers should assure that the practice of carryover of prior designs has adequate safeguards to prevent the carryover of failure-prone features.

Upper managers should assure that the product-development process provides an adequate response to the effects of proliferation.

Upper managers should become knowledgeable about the growing role of the process-capability concept and the methodology behind the concept.

Upper managers should take steps to establish the organizational machinery needed to apply the Santayana review to selected critical macroprocesses.

] *5* [

Quality Control

This chapter provides upper managers with a universal process for conducting operations in ways that will

1. Meet established quality goals
2. Detect departures from planned levels of performance
3. Restore performance to the planned levels

The process presented here is a true universal. It applies to all types of operations, whether in service industries or manufacturing industries. It applies to all levels in the hierarchy, from the chief executive officer to the work force, inclusive.

WHAT IS CONTROL?

We define quality control as a managerial process during which we

1. Evaluate actual performance
2. Compare actual performance to goals
3. Take action on the differences

The concept of control is one of "holding the status quo": keeping a planned process in its planned state so that it remains able to meet the operating goals.

A process that is designed to be able to meet operating goals does not stay that way. All sorts of events can intervene to damage the ability of the process to meet goals. The main purpose of control is to minimize this damage, either by prompt action to restore the status quo or, better yet, by preventing the damage from happening in the first place. (Note that in some European countries, the word *control,* in various spellings, has a meaning synonymous with product inspection.)

THE FEEDBACK LOOP

The control process takes place by use of the feedback loop. The basic elements of the feedback loop and their interrelations are shown in Figure 5–1.

The flow of events progresses as follows:

1. The sensor (which is "plugged into the process") evaluates actual performance.

2. The sensor reports this performance to an umpire.

3. The umpire also receives information on what the goal or standard is.

4. The umpire compares actual performance to the goal. If the difference warrants action the umpire energizes an actuator.

5. The actuator makes the changes needed to bring performance into line with goals.

Control at All Levels

All company employees, from the chief executive officer (CEO) down to the workers, are active in quality control, and all make use of the feedback loop. However there are differences. One such difference is in the *subject matter* of control. At the worker level the goals consist mainly of numerous product and process features that are set out in specifications and procedures manuals. At managerial levels the goals are broader. They tend to become business

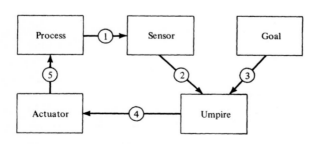

FIGURE 5–1   The feedback loop

oriented, and the emphasis is often on being competitive in the marketplace. In turn, the differences in subject matter require additional differences:

Sensors. At the worker level, these tend to be "technological"—that is, related to the process itself. Technological sensors may be instruments that measure physical, chemical, or electrical properties. Or they may be information generated in the course of providing a service, like counts of units, or chronological time. At managerial levels, the sensors tend to be summary data systems.

The scope of decision making. At the worker level this tends to be limited to decisions and actions that are relevant to conformance to specifications and procedures. At managerial levels the responsibility widens considerably.

These differences can be summarized as follows:

	AT WORK-FORCE LEVELS	AT MANAGERIAL LEVELS
Control goals	Product and process features in specifications and procedures	Business oriented: product salability; competitiveness
Sensors	Technological	Data systems
Decisions to be made	Conformance or not?	Meet customer needs or not?

Self-control

Ideally, responsibility for control should be assigned to individuals. Such assignment is inherently clear. It also confers status—a form of "ownership" that responds to some basic human instincts.

Ideally, responsibility should also be coextensive with authority. Applied to quality control this requires meeting the criteria for self-control—that is, providing the operating forces with the following:

1. *A means of knowing what the goals are.* This criterion is met by publishing the goals and standards.

2. *A means of knowing what the actual performance is.* This criterion is met by establishing the system of measurement, the frequency of measurement, and the means for interpreting the measurements.

3. *A means for changing the performance in the event that performance does not conform to goals and standards.* To meet this criterion requires an operating process that is inherently capable of meeting the goals and is provided with features that enable the operating forces to change the performance as needed to bring it into conformance with the goals.

The concept of self-control is also universal. It applies to everyone in the company, from the CEO to the worker level, inclusive.

The importance of the self-control concept goes beyond its value in establishing clear responsibility and ownership: self-control is a necessary prerequisite to motivation.

To hold someone "responsible" in the absence of controllability (see the following section) creates the risk of unwarranted blame and of divisiveness. In this way one of the tests of completeness of planning for control is whether the criteria for self-control have been met.

THE CONTROL PYRAMID

Any company has a huge number of things to control: the myriad features of the various products, as well as the myriad features of the various processes. There is no possibility for the managers and professional specialists to do all that control work. Instead the company designs a plan of delegation somewhat as depicted in Figure 5–2.

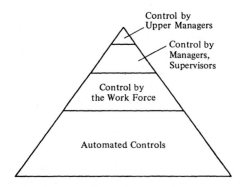

FIGURE 5–2 The pyramid of control

Control by Nonhuman Means

At the base of the pyramid are the *error-proof (foolproof) and automated processes* designed to keep on producing products that conform to goals. These processes control most of those myriad features. Yet they do so through feedback loops that operate with little or no human intervention other than maintenance of the facilities (which is, however, an essential control).

The remaining controls in the pyramid do require human intervention, at several levels.

Control by the Work Force: Controllability

Most human control is exercised by *the work force*—the clerks, factory workers, salespersons, etc. Many of these have been put into a state of self-control, so that they are able to detect and correct nonconformances. In addition they often are able to do this on a "real-time" basis—that is, the corrective actions do not lag significantly behind the detection of the nonconformances.

There also exist a great many operations for which the criteria for worker self-control have not been fully met. In such cases it is risky for managers to hold the workers "responsible" for quality. What is required in such cases is recognition of the concept of *controllability*.

If all the criteria for self-control have been met at the worker level, any resulting product nonconformances are said to be worker controllable. If any of the criteria for self-control have not been met, then management's planning has been incomplete. The nonconforming products resulting from such planning deficiencies are then said to be management controllable.

In the minds of workers and managers alike, responsibility for results should be keyed to controllability. However, in the past many upper managers have not understood the state of controllability as it prevailed at the worker level. Numerous studies conducted in the 1950s and 1960s showed that for operations at the worker level the proportion of management-controllable to worker-controllable nonconformances was of the order of 80 to 20. That ratio helps to explain the failure of so many programs that tried to solve the company's quality problems solely by motivating the work force.

There remains a considerable residue of management controllability for operations at the worker level. The extent of this should be evaluated by managers so that allocation of responsibility is in harmony with the state of controllability. To this end upper managers, as part of their auditing of managing for quality, should assure that allocation of responsibility for producing nonconforming products at the worker level is in *accordance with the state of worker controllability.*

Control by Supervisors and Middle Managers

These levels in the hierarchy make up the second layer of human control in the control pyramid (see Figure 5–2). At these levels quality control of specific product and process features is limited to the "vital few" under the Pareto principle. Most of the quality-control effort at these levels relates to groupings and composites of features and is based on data summaries. As a result, their control is after the fact rather than real-time.

The material that follows will elaborate on the way in which the feedback loop is utilized by these layers of human control.

ROLES FOR UPPER MANAGERS

Upper managers have two major roles relative to quality control:

1. *To personally exercise control with respect to the strategic goals represented by the apex of the control pyramid* (Figure 5–2). We shall look at this role in detail in Chapter 6, "Strategic Quality Management."

2. *To assure that a control system is established for the rest of the control pyramid.* The nature of this control system is spelled out in this chapter. Upper management's assurance of the adequacy of the control system is derived mainly through the auditing process. Here and there in this chapter, we shall identify specific features of the control system that merit such upper-management auditing. In addition we shall discuss upper management's auditing of the overall control process in the section An Assurance Role for Upper Management.

PLANNING FOR CONTROL

The feedback loop is fundamental to all control. However, it takes a good deal of planning to provide the operating forces with the means of applying the feedback loop to specific control situations.

Planning for control is preceded by product development and process development. These activities establish the product features required to meet customer needs, and the processes required to produce those product features. For a discussion of this, see chapter 4, the sections Product Development and Process Development, respectively.

In most companies the quality-control system is designed to go beyond control of product features and process features; the system is also used to control the quality performance of organizations and individuals, for example, departments and department heads. Such control is also carried out by use of the feedback loop. For example, many companies prepare and regularly publish scoreboards showing summarized quality performance data for various market areas, product lines, and operating functions. These performance data are often used as measures of the quality performance of the managers in charge. Planning for this form of control requires special design of goals and measures in order to apply the feedback loop.

Control Subject

Each feature of the product or process becomes a *control subject:* a center around which the feedback loop is built. The quality planner or planners identify each such control subject and enter each in one of the horizontal bands of the control spreadsheet. Figure 5-3 is an example of such a spreadsheet.

Additional sources of control subjects may be derived from government regulations, industry standards, mandates from customers, and so forth.

QUALITY GOALS

For each control subject it is necessary to establish a quality goal (objective). A quality goal is an aimed-at quality target: an achieve-

Control Subject ╲ Process Control Features	Unit of Measure	Type of Sensor	Goal	Frequency of Measurement	Sample Size	Criteria for Decision Making	Responsibility for Decision Making	...
Wave solder conditions:								
Solder temperature	Degree F	Thermo-couple	505 Deg.F	Continuous	N/A	510 Deg.F reduce heat 500 Deg.F increase heat	Operator	...
Conveyor speed	Feet per minute (fpm)	fpm meter	4.5 fpm	1/hour	N/A	5 fpm reduce speed 4 fpm increase speed	Operator	...
Alloy purity	% Total contam-inants	Lab chemical analysis	1.5% max.	1/month	15 grams	At 1.5%, drain bath, replace solder	Process engineer	..
.	.	.	.	.	.	.	.	

FIGURE 5-3   A quality-control spreadsheet

ment toward which effort is expended. Here are some familiar examples of control subjects and the associated goals:

CONTROL SUBJECT	GOAL
Vehicle mileage	Minimum 25 miles per gallon
Delivery time	85% within 24 hours
Reliability	Minimum 10,000 hours mean time between failures
Temperature	Maximum 140°C
Departmental error rate	Maximum 3 per 1000 documents
Competitiveness in performance	At least equal to the average of the top three competitors

When quality goals are established for departments and persons, the performance against those goals becomes an input to the company's reward system. Such goals should meet certain criteria. The goals should be

1. *Legitimate,* i.e., have undoubted official status

2. *Measurable,* so that they can be communicated with precision

3. *Attainable,* so that they can be met by application of reasonable effort

4. *Equitable,* i.e., attainability should be reasonably alike for all individuals at the same level of responsibility

Bases for Quality Goals

Quality goals are established from a combination of two bases:

1. Goals for product features and process features are largely based on *technological* analysis.

2. Goals for departments and persons are largely based on *historical* performance. (Such goals are attainable, since they have already been attained.)

However, many of these goals include provision for some improvement over history.

Quality goals at upper management levels are still in the early stages of development. The emerging practice is to base these goals on (1) customers' changing needs, (2) competitors' performance in the marketplace, and (3) outdoing historical performance through accelerated rates of improvement.

MEASUREMENT OF QUALITY

Attaining good quality requires precise communication among customers, processors, and suppliers. Such precision is best achieved when they "say it in numbers." To say it in numbers requires creating a system of measurement, consisting of

1. *A unit of measure*—a defined amount of some quality feature—that permits evaluation of that feature in numbers

2. *A sensor*—a method or instrument—that can carry out the evaluation, and state the findings in numbers, in terms of the unit of measure.

The Unit of Measure

The most widely used units of measure are basic technological units such as time in hours or temperature in degrees. Also widely used are units of measure for product features such as fuel efficiency in miles per gallon. A further widely used category is units of measure for deficiencies, for example, maintenance hours per one thousand operating hours, or percent defective.

Less frequently used but of increasing importance to managers are units of measure for departmental performance. Here are some examples:

FUNCTIONAL DEPARTMENT	EXAMPLES OF UNITS OF MEASURE
Product development	Months required to launch new products
Purchasing	Cost of poor quality (from suppliers) per dollar of purchases
	Percent of reorders due to poor quality
Manufacture	Cost of poor quality per dollar of manufacturing cost
Materials management	Percent of stock-outs
Sales	Percent of orders canceled
Credit	Ratio of bad debts to sales
Field service	Percent of service calls requiring second call

As companies get into strategic quality management, they find it necessary to establish units of measure for very broad aspects of performance:

QUALITY FEATURES	UNIT OF MEASURE
Competitiveness in the marketplace	Ratio of product performance to that of leading competitors
Cost of poor quality	Ratio of cost of poor quality to sales

(For further elaboration see chapter 6, "Strategic Quality Management," the section Measures of Quality for SQM.)

(Note that units of measure and sensors are needed and applied during all three processes of the Juran Trilogy. However, the basic methodology is discussed solely in this chapter, in order to minimize duplication.)

The Sensor

A sensor is a specialized detecting device. It is designed to recognize the presence and intensity of certain phenomena, and to convert this sensed knowledge into "information." This information then becomes the means of evaluating actual performance.

The wide variety of control subjects has given rise to a correspondingly wide variety of sensors. The best known are the numerous technological instruments used to measure product features and process features. Another major category of sensors is the data systems and associated summarized reports that supply information to the managerial hierarchy. There is also extensive use of human beings as sensors. Questionnaires and interviews (to evaluate quality of service) are also a form of sensor.

Human Sensing

Human sensing takes place at all levels of the hierarchy of measurement. At the basic data level, human workers must evaluate product and process features of a sensory nature, for example, taste, smell, and feel. Similarly, human workers must decide: Which accounts should be charged with these hours of time or this material requisition? How should this field failure be classified? At higher levels human beings must evaluate the performance of other human beings with respect to various criteria, some of which are not measurable. Still other evaluations must be based on incomplete data.

All human sensing is subject to human errors, which stem from various sources: inadvertence, lack of technqiue, conscious errors. A great deal of work has been done by behavioral scientists, quality specialists, and others to study the nature of human error and to provide remedies. Figure 5-4 lists the more common types of errors in human sensing, along with the available remedies. (For elaboration, see Juran 1988a, *Planning for Quality,* pages 89-96.)

Managers should understand that these errors exist and should also understand the nature and extent of such human errors, including their own. Therefore, upper management's auditing of the quality-control process should include *an examination of the provisions that have been made to deal with human sensing errors.*

If No Means of Measurement Exists

There may exist no means of measurement as a result of the lack of a unit of measure or of a sensor. The answer is to establish clear responsibility for creating the missing element or elements. This can be done by use of the conventional quality-improvement process. An improvement project is defined, for example, "Develop a unit of measure and a sensor for measuring phenomenon X." A

ERROR TYPES	REMEDIES
Misinterpretation	Precise definition; glossary Check lists Examples
Inadvertent errors	Aptitude testing Reorganization of work to reduce fatigue and monotony Fail-safe designs Redundancy Foolproofing (errorproofing) Automation; robotics
Lack of technique	Discovery of knack of successful workers Revision of technology to incorporate the knack Retraining

Conscious errors:
  coloration
  bias
  futility
	Design review of data-collection plan
	Removal of atmosphere of blame
	Action on reports, or explanation of why not
	Depersonalize the orders
	Establish accountability
	Provide balanced emphasis on goals
	Conduct quality audits
	Create competition, incentives
	Reassign the work

FIGURE 5–4 Human error types and remedies

quality-improvement team is then given the responsibility to carry out that mission.

Information for Decision Making

The ultimate purpose of sensing is to provide information for making decisions. These decisions cover a wide variety of subject matter, and take place at all levels of the hierarchy. The planning for quality control should provide an information network that can serve all decision makers. At the lower levels the information network should provide real-time information to permit prompt detection and correction of nonconformance to goals. At the higher levels, the information network should provide summaries that enable managers to exercise control over the vital-few control subjects. In addition the information should enable managers to (1) detect major trends, (2) identify threats and opportunities, and (3) evaluate performance of organizational units and managers.

] 156 [

To provide information that can serve all those purposes requires planning—planning which is directed specifically to the information system. Such planning is beyond the scope of those whose responsibility is to develop specific products or processes. Instead, the planning of the quality-information system should be done by a broad-based multifunctional team whose mission is dedicated to the quality-information system. Such a team properly includes the customers as well as the suppliers of the information. During its auditing of the quality-control process, upper management should assure that the organizational machinery for planning the quality-information system *includes the customers as well as the suppliers.*

ADJUSTMENT CAPABILITY

The planners should provide the operating forces with the means for adjusting the process to bring it into conformance with goals. Such adjustments are usually needed at start-up of the process, and are periodically needed during running of the process. Ideally, this aspect of planning for quality control includes meeting the following criteria:

Each product feature should be linked to a single process variable.

Means should be provided for convenient adjustment of the process setting for that variable.

There should be a predictable, precise relationship between the amount of change in the process setting and the amount of effect on the product feature.

To meet these criteria the planners must first acquire in-depth knowledge of the relationships between the process variables and the product results. To acquire such knowledge it is necessary to conduct designed experiments. These experiments not only can disclose the relationships; they also can provide the information needed to optimize product performance and process yields.

These statistically designed experiments are often part of a process-capability study. During the process-capability study, the process engineers and work force strive to determine the optimum performance of the process in everyday operation. This study includes

1. Determining what are the key process parameters
2. Determining how to control these parameters
3. Determining the levels of these parameters that will lead to optimum performance
4. Understanding the natural variability of the process

If the planners lack in-depth knowledge, the resulting products and processes impose chronic hardships on the operating forces:

1. Product performances are chronically below optimal levels.
2. Process yields are chronically low.
3. Corrective actions require extensive cut and try.

A major limiting factor in securing this critical knowledge has been the lack of training in statistical design of experiments. In the United States, the planners (e.g., product designers and process designers) have lacked training in this specialty. In large companies certain specialists, such as quality engineers, do have such training. However, it has been difficult to secure the needed collaboration between the respective departments and individuals.

The optimum solution is to train the planners in how to use statistical design of experiments. The training courses have long been available, but only a relative few planners have volunteered to take them. It has become necessary to go beyond voluntarism, and the emerging trends include mandating training in the design of experiments for the planners and making such training a prerequisite for advancement.

During its auditing of the quality-planning process, upper management should assure that the training of planners in statistical design of experiments is sufficient to enable them to *optimize performance and to provide the operating forces with process-adjustment capability.*

PROOF THAT THE PROCESS IS
CONTROLLABLE

Transfer from planning to operations includes transfer of responsibility for control. The operating forces become responsible not only for producing the product but also for maintaining the process at its planned level of capability. To carry out the latter responsibility requires that the process be controllable—that the planning has provided the means for carrying out the activities within the feedback loop.

An important part of this proof can be supplied by the quality-control spreadsheet (Figure 5-3). This spreadsheet makes it possible for the operating forces to understand, in considerable detail, the actual scope of the planning.

For *critical* processes, proof of controllability is best provided by demonstration. In consequence, the planning should include defining the terms of the demonstration, that is, the criteria to be met by the operating forces when faced with crises of the type that might arise during conduct of operations. These criteria consist of such matters as time of response to alarm signals, accuracy of diagnosis, and adequacy of remedial action.

ALLOCATION TO CONTROL STATIONS

Organization for control usually starts by defining specific "control stations." In the lower levels of organization, a control station is usually confined to a single physical area. Alternatively the control station takes such forms as a patrol beat or a "control tower." At higher levels a control station may be widely dispersed geographically, for example, the scope of a manager's responsibility.

A review of numerous control stations shows that they are usually designed to provide evaluations and early warnings in the following ways:

1. At changes of jurisdiction, where responsibility is transferred from one organization to another

2. Before embarking on some significant irreversible activity

3. After creation of a critical quality feature

4. At dominant process variables

5. At areas ("windows") that allow economical evaluation to be made

Definition of Work

The spreadsheet in Figure 5-3 summarizes this definition. The control subjects are listed in the left-hand column. The vertical columns then set out information such as

1. The goals for the product and process features

2. The evaluations to be made: the instruments to use; the frequency of measurement; the measurement procedures; the data to record

3. Interpretation: how to analyze the data; guides to interpretation

4. Decision making: what decisions to make; criteria for decision making

5. Actions to take; criteria for choice of actions

Who Does What

Usually there are multiple people associated with each control station: the work force, the supervision, planners (e.g., process engineers), inspectors, data collectors. Even within the work force there can be multiple categories: setup specialists, operators, maintenance specialists. In such cases it is not possible to answer the question, Who is responsible for quality? Instead it is necessary to assign responsibility in detail: who should make which decisions; who should take which actions.

A special spreadsheet is used to help decide who does what. For an example, see Figure 8–3 in chapter 8.

The essential decisions and actions are listed in the left-hand column. The remaining columns are headed up by the names of the job classifications associated with the control station. Then, through multidepartmental discussion, agreement is reached on who is to do what.

EVALUATION OF PERFORMANCE

The starting point is the measurements and observations made by technological and human sensors. The resulting data undergo processing to provide information for decision making. At the lower levels this information is often on a real-time basis and is used for current control. At higher levels the information is summarized in various ways to provide broader measures, detect trends, and identify the vital-few problems.

There is additional need to define who does what: who is to interpret the data; who is to determine what actions to take; who is to take the actions. In large organizations it is quite common to divide such responsibilities among different functions and levels.

Interpretation: Statistical Significance

In some cases the data are conclusive on what action should be taken. In other cases there is need for interpretation. In these latter cases it is usually helpful and sometimes necessary to provide the responsible parties with tools that simplify making interpretations.

A frequent problem is to interpret observed differences. The data may show that the present product or process differs from the previous evaluation. Such an observed difference can be the result of (a) a real change in the product or process, or (b) an apparent change arising from chance variation.

An apparent change is a sort of false alarm. It is a waste of time to look for the cause: the cause is not "findable." It is therefore useful to distinguish somehow between false alarms and real changes before trying to discover causes. An elegant tool for this purpose is the Shewhart control chart (or just control chart) shown in Figure 5–5.

Figure 5–5 shows a typical control chart. The horizontal scale is usually time, or some time-related variable. The vertical scale is performance. The plotted points show successive performances over time.

The chart also exhibits three horizontal lines. The middle line is

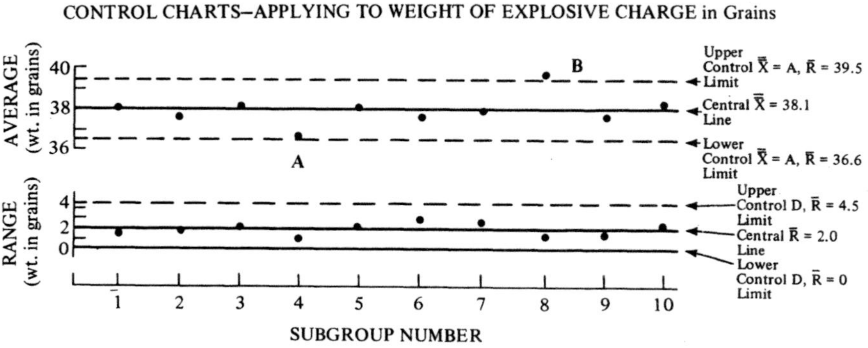

CONTROL CHARTS–APPLYING TO WEIGHT OF EXPLOSIVE CHARGE in Grains

FIGURE 5–5   Shewhart control chart

the average performance over some earlier span of time. The other two lines are "limit lines." They are drawn to separate false alarms from real changes, based on some chosen level of odds, for example, 1000 to 1.

Point A on the chart differs from the historical average, but this difference could be due to chance variation (at odds of less than 1000 to 1). Hence it is assumed that there has been no real change. Point B also differs from the historical average, but now the odds are heavily against this having been caused by chance (over 1000 to 1). Hence it is assumed that there was a real change, and that the cause is findable.

There are many types of control charts. The most important types (recent nonconforming; number nonconforming; average and range; average and standard deviation; number of nonconformities) are usually covered thoroughly in basic courses in statistical quality control or statistical process control.

Interpretation: Economic Significance

Ideally all real changes should stimulate prompt action to restore the status quo. In practice some real changes do not result in such action. The usual reason is that the indicated changes have appeared in such numbers that the available personnel cannot deal with all of them. Hence priorities are established based on economic significance or on other criteria of importance. Some changes at low levels of priority may wait a long time for corrective action.

Interpretation: Trends and the Vital Few

Discovery of trends is a useful aid in decision making. Trends are "leading indicators" that help to predict future events.

A graphic aid to discovery of trends is the cumulative-sum chart. Figure 5–6 shows the same data plotted as a simple time graph (a) and in cumulative-sum form (b). The cumulative-sum chart is more sensitive to trends than the Shewhart control chart but is slower to detect sudden shifts.

Numerous other types of analysis are used to aid interpretation. One of the most common is the familiar Pareto analysis used to separate the vital-few problems from the rest. Correlation analysis can be used to discover relationships between variables. We

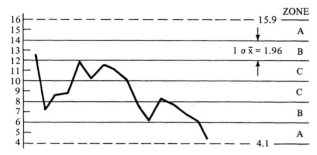

(a) Shewhart control chart of water absorption in common building brick

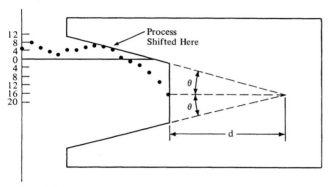

1 2 3 4 5 6 7 8 9 10 11 12 13 14 15 16 17 18 19 20

(b) Cumulative sum-control chart of same data as in (a). (Note that the data are expressed as the cumulative sums of the deviations from the target value. A special mask is used to interpret the data.)

FIGURE 5–6   Comparison of simple time graph with cumulative-sum graph
Source: Juran 1988b, p.24.29.

shall look at some of the principal tools of analysis in chapter 10, "Training for Quality."

DECISION MAKING

During conduct of operations certain cardinal decisions must be made, over and over again:

The process—should it run or stop?
The resulting product—does it conform to goals?
Nonconforming product—what disposition should be made?

The role of the managers is not to make all these huge numbers of decisions. Their role is to

1. Make the vital-few decisions

2. Delegate the rest under a well-designed decision-making process that provides the essential tools and training

3. Provide criteria to distinguish the vital-few decisions from the rest

Factual Determination

Ideally, factual determinations relative to product and process performance should be made at the very bottom of the hierarchy— by the work force with the aid of the instruments. Usually these same facts are needed as a feedback to the workers who perform the operations. There is no shorter feedback loop. Under this ideal arrangement the workers become the umpires: there is no need for additional personnel to serve as umpires (for example, checkers or inspectors).

Determining Process Conformance

The decision of whether the process conforms to the process goals is based on a factual comparison: measurement of process conformance compared with process goals. This decision is almost universally delegated to the operating personnel, and mostly to the work-force levels.

Sometimes this decision is delegated to designated umpires (for example, checkers or inspectors). Use of designated umpires is for reasons such as

1. The process is critical to safety, health, or the environment.

2. Quality does not have top priority.

3. There is incomplete mutual trust between management and the work force.

To enable the work force to carry out its delegations requires training in

1. The nature of the product and process involved

2. How to interpret the specifications and procedures

3. How to use the instruments

4. The consequences of nonconformance

Once these training needs are met, managers can delegate the conformance decision to the people at the bottom of the organization.

When making this delegation the managers should establish criteria for decision making. The need for such criteria is evident from Figure 5–7.

The criteria for quadrants A and C are universally clear:

1. If both process and product conform to their respective goals, the process may continue to run.

2. If neither process nor product conform to their respective goals, the process should stop, and remedial action should be taken. (See the section Corrective Action, which follows.)

The criteria for quadrants B and D are often vague, and this vagueness has been the source of a good deal of confusion. Upper management should insist that *clear criteria be established.* In most cases the decision making for these quadrants should be delegated to the supervision rather than to the work force.

The above discussion on process conformance is applicable to intradepartmental processes in which the departmental personnel are in a position to secure direct process and product feedback. Multidepartmental processes introduce complications, since prod-

		PRODUCT	
		Conforms	Does Not Conform
PROCESS	Does Not Conform	B Vague	C Clear
	Conforms	A Clear	D Vague

FIGURE 5–7   Example of areas of decision making

] *165* [

uct evaluation may take place late in the macroprocess. In such cases the product evaluation is at best only a lagging indicator for the earlier steps in the process. Such early control stations may be forced to base their control solely on process conformance to process goals.

Determining Product Conformance: Self-inspection

Whether *product* features conform to *product* goals also involves a myriad of decisions that must be delegated to the lowest levels of the organization. The training prerequisites are similar to those for process conformance. However, some additional considerations influence the plan of delegation.

It is virtually universal for the managers to establish policies to the effect that products that are found to conform to specification may be sent on to the next destination. The assumption is that product that conforms to specification is also fit for use, and this assumption is valid in the great majority of cases.

In many companies the product-conformance decision has traditionally *not* been delegated to the operating forces. Instead it has been delegated to a separate inspection department. The reasons have generally been that quality has not had top priority. In such cases there is a risk that evaluation of product conformance will be biased in ways that result in meeting the top-priority parameter (whatever that is) but not the quality parameter.

Ideally the operating forces at the lowest levels of the organization *should* make the product-conformance decision. However, some prerequisite criteria must be met:

Quality is number one. Quality must have undoubted top priority.

Mutual confidence. The managers must trust the work force enough to be willing to make the delegation, and the work force must have enough confidence in the managers to be willing to accept the responsibility.

Self-control. The conditions for self-control should be in place so that the work force has all the means necessary to do good work.

Training. The workers should be trained to make the product-conformance decisions and should also be tested to assure that they make good decisions.

Certification of Measurement

One of the goals of the measurement process should be to establish a record such that the results of measurement are accepted as valid by subsequent customers. Attainment of such a goal normally requires undergoing a test period during which the customer (external or internal) confirms that the supplier's measures can be relied upon. Following such confirmation, the supplier's measurements are regarded as "certified," that is, the supplier is placed on an approved list (formal or informal) so far as measurement is concerned. This certification opens the way to some important benefits such as

1. The elimination of duplicate measurements by subsequent customers
2. The removal of a major obstacle to "just-in-time" operations
3. The increase of mutual confidence between supplier and customer, leading to better teamwork

Disposition of Nonconforming Products

Many nonconforming products are so obviously unfit for use that they are discarded (or repaired) as a matter of course. Other nonconforming products are not so obviously unfit for use. In some such cases, the optimal decision may be to use the product as is.

To make this "fitness-for-use" decision requires acquiring certain additional pertinent information, such as,

How will this product be used? What will be the environment of use?

Who will be the user?

Are there any potential dangers to human safety or health?

Are there any potential violations of obligations to society?

What is the urgency for delivery?

How do the available alternatives affect our economics?

How do these alternatives affect the users' economics?

Some companies must deal with numerous cases of nonconforming products. In such companies it is usual to establish a standing committee (e.g., material review board) specifically to deal with disposition of nonconforming products.

Improper disposition of nonconforming products is a potential trouble area. Failure to use products that meet customer needs is a waste. Sending out products that do not meet customer needs is worse. In view of such potential problems, upper managers should, as part of their auditing of the quality system, assure that decisions on the disposition of nonconforming products are made by persons *with the information needed to balance the considerations of cost and customer satisfaction.*

CORRECTIVE ACTION

The final step in closing the feedback loop is to actuate a change that restores a state of conformance with quality goals. This step is popularly known as troubleshooting or fire fighting.

The term *corrective action* has been loosely applied to two very different activities:

1. *The elimination of* chronic *sources of deficiency.* The feedback loop is *not* a suitable means for dealing with such chronic problems. Instead the need is to employ the quality-improvement process as set out in chapter 3.

2. *The elimination of* sporadic *sources of deficiency.* The feedback loop is well designed for this purpose.

Most corrective actions consist of making adjustments to the technological processes, such as inserting a new battery or resharpening a tool. Such corrective actions are delegated to the work force.

The really troublesome problems of corrective action involve sporadic changes for which the causes are not immediately obvious. In such cases corrective action consists of two actions:

1. Discovering the *cause (or causes)* of the sporadic change

2. Providing a *remedy* for the change

Usually the main obstacle to restoring the status quo is diagnosing the cause.

Diagnosis

Diagnosis of sporadic troubles makes use of methods and tools such as

1. *Autopsies* to determine with precision the nature of the deficiencies
2. Comparison of *products* made before and after the trouble began, to see what has changed; also comparison of good and bad products made since the trouble began
3. Comparison of the *process* before and after the problem began to see what process parameters have changed
4. *Reconstructing the chronology.* This consists of logging on a time scale (of hours, days, etc.)
   a. The events that took place in the process before and after the sporadic change: rotation of shifts, new employees on the job, maintenance actions, etc.
   b. The time-related product information: date codes, cycle time for processing, waiting time, move dates, etc.

Analysis of this chronology usually clears away a good deal of shrubbery: certain theories are denied; other theories survive to be tested further. (For further elaboration, see Juran 1988b, chapter 22, the section Troubleshooting.)

Remedy

Once the cause or causes of the sporadic trouble is known, the worst is over. For the great majority of sporadic troubles the remedy involves going back to what was done once before. This is a return to the familiar, not a journey into the unknown (as is often the case when we are dealing with chronic troubles). The needed technology is usually known to the local people, and they can take the necessary action to restore the status quo.

THE ROLE OF STATISTICAL METHODS

An essential activity within the feedback loop is the collection and analysis of data. This activity falls within the scientific discipline known as statistics. The methods and tools used are often called statistical methods. These methods have long been used to aid in data collection and analysis in many fields, such as biology, government, economics, finance, and management.

During this century much has happened to apply statistical methodology to quality-oriented problems. This has included development of special tools such as the Shewhart control chart. An early wave of such application took place during the 1920s, largely within the Bell System. A second and broader wave was generated during the 1940s and 1950s. It came to be known as statistical quality control. A third wave, broader still, emerged during the 1980s, and came to be widely known as statistical process control.

Statistical Process Control

The term *statistical process control* (SPC) has multiple meanings, but in most companies it is considered to include the use of

1. Basic data collection

2. Analysis through such tools as frequency distributions, the Pareto principle, the Ishikawa (fish bone) diagram, and the Shewhart control chart

3. Application of the concept of process capability

Advanced tools such as design of experiments and analysis of variance are a part of statistical methods but are normally not considered to be a part of statistical process control.

The Merits

These statistical methods and tools have contributed importantly to quality control and also to the other processes of the Juran Trilogy: quality improvement and quality planning. For some types of quality problems the statistical tools are more than useful: the problems cannot be solved at all without using the pertinent statistical tools.

The SPC movement has resulted in the training of a great many supervisors and workers in basic statistical tools. The resulting increase in statistical literacy has made it possible for these employees to increase their understanding of the behavior of processes and products. In addition many of them have learned that decisions based on data collection and analysis will yield superior results. At higher levels there has been a parallel development. (For additional discussion on the use of statistical tools to aid the work force in decision making, see chapter 8, the section Statistical Tools: Aids to Decision Making.)

The Risks

There is danger in taking a tool-oriented approach to quality instead of a problem-oriented or results-oriented approach. (During the 1950s this preoccupation became so extensive that the entire statistical-quality-control movement collapsed; the word "statistical" had to be eliminated from the names of the departments.) The proper sequence in managing is first to establish the goals and then to plan how to meet those goals, including the choice of the appropriate tools. Similarly, in dealing with problems—threats or opportunities—sensible managers start first by identifying the problems and then try to solve those problems by various means, including the choice of the proper tools.

During the 1980s numerous companies did in fact try a tool-oriented approach. For example, many companies trained large numbers of their personnel in statistical tools that can be useful in making quality improvements. However, there was no effect on the pace of improvement. The reason was that there was in place no organization to identify which projects to tackle, to assign clear responsibility for tackling those projects, to provide the needed resources, and to review progress.

Upper managers should be on the alert to assure that *the statistical tools do not become an end in themselves*. A major form of such assurance is through the measures of progress. These measures should be designed to evaluate the effect on operating results, for example, improvement in product performance and customer satisfaction, and reduction in cost of poor quality. Other measures (numbers of courses conducted, numbers of people trained) do not evaluate the effect on operations and hence should be regarded as subsidiary in nature.

AN ASSURANCE ROLE FOR UPPER MANAGEMENT

The huge number of control subjects precludes upper management's becoming involved with any except a select vital few. However, upper management can and should assure that *the system of quality control is adequate.* A widely used and effective way of securing this assurance has been for upper managers to

1. Mandate the creation of a quality control manual to define the system
2. Approve the final draft
3. Audit to assure that the system is followed

The goal of the quality-control system is to provide the organization with a comprehensive set of plans for applying the feedback loop to a wide array of control subjects. The quality control manual defines those plans in ways that make them

1. *Optimal:* the plans are the result of multifunctional discussion and agreement.

2. *Repetitive-use:* they reduce the need for replanning, over and over again.

3. *Official:* they are approved at the highest levels of the organization.

4. *Readily findable:* they are assembled into a well-known reference source rather than being scattered among many memoranda, oral agreements, reports, and minutes.

5. *Stable:* they survive despite lapses in memory and employee turnover.

Such quality control manuals abound. The general sections exhibit much commonality, and include

1. A statement by the general manager relative to the official status of the manual. It includes the signatures that confer legitimacy.

2. The purpose of the manual; the intended use; how to use it.

3. The pertinent company (or divisional) quality policies. Often these may be incorporated by reference to the policy document.

4. The organization charts and tables of responsibility relative to the quality function.

5. Provision for the auditing performance against the mandates of the manual.

Additional sections of the manual deal with applications to various functional departments, macroprocesses, and technological products and processes. (For further elaboration, see Juran 1988b, the subsection "The Quality Manual.")

Upper managers are in a position to exercise considerable influence over all this in several ways:

1. Establish the criteria to be met by those who draft the manual. These criteria should include (a) clear definition of who is to be responsible for carrying out each step of the feedback loop, (b) qualification standards for those who are to be responsible, and (c) provision for periodic auditing of conformance to the manual.

2. Approve the final draft of the manual to make it official.

3. Periodically conduct an audit that reviews the up-to-dateness of the manual as well as the state of conformance to the manual.

The periodic audit by upper management is normally a part of the broader audit discussed in chapter 6, the section Quality Audits.

Applied to the auditing of the quality-control system, one element of prior preparation is to summarize the findings of the regular audits conducted at lower levels. Such summaries then provide useful inputs regarding the prevailing state of conformance and the adequacy of the manual as well. When nonconformances are frequent, the reasons are usually traceable to inadequacies in the system.

CONTROL THROUGH THE REWARD SYSTEM

A major influence on quality control is the extent to which the reward system (e.g., merit rating) emphasizes quality in relation to other parameters. This aspect of quality control is discussed in chapter 9, "Motivation for Quality."

HIGH POINTS OF CHAPTER 5

All company employees, from the chief executive officer (CEO) down to the workers, are active in quality control, and all make use of the feedback loop.

The concept of self-control is also universal. It applies to everyone in the company, from the CEO to the worker level, inclusive.

Self-control is a necessary prerequisite to motivation.

It is risky for managers to hold workers "responsible" for quality unless the workers are in a state of self-control.

Managers should understand the existence, nature, and extent of human errors, including their own.

The optimum solution for acquiring in-depth knowledge of the relationships between process variables and product results is to train the planners in how to use statistical design of experiments.

The proper sequence in managing is first to establish the goals and then to plan how to meet those goals, including the choice of the appropriate tools.

Measures of progress should be designed to evaluate the effect on operating results, such as improvement in product performance and customer satisfaction, and reduction in cost of poor quality.

TASKS FOR UPPER MANAGERS

Upper managers, as part of their auditing of managing for quality, should assure that allocation of responsibility for producing nonconforming products at the worker level is in accordance with the state of worker controllability.

Upper management's auditing of the quality-control process should include an examination of the provisions that have been made to deal with human sensing errors.

During its auditing of the quality-control process, upper management should assure that the organization machinery for planning the quality information system includes the customers as well as the suppliers.

During its auditing of the quality-planning process, upper management should assure that the training of planners in the statistical design of experiments is sufficient to enable them to optimize performance and to provide the operating forces with process-adjustment capability.

Upper management should insist that clear criteria be established as guides to actions on cases of nonconformance.

Upper managers should, as part of their audit of the quality system, assure that decisions on disposition of nonconforming products are made by persons with the information needed to balance the considerations of cost and customer satisfaction.

Upper managers should be on the alert to assure that the statistical tools do not become an end in themselves.

Upper managers should exercise control over the quality-control *system* by:

1. Mandating creation of a quality control manual
2. Establishing the criteria to be met by the manual
3. Approving the final draft
4. Auditing periodically the up-to-dateness of the manual and the state of conformance.

] *6* [

Strategic Quality Management (SQM)

The purpose of this chapter is to provide upper managers with a structured approach for managing quality throughout the company. To this end, the chapter

1. Defines the nature of this structured approach (we shall call this strategic quality management, or SQM)
2. Points out the pros and cons of SQM
3. Explains how to introduce SQM into a going company
4. Sets out the specific roles to be played by upper managers

This chapter is central to the entire subject of making quality happen. All else is supportive.

WHAT IS STRATEGIC QUALITY MANAGEMENT (SQM)?

SQM is a systematic approach for setting and meeting quality goals throughout the company.

SQM is the apex of the broader system of managing quality throughout the company. This broader system is variously called companywide quality management, total quality management, and so forth. The relation of SQM to the broader system is shown in Figure 6–1.

In this book the apex (SQM) is discussed in the present chapter. The middle sector of the pyramid is discussed in the next chapter, "Operational Quality Management." The base of the pyramid is discussed in chapter 8, "The Work Force and Quality."

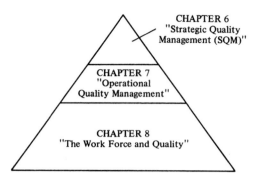

FIGURE 6-1 Relation of strategic quality management to companywide quality management

In this connection it is instructive to look at the list of features of Japanese companywide quality management as identified by a committee of Japanese experts (Ikezawa and others 1987). Their list is set out in Figure 6-2.

The Finance Parallel

The methodology of SQM is quite similar to that long used to establish and meet other broad company goals, notably financial goals. The similarity is so striking that it is worthwhile to review briefly the well-known approach to companywide financial management, before getting deeply into the corresponding means for SQM.

Many companies manage for finance by use of a structured, coherent approach that can be described as companywide financial management. This approach consists of establishing financial

1. President-led QC Activities in which All Departments and All Personnel participate
2. Top Priority consistently assigned to Quality by Management
3. Policy Dissemination and Control by Delegation
4. QC Audits and Their Implementation
5. Quality Assurance Activities ranging from Planning and Development to Sales and Servicing
6. QC Circle Activities
7. QC Education and Training
8. Development and Implementation of QC Techniques
9. Extension of Applications from Manufacturing to Other Industries
10. Nationwide QC Promotion Activities

FIGURE 6-2 Features of Japanese companywide quality management

goals, planning to meet the goals, providing the needed resources, establishing measures of performance, reviewing performance against goals, and providing rewards based on results.

Certain features of this approach are generic: they can be applied to other functions, including the quality function. These generic features consist largely of the following:

A Hierarchy of Goals. The major financial goal—the corporate budget—is supported by a hierarchy of financial goals at lower levels, such as divisional and departmental budgets, sales quotas, cost standards, and project cost estimates.

A Formalized Methodology for establishing the goals and for providing the needed resources.

An Infrastructure that (usually) includes a finance committee, a full-time controller, and supporting personnel.

A Control Process that includes systems for data collection and analysis, financial reports, and reviews of financial performance against goals.

Provision of Rewards. Performance against financial goals is given substantial weight in the system of merit rating and recognition.

Universal Participation. The financial goals, reports, and reviews are designed in hierarchical form to parallel the company's organizational hierarchy. These hierarchical designs make it possible for managers at all levels to support upper managers in managing for finance.

A Common Language. This is centered on a major, common unit of measure: money. There are also other common units of measure, for example, ratios such as return on investment. In addition, key words (such as *budget, expense,* and *profit)* acquire standardized meanings, so that communication becomes more and more precise.

Training. It is common for managers at all levels to undergo training in various financial concepts, processes, methods, and tools. Companies that have so trained their managers, in all functions and at all levels, are well poised to outperform companies in which such training has been confined to the finance department.

Application to SQM

Quite obviously, the approach used to establish companywide financial management is applicable to the establishment of companywide quality management. The basic trilogy of processes (planning, control, and improvement) is identical. The generic features inherent in managing for finance are likewise applicable to managing for quality.

To apply such a generic approach to managing for quality involves profound changes, some of which may be unwelcome. The major changes include

1. The establishment of broad quality goals as part of the company's business plan

2. The adoption of cultural changes (for example, big Q in place of little Q) that disturb long-standing beliefs and habits

3. The rearrangement of priorities, with resulting upgrading of certain skills and downgrading of others

4. Creating a new infrastructure, including a quality council and a quality controller, and fitting it in place

5. Extensive training for the entire hierarchy

6. Upper-management participation in managing for quality, to an unprecedented degree

The foregoing list is obviously an extensive array of changes. It is also a lot of work: there is a significant price to be paid. Therefore before rushing into SQM it is useful to have a look at the pros and cons of SQM. Is it worth the price?

WHY GO INTO SQM?

Factual Premises

Advocacy for SQM starts with some premises that have a sound, factual base:

1. Many of our industries are no longer among the quality leaders in the marketplace.

2. Some of our industries are in a crisis due in large part to a lack of competitiveness in quality.

3. All our industries are enduring huge wastes consisting of re-doing prior work.

Assertions Regarding Causes

Explanations of why our industries are in this state of affairs center on the "methods of the past," practices such as the following:

1. Each department has been pursuing departmental goals, with a resulting failure to optimize the overall quality performance. For example:

a. Error-prone clerical processes were computerized, error proneness and all. Result: a manual mess became a computerized mess.

b. Failure-prone features of goods (e.g., automobiles and copiers) were carried over, model after model.

2. Quality planning has largely been done by untrained amateurs. Planners within the various functions have lacked training in quality concepts, methods, skills, and tools. This lack of training has contributed to an outpouring of deficient products and processes. Collectively these deficiencies account for much of that huge, chronic cost of poor quality that is a continuing burden on our companies.

3. Multifunctional planning projects have suffered delays and wastes as a result of inadequate participation and to lack of early warnings. A widespread example has been new product developments that often met the needs of external customers but not the needs of internal customers. The designs were "thrown over the wall" without having undergone reviews by internal customers to provide early warning of trouble ahead.

4. There has been no clear responsibility for reducing the major chronic quality wastes. This responsibility has been clear only for the local (intradepartmental) wastes. However, the major quality problems are mostly interdepartmental. Instead of tackling these major wastes, the companies hid them in the cost standards. The alarm signals were disconnected.

5. Quality was assumed to apply only to manufactured goods and manufacturing processes (i.e., little Q). The need is to extend the concept of quality to all products and processes (big Q). Cus-

tomers are irritated not only by receipt of defective goods; they are also irritated by receiving incorrect invoices or late deliveries. The business processes that produce invoices and deliveries should also be subject to modern quality planning.

The Super Cause and Proposals for Remedies

From the foregoing catalog of causes there emerges a *supercause:* the deficiencies of the past have their origin in the lack of a systematic, structured approach such as already exists in managing for finance.

The existence of this supercause then leads logically to a proposal for a remedy—a remedy that will put managing for quality on the same companywide structured basis as is already used in managing for finance. This structured approach would consist essentially of the changes listed in the section Application to SQM, earlier in this chapter.

OBJECTIONS TO SQM

Prior to the 1980s the asserted benefits of SQM were generally not persuasive to upper managers. Most of the reasons are implied in that same list of changes:

1. Going into SQM is a lot of work.

2. It adds to the work load of upper managers as well as lower levels.

3. It is quite disturbing to the established cultural pattern.

Challenge to the Rationale

A good many respected managers are wary about going into SQM solely on theoretical or logical grounds. They are wary because they have endured too many prior experiences in which the results did not come up to what the advocates had promised. We shall classify these managers as "conservatives."

The conservatives (who constitute most of humanity) do not oppose change on principle. They are quite willing to change once it has been demonstrated that the change does in fact produce results. This insistence on results before change is actually a valuable stabilizer.

The views of these conservatives can be summed up as follows: The asserted benefits of the proposed structured approach are untested theories as applied to our company. We have in the past mandated a number of programs (i.e., drives) based on untested theories. Collectively the results have been so limited that we should be skeptical about mandating a new program until we have demonstrated that it will produce useful results in our company.

The Time Demand

The nature of this demand is readily seen by looking sideways at managing for finance. It takes time to participate in the budget preparation meetings, in meetings to plan for resources, in other preparatory steps. It then takes time to review the periodic performance reports and to act on the findings.

It is the same with SQM. It takes time to participate in the annual start-up; to make the subsequent periodic reviews of results; to take the appropriate actions. In most companies this time demand will be at its greatest during the first few years as a result of the awkwardness of start-up and of the big backlog of chronic wastes.

Disruptions

Disruptions are intangible, but they can become a greater obstacle than the tangibles.

Fitting in the added work is an obvious disruption. Usually this work is superimposed on the schedules of people who are already overburdened. They are faced with delegating some existing activities, slowing up others, and bringing still others to a halt.

Another form of this disruption arises from the change in priorities. To make quality the number one priority means outwardly downgrading the former number one down to something lower than number one. This downgrading is particularly disruptive to those who have been specially associated with the former top-priority goal.

Probably the biggest disruption is due to imposing a structured approach on those who prefer not to have it. Resistance to the structured approach is evident at the very outset. What becomes obvious to upper managers is a conflict between two contesting schools of thought: (1) the advocates who point to the asserted benefits to be derived from SQM, and (2) conservative managers who point out that these benefits are unproven in this company and that hence it may all end up as just another unsuccessful drive.

This conflict is seldom resolved by debate. More often it is resolved by the results achieved at some test site, as discussed in the section Establishing SQM, which follows later in the chapter.

Objections to "Big Q"

The recent emphasis on quality has included proposals to broaden the area of application of the term *quality* in various directions, principally as follows:

	AREA OF APPLICATION	
SUBJECT MATTER	FORMER (LITTLE Q)	NEW (BIG Q)
Quality of products	Products sold to clients	All products
Quality of processes	Manufacturing processes	Manufacturing and business processes
Customers	External	External and internal

(For further elaboration, see chapter 3, Figure 3–7.)

These efforts to crowd so much under the banner of "quality" run into understandable resentments. Some managers of business processes have long been active in trying to improve their quality—they are quite aware of the merits of good quality. What they resent is the change in nomenclature. Their terminology for high quality has used terms such as "low error rates" and "low downtime." Such managers perceive the change in terminology as a form of intrusion into their territory or downgrading of their prior efforts.

Cultural Resistance

A shift of responsibility for planning (from a functional level to a divisional or corporate level) readily runs into resistance from the function that previously "owned" the responsibility. Some of this resistance is cultural in nature. It results from the effect of the change on the status, beliefs, practices, and habits of those affected.

To deal with cultural resistance the behavioral scientists have developed some helpful rules of the road. (For elaboration, see chapter 9, the section Dealing with Cultural Resistance.)

Rejection by the "Immune System"

All large organizations exhibit some of the features of a biological organism. Invariably one of those features is the immune reaction when something alien is introduced. The organism senses the intrusion of the alien and mobilizes to reject it.

In biological systems the immune reaction can be lessened by (1) introducing only those transplants that are genetically alike, that is, from oneself or from an identical twin, or (2) chemically altering the response of the immune system.

The introduction of SQM is analogous to an alien transplant, and it stimulates an immune reaction. This reaction can be reduced in ways that are similar to those used for the biological organism: (1) design SQM so that it resembles oneself—that is, so that it closely parallels the existing business planning structure—and (2) alter the reward system in ways that will stimulate the managers to accept the new quality goals.

BRIDGING THE VIEWPOINTS: PILOT TESTS

In many companies the differences in viewpoints (advocates versus those on the receiving end) will preclude reaching a meeting of the minds solely through discussion. In such companies (barring a mandate by the upper managers), progress will depend on the results of a pilot test. If the results are favorable, the new approach is scaled up because the results are so attractive.

The pilot test takes place in the area of some manager—an "explorer"—who is willing to make that area a test site. There are always some managers who are willing to accept that responsibility.

Companies are normally unable to move in a new direction across a broad front. Instead they move in single file: one division after another, one department after another, one new product after another. This tends to be true even if there has been an upper-management mandate requiring all to move. In part, the single file results from bottlenecks in essential services, for example, capacity for training. In part, the single file results from differences in priorities and enthusiasm among the various parts of the organization.

The single file phenomenon means that little is lost by deliberately designing a pilot test to be conducted in the organization units of the "explorers." These explorers will likely be at the head of the single file anyway. The resulting pilot tests become the means for converting the skeptics into believers.

ESTABLISHING SQM: THE QUALITY COUNCIL

The elements needed to establish SQM are generally alike for all companies. However, each company's uniqueness will determine the sequence and pace of application as well as the extent to which additional elements must be provided.

A fundamental step in establishment of SQM is the creation of the quality council (or committee). The quality council is the key element in the company's infrastructure for SQM. It exercises complete oversight with respect to establishment and maintenance of SQM.

The quality-council membership typically consists of the senior managers. In large organizations there may be quality councils at multiple levels of the organization. In such cases the councils are "networked," that is, members of upper-level councils serve as chairpersons for lower-level councils. The arrangement is quite similar to that used for quality-improvement councils. (See Figure 3–8 and the associated explanation. Generally the quality-improvement council is identical with, or an arm of, the quality council.)

If the needed quality councils are not already in existence, *the upper managers must create them.* Once created, the quality council or councils have the responsibility to incorporate the Juran Trilogy into strategic business planning. In addition the council has the responsibility to assure that a corresponding pattern is introduced at the subordinate levels of organization.

QUALITY POLICIES

Policy, as used here, is a guide to managerial action. Published policy statements are the result of a good deal of deliberation in high places, followed by approval at the highest level. The quality council plays a major role in this process.

Policy declarations are a necessity during a period of severe change, and companies have acted accordingly. The 1980s have seen an unprecedented surge of activity of thinking through and publishing quality policies. Although the details vary, the published policies have much in common.

Without exception, all published quality policies declare the intention to *meet the needs of customers.* The wording often includes identification of specific needs to be met—for example, that the company's products *should provide customer satisfaction.*

Most published policies include language relative to competitiveness in quality—for example, that the company's products *shall equal or exceed competitive quality.*

A third frequent area of published quality policy relates to quality improvement—for example, that the published statements declare the intention to *conduct improvement annually.*

Some quality policy statements include specific reference to internal customers—for example, that quality should *extend to all phases of the business.*

Enforcement of quality policies is a comparatively new problem owing to the relative newness of written quality policies. In some companies provision is made for independent review of adherence to quality policies.

In IBM there is a quality policy requiring that new models of products must have a reliability at least equal to the reliability of the models they replace, and also at least equal to the reliability of the models of competitors. The product-development departments are required to demonstrate that this policy has been met. In addition, the quality-assurance department has the responsibility to review the demonstration.

As a part of introducing SQM, upper management should assure that the prevailing quality policies correctly reflect the company's intentions with respect to quality, that is, "the party line." If the policies are found to be out of date upper management should take steps to *assure that the quality-policy statements are updated.*

STRATEGIC QUALITY GOALS

As used here, *a quality goal* is an aimed-at quality target. A goal is specific. It is usually quantified and is to be met within a specific period of time.

An essential element of SQM is the establishment of broad quality goals as part of the business planning, along with goals for sales, investment, and profit. Here are some actual examples of corporate level quality goals:

> Make the Taurus/Sable models at a level of quality that is best in class. This goal was established by Ford Motor Company.
>
> Cut in two the time to fill customer orders. [Becton Dickinson and Company]
>
> Reduce the cost of (poor) quality by 50 percent by 1987. [This goal was established in July 1982, by 3M Corporation.]
>
> Reduce billing errors by 90 percent. [Florida Power and Light Company]

(Note that all the foregoing goals relate to "macroprocesses," namely new product launching, customer service, reduction in chronic waste, and billing.)

Subject Matter of Quality Goals

Despite the uniqueness of specific industries and companies, certain subjects for quality goals are widely applicable:

Product performance. This goal relates to performance features that determine response to customer needs: promptness of service, fuel consumption, mean time between failures, courtesy. These features directly influence product salability.

Competitive performance. This has always been a goal in market-based economies, but seldom a part of the business plan. The trend to make competitive quality performance a part of the business plan is recent but irreversible.

Quality improvement. This goal may be aimed at improving product salability or reducing the cost of poor quality. Either way, the end result after deployment is a formal list of quality-improvement projects with associated assignment of responsibilities.

Cost of poor quality. The goal of quality improvement usually includes a goal of reducing the costs due to poor quality. Although these costs are not known with precision, they are known to be very high. Despite the lack of complete figures, it is feasible, through estimates, to bring this goal into the business plan and to deploy it successfully to lower levels.

Performance of macroprocesses. This goal has only recently entered the strategic business plan. The goal relates to the performance of major processes that are multifunctional in nature, such as new product launching, billing, and purchasing. For such macroprocesses, a special problem is: Who should have the responsibility for meeting the goal? We shall discuss this shortly, in the section Deployment to Whom?

Nominations of Quality Goals

The goals selected to enter next year's business plan ideally are chosen from a list of nominations made by all levels of the hierarchy. Only a few of these nominations will survive the screening process and end up as part of the corporate business plan. Other nominations may instead enter the business plans of lower levels in the hierarchy. Many nominations will be deferred: they were unable to secure the necessary priority.

Upper managers should become an *important source of nominations for strategic quality goals,* since they receive important inputs from sources such as

1. Membership on the quality council
2. Contacts with customers
3. Periodic reviews of performance against quality goals
4. Quality audits conducted by upper managers (see the section Quality Audits which follows later in this chapter)
5. Contacts with upper managers in other companies

Bases for Setting Quality Goals

An important consideration in setting quality goals is the choice of the proper base.

At the lowest level of the hierarchy the quality goals are established largely on a *technological* basis. Most of these goals are published in the procedures and specifications that define the quality targets for the work force.

Goals for quality with respect to features that affect product salability should be based primarily on *the market*—meeting or exceeding marketplace quality. Some of these goals relate to projects that have a long lead time, for example, a new-product development involving a cycle time of several years, computerizing a major business process, or a large construction project that will not come on stream for several years. In such cases the goal should be set so as to meet the competition estimated to be prevailing when the project is completed.

In industries that are natural monopolies (e.g., certain utilities) the companies often are able to make comparisons through the use of industry data banks. In some companies there is internal competition as well: the performances of regional branches are compared with each other.

Some internal suppliers are also internal monopolies. However, most internal monopolies have potential competitors: outside suppliers who offer to sell the same service. Therefore the performance of the internal supplier can be compared with the proposals offered by an outside supplier.

A third and widely used basis for setting quality goals has been *historical* performance; that is, the goals parallel past performance. (Sometimes this is tightened up in order to stimulate improvement.) For some products and processes the historical basis is an aid to needed stability. For other cases—notably those involving high chronic cost of poor quality—the historical basis has done a lot of damage by helping to perpetuate a chronically wasteful performance.

During the goal-setting process, upper managers should be on the alert for such misuse of historical basis. Goals for cases of chronically high cost of poor quality should be based on *planned breakthroughs using the quality-improvement process.*

Deployment of Quality Goals

At the outset, a list of quality goals is a "wish list." To convert this list into potential realities requires identifying some essential specifics, such as what tasks need to be performed, and by whom. The process for identifying these specifics will be referred to as *deployment of quality goals.*[1]

"Deployment" as used here means subdividing the goals and allocating the subgoals to lower levels. Such deployment accomplishes some essential purposes:

1. The subdivision continues until it identifies specific deeds to be done.

2. The allocation continues until it assigns specific responsibility for doing the specific deeds.

3. Those who are assigned to be responsible respond by determining the resources needed and communicating this to higher levels.

Such deployment also provides an opportunity for participation by lower levels, as well as communication both up and down the hierarchy. Strategic quality goals may be proposed at the top. The lower levels then identify the tasks that, if performed, will collectively meet the goals. The lower levels also submit the bill: to perform these tasks, we need the following resources. The subsequent negotiations then arrive at an optimum that balances the value of meeting the goals against the cost of doing so.

The two-way communication feature of the deployment process (a Japanese term is "catch ball") has turned out to be an important aid in getting results. Feedback from companies using this process suggests that it outperforms the process of unilateral goal setting by upper managers.

This same two-way–communication feature requires that the recipients be trained in how to respond. The most useful training is prior experience in quality-improvement projects.

Many of the quality goals represent "elephant-sized" quality-improvement projects and must be broken down. For example:

1. A quality goal of reducing the cost of poor quality by X million dollars must in due course be broken down into "bite-sized" projects, using the tools of the quality-improvement process.

---

[1]*A note on terminology:* Some companies use the term "policy deployment" to designate deployment of quality goals. This usage seems to be the result of difficulties in translation from the corresponding Japanese term.

The Pareto principle must then be used to separate out the vital-few projects, and so on.

2. An airline goal of attaining Y percent on-time arrivals required projects to look into such matters as the policy of delaying departures in order to accommodate delayed connecting flights, the organization for decision making at departure gates, the need for revisions in departmental procedures, and the state of employee behavior and awareness.

3. Any goal of improving timeliness of service requires a breakdown of the macroprocess into its components, identifying the vital few and then considering each as a project, along with the macroprocess itself.

Brunetti (1987) describes how Florida Power and Light Company uses "policy deployment" to convert the corporate vision and corporate objectives into specific action projects.

Deployment to Whom?

The deployment process exhibits some of the features of the quality-planning process. It starts with the needs of the company and the upper managers. It determines what deeds are required to meet those needs. It arrives at an optimum through consideration of the resources required.

The bulk of this planning must be done at levels below the upper-management level.

The Ford Taurus-Sable goal of "best in class" ended up with over four-hundred specific subgoals, each related to a specific product feature. The total planning effort was enormous.

To a degree, deployment can follow hierarchical lines: corporate to division, division to functional department, and so on. However, this simple arrangement fails when goals relate to macro-processes.

Major activities of companies are carried out by use of interconnecting networks of macroprocesses. Each macroprocess is a multifunctional system consisting of a series of sequential operations. Being multifunctional in nature, there is no single "owner" and hence no obvious answer to the question, Deployment to whom?

We shall have a detailed look at ownership of macroprocesses in chapter 7, "Operational Quality Management." At this point what is pertinent is that there should be no vagueness with respect to deployment. In deploying goals that involve macroprocesses, upper managers should *squarely face the question, Deployment to whom?*

Deployment to teams has taken on new dimensions as a result of the trend to establish teamwork relations with external suppliers. There are numerous cases in which the assigned team should include the impacted supplier or suppliers, and still other external agencies. (For an example of a joint supplier-customer project, see Kegarise and Miller 1986.)

The Effect of Big Q

The growing adoption of the concept of big Q has brought some new elements into business planning, for example, quality performance of major functions and quality performance of macroprocesses. Traditionally these elements have been among the monopolies delegated to functional managers.

Generally these elements are regarded as "business processes." Obvious examples include billing, recruitment, and payroll. Beyond these obvious examples it is instructive to note the wide range of some of the goals that have been making their way into business planning:

1. Shortening the time for the new-product launch cycle (Pisano 1987)

2. Improving the accuracy of the sales forecast (Wolf 1985)

3. Establishing supplier relations on a teamwork basis (Branco and Willoughby 1987)

This same concept of big Q has promise of becoming a unifying force for dealing with the contention that "my industry (or company, function, etc.) is different." The technologies and markets certainly differ. However, the business processes and macroprocesses are quite similar for all industries. In addition, the areas of similarity are much greater than the areas of difference.

PROVISION OF RESOURCES

Resources are the price to be paid for the benefits of SQM. These resources parallel those required to establish and maintain the systems of companywide financial management. More specifically, the resources include

1. The effort needed to establish the basic SQM system, including processes for goal setting and deployment, evaluation of results, and recognition and rewards
2. Training in operation of the system
3. The effort required, at all levels, to administer the system on a continuing basis

In the absence of some form of SQM, a major obstacle to meeting quality goals has been lack of resources. This has been widely demonstrated in efforts to go into quality-improvement projects. To bring such projects to completion requires various resources: time for project team members to guide the projects, support from technicians and specialists, training in several directions. With the exception of some aspects of training, these resources have not been provided adequately. In turn, lack of the resources has starved out many efforts to improve quality on a scale that offered major benefits.

The SQM approach, being tied into companywide business planning, offers a way to provide the resources. Companywide business planning has long included a positive approach to bringing out into the open the resources required to meet the corporate business goals. Those who are apprehensive about "corporate interference" (see the next section) should note that SQM provides a channel for dealing with the problem of securing resources.

Corporate Interference

In some companies SQM faces resistance from the autonomous divisions (or from the functional departments) on the grounds of "corporate interference." It is a fact that adoption of SQM takes away some of the autonomy previously enjoyed by these divisions and departments. Such reduction in autonomy is never welcomed, even if the associated human relations are harmonious. Where they are less than harmonious, the problem can become severe.

The nature of this reduction in autonomy becomes evident if we look sideways at the finance function. In virtually all large companies the corporate headquarters office "inteferes" in divisional financial affairs in three major ways:

1. Approval of the divisional financial budgets

2. Approval of the divisional financial plans for meeting their budgets

3. Review of divisional financial performances against budgets

The parallel "interference" with respect to quality consists of actions taken by the corporate headquarters office to

1. Approve divisional quality goals

2. Approve divisional plans for reaching the quality goals

3. Review of divisional quality performance

The major difference is that in the case of finance the practice is of long standing, whereas in the case of quality the practice is just beginning. However, SQM does in fact interfere with some prior monopolies, and this is one of the prices to be paid.

QUALITY CONTROL AT UPPER-MANAGEMENT LEVELS

As used here, *quality control* has the same meaning as that set out in chapter 5. We define quality control as a managerial process during which we

1. Evaluate actual performance

2. Compare actual performance to goals

3. Take action on the difference

Quality control at upper-management levels makes use of the same feedback loop as is employed for all other controls. The feedback loop diagram appears in Figure 6–3.

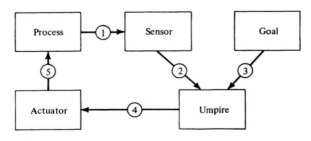

FIGURE 6–3 The feedback loop

ELEMENT	APPLICATION TO WORK-FORCE QUALITY CONTROLS	APPLICATION TO MANAGERIAL QUALITY CONTROLS
Control subjects	Physical, chemical, procedural specification requirements	Summarized performance for product lines, departments, etc.
Units of measure	Natural, physical, chemical (ohms, kilograms, etc.)	Various: money; indexes; ratios
Sensing devices	Physical instruments, human senses	Summaries of data
Who collects the sensed information	Workers, inspectors, clerks, automated instruments	Automated information systems; various statistical departments
When is the sensing done	During current operations	Days, weeks, or months after current operations
Standards used for comparison	Engineered specifications; specified procedures	History; the market; the plan
Who acts on the information	Servomechanisms, nonsupervisors, first-line supervisors	Managers
Action taken	Process regulation, repair, sorting	Replanning; quality improvement; motivation

FIGURE 6–4 Work-force quality controls compared with managerial quality controls

What differs is the control subjects. This difference in turn affects all other elements of the feedback loop. Figure 6–4 contrasts the application of the feedback loop to work-force quality controls with the application to managerial quality controls.

Until the 1980s upper managers had little involvement with quality control. The prevailing organizational forms classified work into broad functions (finance, marketing, operations, and so forth) and then delegated wide responsibility to the functional managers. The delegated responsibility included responsibility for control of quality in the respective functions. For products to be sold it was common practice to superimpose added quality controls in the form of independent inspections and audits.

The big-Q approach has required upper managers to participate much more actively in the quality-control process. This participation necessitates application of every element of the feedback loop to those control subjects that require upper-management attention.

Control Subjects

An earlier section, Subject Matter of Quality Goals, included five major quality goals:

1. Product performance
2. Competitive performance
3. Quality improvement
4. The cost of poor quality
5. The performance of macroprocesses

Every one of these goals becomes a control subject for upper managers. The subgoals become control subjects at lower levels in the hierarchy.

In addition, under the concept of big Q, the control subjects for upper managers often include

1. The quality performance of organizational units in the upper hierarchy
2. The quality performance of managers

The foregoing lists of control subjects apply to a wide spectrum of companies. However, the actual choice must be tailored specifically to each company's needs. In addition, each company is sufficiently unique to require a special look to determine what control subjects warrant upper management's attention. To meet this need requires specific action. Upper managers should place on the agenda of the quality council the question: *What quality-control subjects warrant upper management's personal attention?*

· MEASURES OF QUALITY FOR SQM

To establish measurement for SQM requires creating units of measure and sensors for each pertinent control subject. Figure 6–5 shows a sample of "new" control subjects stimulated by the shift to big Q, along with associated units of measure.

Product Performance

Product features are very numerous, but for the great majority, there exist units of measure in such forms as: delivery time, mean time between failures, weight, and fuel consumption. Also, for the

CONTROL SUBJECT	UNIT OF MEASURE
Promptness of service	Days; percent of responses within target goals
Competitiveness in quality	Performance versus top three competitors
Avoidable changes in engineering drawings, purchase orders, etc.	Percent of all changes; cost of correction
Document quality	Percent of pages in error
Software quality	Errors per 1000 lines of code; cost to correct errors
Invoicing errors	Percent in error; cost of corrections
Quality improvement	Project data: undertaken, in progress, completed; results of projects collectively; status of major projects individually; percent of managers assigned to projects
Strategic quality management: actual performance against goals	Various

FIGURE 6–5   Control subjects and associated units of measure

great majority of these features there exist technological sensors to provide product evaluation in terms of the unit of measure.

Upper managers are of course in no position to control these numerous product features individually. Instead upper managers must limit their control to the vital-few product features. The vital few may be chosen based on the key features as perceived by customers. Alternatively the vital few may be based on data summaries. Each of these vital-few product features then requires a unit of measure and a sensor.

For some products, the units of measure are common across multiple product lines. In such cases measures of performance for control by upper managers consist largely of summaries of basic data. If the units of measure are unlike, it becomes necessary to convert the data to some common index, for example, percent of goal attained.

For the most part, the sensors at upper-management levels consist of the data systems that condense the useful-many facts into the vital-few summaries. These data systems are supplemented by human sensing—for example, by auditors—and include sensing by the upper managers themselves.

Note that for product performance, a major data source is external customers. These customers usually take the initiative in providing feedback on product deficiencies but not on product performance. Instead the supplier must take the initiative in acquiring the needed data through negotiation, persuasion, purchase, or other means.

Competitive Quality

This control subject usually relates to those qualities that influence product salability—for example, fuel consumption, mean time between failures, promptness of service, and courtesy. For some product features, the needed data must be acquired from customers, again through negotiation, persuasion, purchase, or other means. For other product features, it is feasible to secure the data through laboratory tests. In still other cases it is necessary to conduct market research.

The recent increase in the pace of competition has required a corresponding increase in the frequency and depth of evaluation of competitive quality:

In many product lines, competitive quality must now be evaluated every year or two in order to keep up with the pace of change.

Customers now must be asked to identify the key product features, rank these features in their order of importance, and evaluate performance relative to competitive features.

Trends must now be studied so that goals for new products can be set to correspond to the state of competition at the time of launch.

Some companies operate as natural monopolies, for example, regional public utilities. In some such cases, the industry association gathers and publishes performance data. In the case of internal monopolies (e.g., payroll preparation and transportation) it is sometimes feasible to secure competitive information from companies who offer similar services for sale.

Performance on Quality Improvement

This evaluation is important to companies that go into quality improvement on a project-by-project basis. As a result of the lack of commonality among the projects, collective evaluation is limited to such features as

1. *Summary of numbers of projects:* undertaken, in-process, completed, aborted

2. *Summary of financial results:* amounts gained, amounts invested, returns on investment

3. *Summary of persons involved as project team members.* Note that *a key measure* is the proportion of the company's management team that is actually involved in improvement projects. Ideally this proportion should be over 90 percent. In the great majority of Western companies the actual proportion has been less than 10 percent.

(For further elaboration, see chapter 3, the section Progress Review.)

Cost of Poor Quality

We define cost of poor quality as those costs that would disappear if our products and processes were perfect. Those costs are huge. As of the 1980s, about a third of the work in the United States economy consisted of redoing prior work because products and processes were not perfect.

The costs are now known with precision. In most companies the accounting system provides only a minority of the information needed to quantify this cost of poor quality. It takes a great deal of time and effort to extend the accounting system to provide full coverage. Most companies have concluded that such effort is not cost-effective.

What can be done is to fill the gap by *estimates* that provide upper managers with approximate information as to the total cost of poor quality and as to which are the major areas of concentration. These concentrations then become the target for quality-improvement projects. Thereafter the completed projects do provide fairly precise figures on quality costs before and after the improvements.

Product and Process Deficiencies

Even though the accounting system does not provide for evaluating the cost of poor quality, much evaluation is available through measures of product and process deficiencies, either in natural units of measure or in money equivalents. As it happens, the prevalence of most deficiencies can be expressed by one simple generic fraction:

$$\text{Quality} = \frac{\text{frequency of deficiencies}}{\text{opportunities for deficiencies}}$$

Applied to upper-management levels this fraction is transformed into such terms as

Errors per 100 documents

Defective parts per million

Software errors per 1000 lines of code

Rework hours to total hours

Warranty charges per 1000 units under warranty

Cost of poor quality per dollar of sales, dollar of cost of sales, hours of work, or units shipped

Most such measures lend themselves to summation at progressively higher levels. This feature enables goals in identical units of measure to be set at multiple levels: corporate, divisional, and departmental.

Performance of Macroprocesses

Despite the wide prevalence and importance of macroprocesses, they have been only loosely controlled with regard to performance. A contributing factor is their multifunctional nature. There is no obvious owner and hence no clear, sole responsibility for their performance. Responsibility is clear only for the subordinate microprocesses.

We shall look at these macroprocesses in some detail in the next chapter, "Operational Quality Management," in the section Quality Management for Macroprocesses. Right now we should notice that the system of upper-management controls should include control of the macroprocesses. That requires establishing goals and means for evaluating performances, such as cycle times and deficiencies.

Performance of Organizational Units

In many manufacturing companies it has been a long-standing practice to summarize quality data in ways that match the organizational structure—that is, summaries by processing departments, product families, factory location, and so forth. Often this practice has been extended to evaluation of supplier quality. Generally this long-standing practice has been restricted to what we now call little Q.

We are in the early stages of extending this practice to big Q. Being early, there is need to pioneer and experiment. To make matters worse, the macroprocesses are multifunctional and hence do not neatly match the hierarchical structure.

Performance of Managers

How to evaluate the performance of managers with respect to quality has until recently not been a matter that received upper managers' attention. In manufacturing operations the quality performance of the products made by an organizational unit has generally been regarded as the quality "rating" of the manager of that unit. Now it has become necessary to rethink the entire approach to evaluating the quality performance of managers. The reasons are compelling:

1. For quality to have top priority requires that quality receive the greatest weight in evaluating the performance of managers.

2. To go from little Q to big Q requires new thinking in how to deal with activities not previously subject to quality evaluation.

3. Going into annual quality improvement requires new thinking in how to evaluate the contributions made by individuals to team projects (McGrath 1986).

4. The new attention being given to macroprocesses requires new thinking because there is no obvious "owner" of the macroprocess.

Meanwhile companies are beginning to test out various alternatives. It will take time for these tests to be published and discussed in the forum of managerial opinion. We are at least a few years away from reaching any kind of consensus.

THE REPORT PACKAGE

To enable upper managers to "know the score" relative to quality, it is necessary to design a special report package. In effect, the choice of control subjects identifies the instruments needed on the upper-management instrument panel. The system of reports is what connects these instruments to the data sources.

Contents

The report package consists of several conventional components:

1. Quantitative reports on performance, based on data systems
2. Narrative reports on such matters as threats, opportunities, and pertinent events
3. Audits conducted

These conventional components are supplemented as required to deal with the fact that "each company is different." The end result should be a report package that assists upper managers in meeting quality goals in much the same way that the financial report package assists the upper managers in meeting financial goals.

The quality council has the ultimate responsibility for the designing of such a report package. In large organizations, the designing of such a report package requires inputs from the corporate offices and divisional offices alike. At the divisional level the inputs should be from multifunctional sources.

Format and Frequency

The report package should be specially designed to read at a glance, and to permit easy concentration on those exceptional matters that call for attention and action. Reports in tabular form should present the three essentials: goals, actual performances, and variances. Reports in graphic form should show minimally the trends of performances against goals. The choice of format should be made only after learning what the preferences of the upper managers—that is, the customers—are.

Publication of managerial reports on quality is usually on a monthly or quarterly basis. The schedule is typically established to be in synchronism with the meeting schedule of the quality council or other key reviewing body.

The editor of the quality-report package is usually the director of quality (quality manager, and so forth), who is usually also the secretary of the quality council.

In Texas Instruments the quality report package (the "Quality Blue Book") was deliberately designed to parallel the company's financial reporting system, down to the color of the cover (blue). The report battery is organized into

1. Leading indicators, e.g., quality of purchased components

2. Concurrent indicators, e.g., product test results, process conditions, and service to customers

3. Lagging indicators, e.g., data feedback from customers and returns

4. Data on cost of poor quality

The report is issued monthly, and is the basis for annual performance appraisal of managers' contribution to quality (Onnias 1986).

Review of Performance

Reviews of the reports, both quantitative and narrative, should be on a scheduled, formalized basis. Formality adds legitimacy and status to the reports. The scheduled reviews add visibility. The fact that upper managers personally participate in the reviews sends its own message to the rest of the organization.

QUALITY AUDITS

An essential part of upper managers' system of quality controls is quality audits. As used here a *quality audit* is an independent review of quality performance. (To be "independent" the auditor should not have any close responsibility for the adequacy of the performance.)

The purpose of audits is to provide independent, unbiased information not only to the operating heads but also to others who have a need to know. For certain aspects of quality performance, those who have a need to know include the upper managers.

Subject Matter

Traditionally, quality audits have been used to provide assurance that products conform to specifications and that operations conform to procedures. At upper-management levels the subject matter of quality audits expands to provide answers to such questions as

Are our quality policies and quality goals appropriate to our company's mission?

Does our quality provide product satisfaction to our clients?

Is our quality competitive with the moving target of the marketplace?

Are we making progress in reducing the cost of poor quality?

Is the collaboration among our functional departments adequate to assure optimizing company performance?

Are we meeting our responsibilities to society?

Questions such as the foregoing are not answered by conventional technological audits. Moreover, the auditors who conduct technological audits seldom have the managerial experience and training needed to conduct business-oriented quality audits. In consequence, companies that wish to carry out quality audits oriented to business matters usually do so by using upper managers or outside consultants as auditors. The widest use of this concept is in the major Japanese companies.

A time-tested body of subject matter is the list of criteria used in Japan to award the Deming Application Prize. This list has been in evolution since 1951. As of 1987 it could be summed up as follows:

Policies and objectivies

Organization and its operation

Education and its dissemination

Information flow and utilization

Product and process quality

Standardization

Control and management

Quality assurance of functions, systems, and methods

Results

Future plans

(For further elaboration, see Ishikawa 1987.)

Conduct of Audits by Upper Managers

Audits by upper managers should be scheduled with enough lead time for preparing the needed information base. The subject matter should likewise be determined in advance, based on prior discussions by the quality council.

Some of these audits are conducted on-site at major facilities or regions. In such cases local managers are able to be active participants through making presentations, responding to questions, and guiding the upper managers during the tour of the facility.

The President's Quality Audit

In some major Japanese companies quality audits are conducted by managers at the highest levels of the company, either by the companywide quality committee or by some other team of upper managers. Where the president personally participates in the audit it is usually called the president's quality audit (Kondo 1988).

Such audits, conducted by upper level managers, can have major impacts throughout the company. The subject matter is so fundamental in nature that the audits reach into every major function. The personal participation of the upper managers simplifies the problem of communicating to the upper levels and increases the likelihood that action will be forthcoming. The very fact that the upper managers participate in person sends a message to the entire organization relative to the priority placed on quality and to the kind of leadership being provided by the upper managers: they are leading, not cheerleading (Shimoyamada 1987). (For further elaboration on quality audits generally, see Juran 1988a, section 9, "Quality Assurance." For further elaboration on quality audits at upper-management levels, see Juran 1988a, section 8, "Upper Management and Quality," under the heading Quality Audits by Upper Managers.)

THE QUALITY MANAGER

An essential resource of SQM is a quality manager, the quality equivalent of the financial controller. The need for such a quality manager is better understood if we first look sideways at the roles played by the financial controller's office.

The Financial Analogy

The finance function includes the organizational structure needed to

1. *Establish the strategic financial goals.* These goals are the end result of the budgetary process. A controller (the titles vary) presides over this budgetary process. In large companies a "budget officer" may be specially assigned to administer the budgetary process.

2. *Evaluate performance against financial goals.* The accounting system provides the factual basis for the summarized financial reports. The controller is importantly involved in editing and interpreting these reports.

3. *Conduct audits.* Auditors (both internal and external) are assigned to determine (a) whether the system, if followed, will correctly reflect the company's financial status, and (b) whether the system is being followed.

To carry out the foregoing activities requires resources in the form of controllers, along with support from budget officers, accountants, and others. In those companies that establish a finance committee (at the board level or the upper-management level), the controller sometimes provides a "secretariat" service.

The Quality Equivalent

Virtually all sizable companies have an organizational unit or units devoted full time to quality. These organizations have names such as Quality Assurance and Product Assurance. Their activities parallel some of the financial controllers' activities, but in most cases the orientation is to little Q. How to establish the quality equivalent of the financial controller has not yet been widely thought through, since most companies have not yet gone into SQM.

The orientation to little Q is widely prevalent:

Goal setting. This activity has been largely confined to (a) defining the properties of products that are to be sold to clients, and (b) defining the auxiliary products that directly affect clients, for example, sales contracts and invoices. The broad goals discussed previously, under Strategic Quality Goals, are still in the early stages of development.

Measures of performance. These abound in the form of inspections, checks, and tests on products prior to sale. They are also available, to a lesser degree, on product performance after sale. Measures relative to broader goals such as competitive performance are in the early stages of development.

Quality audits. These are widely used but they are usually narrowly focused on (a) conformance to regulatory provisions and (b) conformance to established procedures and product specifications. They are seldom used to review the adequacy of the elements of SQM, such as broad quality policies, goals, and plans.

The Quality Department of the Future

The indications are that the present functions and structure of this department will undergo substantial change in those companies that are successful in converting to SQM.

Product evaluation. This function is now carried out by inspectors, checkers, and testers, most of whom are in the quality department. In the future this function is destined to be carried out by the operating forces, provided the essential criteria are met:

1. Quality really has top priority among all parameters.

2. The operating forces are placed into a state of self-control.

3. Mutual trust is established between the managers and the work force with respect to the new delegation.

4. The operating forces are trained to carry out the newly delegated function.

Engineering services. This function consists mainly of the specialties of reliability engineering and quality engineering. The clear trend is to transfer this function to line department specialists. A prerequisite to such transfer is training the line department specialists.

Quality goals. Companies that adopt SQM require some form of secretariat to do the detailed work. A logical choice for secretary of the quality council is the quality manager. Such a choice adds a business orientation to the quality manager's activities. Previously the orientation was to technological and departmental goals.

Measures of performance. Here again the adoption of SQM broadens the scope of activities and therefore demands expansion of measures of performance. For further elaboration see the previous section Measures of Quality for SQM.

Quality audits. The traditional quality audits conducted by the quality department have little relation to the auditing needs created by the adoption of SQM. In addition, most of the auditors lack the needed business training and experience. As a result, much of the quality auditing required by SQM must be done by upper managers themselves. (See the previous section Quality Audits.) However, these high-level audits require extensive preparatory work, and some of this will logically be delegated to the quality manager.

The Transition Process

Converting the present quality department to the quality department of the future should be done on a phased basis. Most of the changes are contingent on meeting prerequisites that have lengthy lead times.

The conversion lends itself readily to establishing goals (or milestones) and then defining the steps required to reach the goals.

The Emerging Job of Quality Manager

The job of quality manager will differ radically from the pattern prevailing during the 1980s. This difference is mandated by the array of unprecedented strategic quality goals. One way of summing it up is to say that the emerging job will be business-oriented rather than oriented to technological or departmental goals.

That is a profound change, and many, perhaps most, quality managers will face a considerable problem of adaptation. Some will have difficulty in conceptually grasping the broader role. Some will be reluctant to delegate so many of their familiar functions to the line organizations. Some will be well advised to take supplementary training in business management.

Upper managers should likewise realize that a profound change is involved. The quality manger has a key role to play in SQM. Appointment to this key role should not be automatic. Appointment to the role of quality manager should be to someone who is able to grasp the role conceptually and who in addition is willing to put forth the effort needed to become qualified to carry it out.

UPPER MANAGERS' ROLES IN SQM

Before discussing the roles of upper managers it is a good idea to discard some diversionary baggage. There are schools of thought that try to define the roles of upper management by skillful choice of a label, for example, upper managers should become committed, involved, or aware. Choice of such labels is an exercise in futility. None of these words makes clear to upper managers what they should do that is different from what they have been doing. What is required is a setting out of specifics: exactly what actions are to be taken; exactly what decisions are to be made. Discarding the diversionary baggage makes it easier to concentrate on the specifics.

Serving on the Quality Council

Membership on the quality council exposes the members to essential inputs relative to the quality problems requiring solution, and to the resources needed. The council is seldom effective if the members lack decision-making power over the subject matter. In addition, the rank of the council membership sends a message to the rest of the organization with regard to the priority of the subject matter.

Participating in Policy Formation

Participation in policy formation takes several forms:

1. *Helping to identify the need for quality policies.* A major symptom of such need is repeated questions raised at lower levels, asking for directions on broad issues.

2. *Assigning responsibility* for drafting the policy statements and checking them out with the affected organizational units.

3. *Reviewing, revising, and approving.*

Participating in Goal Setting and Deployment

Establishing the broad quality goals is inherently an upper-management responsibility. It is also an exercise in futility if the "plans" for reaching the goals consist of exhorting subordinates. Instead it is essential to deploy the goals to subordinate levels and then to review and approve their proposls.

Providing the Needed Resources

A major failing of upper managers has been the failure to provide the resources needed to make the plans effective—to carry out the *list of tasks evolved during the deployment process.* Such a failure sends a negative message to the lower levels.

The resources are a price to be paid for meeting the goals. If the resources are not provided, the perception in the lower levels is that the goals lack priority relative to those goals for which resources are provided.

Establishing the Organizational Infrastructure

The major elements inorganizing for SQM consist of

1. The quality council or councils

2. The quality manager (director of quality, etc.) whose role in SQM parallels that of the financial controller in companywide financial management

3. The multidepartmental teams

The major quality problems are all interdepartmental in nature. In consequence, interdepartmental teams are needed, principally to (1) plan multifunctional processes such as the new product launching cycle, and (2) tackle major quality-improvement projects.

Such teams require legitimacy, priorities, and resources that are best provided from upper-management sources.

Reviewing Progress

Reviews of progress are an essential part of assuring that goals are being met. The very fact that upper managers do review progress sends a message to the rest of the organization about the priority given to the quality goals.

These reviews are carried out in two major ways:

1. Summarized reports of actual performance against quality goals

2. Audits of the processes in use, especially the broad business processes

Giving Recognition

Much of this recognition consists of "ceremonial" actions taken to publicize meritorious performance. These ceremonial actions are typically nonfinancial in nature. They usually focus on the activities of an improvement nature rather than on the conduct of operations. In contrast, the reward systems for the successful conduct of operations employ such devices as performance appraisal or merit rating, and focus on the supervisor-subordinate relationship.

It is common practice for upper managers to preside at ceremonial awards of certificates or plaques to persons who have completed training courses. In some companies, upper managers personally and prominently participate in dinner meetings specifically organized to honor teams that have completed their quality-improvement projects. Similar meetings are organized to recognize outstanding contributions made by suppliers. Still other companies establish special awards for teams or individuals whose contributions are judged to be outstanding. These awards are made by upper managers at ceremonial occasions and are publicized through various media, such as the company's newsletter, the bulletin boards, and the local press.

Revising the Reward System

The reward system (merit rating, bonuses, etc.) not only serves its basic purpose of rewarding human performance; it also serves to inform all concerned of the upper managers' priorities. If the goals are revised but the reward system is not, the result as viewed by subordinates is conflicting signals. Most subordinates resolve this conflict by following the priorities indicated by the reward system.

EFFORTS TO AVOID UPPER-MANAGEMENT PARTICIPATION

The foregoing is a formidable list of roles to be assumed by upper managers. These managers have been understandably reluctant to add so extensively to their own work load. This reluctance helps to explain the popularity (during the early 1980s) of efforts to delegate managing for quality to lower levels of management or to the work force. For the most part these efforts to delegate were made with the best intentions. Good managers do delegate extensively. However, the quality function has grown in importance to a point that the grand strategy is no longer delegable; the upper managers must take charge personally.

A Widespread Failure

A widely tested effort to delegate has consisted essentially of

1. *Goal setting by upper managers.* Some of these goals have been specific—for example, "Let's cut the cost of poor quality in two." More usually the goals have been vague—for example, "Do it right the first time."

2. *Exhorting subordinates* to increase "awareness" and to reach the goals.

The Reasons for Failure

Such approaches are doomed to failure because they lack the substantive content needed to compete with the existing order. A number of upper managers, disappointed that such an approach had failed, have complained bitterly to this author that their subordinates had "let them down." This author offered a rather different explanation, which is summarized in Figure 6–6.

It is evident from Figure 6–6 that the existing order has long imposed on the subordinates a clear system of responsibilities based on specific goals, plans, organizational structure, resources, progress reviews, and rewards. These responsibilities do not change when the new approach (the "doomed" approach) is applied. The subordinates are still expected to meet their schedules, budgets, and so forth. The vagueness of the new approach cannot possibly compete with the existing order.

SQM or Not: The Decisive Element

Whether the upper managers should take the company into SQM is a unique decision for each company. What is decisive is the importance of quality relative to the future health of the company. The potential benefits of SQM are clear:

1. The goals become clear; the planning process forces clarification of any vagueness.

	THE EXISTING ORDER	THE "DOOMED APPROACH"
Goals	Clear: budgets; schedules; specifications; etc. Long-standing Legitimate Credible	Usually vague Suspect due to being part of a new drive— "Here comes another one."
Plans for meeting goals	In place: specific	Vague
Definitions of responsibility	Clear: in job descriptions	Vague
Resources	Provided	Seldom provided
Progress review	In place: standardized reports; scheduled reviews	Vague
Motivation	In place through: supervisory review of progress reports; reward system	Exhortation

FIGURE 6–6   Why many efforts to delegate have been doomed to failure

2. The planning process then makes the goals achievable.

3. The control process helps to assure that the goals are reached.

4. Chronic wastes are reduced through the quality-improvement process.

5. The creation of new wastes is reduced through revision of the quality-planning process.

EMBARKING ON SQM: THE SCENARIO

Companies that have successfully instituted SQM have done so through a series of phases, not all at once. Through this phased approach the management hierarchy gradually acquired the experience needed to go into full-scale SQM.

The First Phase: Choice of Strategy

The first phase has usually consisted of the managers collecting their wits and adopting a strategy—a scenario that would lead to SQM. This first phase has commonly consumed a minimum of six months. Sometimes it has taken much longer as a result of false starts. (For further elaboration, see chapter 1, the section Responses to the Impacts.)

Project-by-Project Improvement at a Test Site

The most successful choice of strategy has been to go first into project-by-project improvement. This is itself a structured approach, which is described in detail in chapter 3. Companies that adopt this strategy do not undertake project-by-project improvement all over the company simultaneously. Instead they usually try the concept out at some test site. The test results then become the basis for scaling up companywide.

The pilot test and the associated evaluation of results commonly consume about a year of calendar time. Scaling up then consumes an additional year or two of calendar time.

A major by-product of all these improvement projects is a dramatic rise in the quality-oriented training and experience of the managers who have served on the quality-improvement teams. The learning experience from multiple improvement projects is profound. For most improvements the remedy is to replan the product or the process, so that much is learned about quality planning. For most quality-improvement projects, controls must be established in order to hold the gains. As a result the teams learn much about the control process.

Still another by-product of the improvement projects is a growing atmosphere of teamwork. Major quality-improvement projects are inherently interdepartmental in nature, requiring interdepartmental teams and teamwork for their completion. The resulting spirit of teamwork then carries over into the traditional work of conducting operations.

Scaling Up

The results achieved at the test site open the way for scaling up into quality improvement on a companywide basis. In addition, the experience gained has tended to stimulate the upper managers' interest in bringing managing for quality into the company's business plan. This concept then also goes through a test before scaling up on a companywide basis.

The Total Calendar Time

Managers are dismayed to hear that attainment of SQM runs into years of calendar time. Yet such are the realities, based on experience. The typical intervals have been about as follows:

PHASE	INTERVAL
Choice of strategy	6–12 months
Quality improvement at a test site, plus evaluation of results	1 year
Scaling up to companywide quality improvement; initiating SQM at a test site	2 years
Scaling up SQM	2 years

In all, a minimum of about six years will elapse before SQM is comfortably in place.

TRAINING

To make SQM operative requires extensive training in managing for quality. This need for training affects the entire company hierarchy. Among the most important training needs are those for the following:

1. *Upper managers.* Here the training concentrates on the processes of the Juran Trilogy and on the specific roles of upper managers in getting managing for quality into the company's business plan.

2. *Planners.* The term *planners* includes full-time planners as well as operating managers, to the extent that they participate in the quality-planning process. The purpose of the training is to minimize the extent to which quality planning is done by experienced amateurs, resulting in quality problems thereafter for the customers, external and internal.

3. *Quality-improvement teams.* These teams are assigned specific projects aimed at improving product quality and reducing chronic costs of poor quality. The training serves to arm them with the methodology of quality improvement: the process, the skills, and the tools.

We shall have a closer look at training in chapter 10, "Training for Quality."

HIGH POINTS OF CHAPTER 6

This chapter is central to the entire subject of making quality happen.

Establishing companywide quality management involves profound changes, some of which may be unwelcome.

The "supercause" of the deficiencies of the past is the lack of a systematic, structured approach such as already exists in managing for finance.

Companies are normally unable to move in a new direction across a broad front. Instead they move in single file.

A fundamental step in establishment of SQM is the creation of the quality council (committee, etc.).

Goals for features that affect product salability should be based primarily on the market: on meeting or exceeding marketplace quality.

For cases involving high chronic costs of poor quality, the historical basis for setting quality goals has done a lot of damage by helping to perpetuate a chronically wasteful performance.

The two-way communication feature of the deployment process (a Japanese term is "catch ball") has turned out to be an important aid in getting results.

Those who are apprehensive about "corporate interference" should note that SQM provides a channel for dealing with the problem of securing resources.

The choice of control subjects must be tailored specifically to each company's needs.

In the absence of accounting data, companies can use estimates to provide upper managers with approximate information as to the total cost of poor quality and as to which are the major areas of concentration.

The quality council has the ultimate responsibility for designing a report package for upper managers.

The auditors who conduct technological audits seldom have the managerial experience and training needed to conduct business-oriented quality audits.

Appointment to the role of quality manager should be to someone who is able to grasp the role conceptually and who in addition is willing to put forth the effort needed to become qualified to carry it out.

Resources are a price to be paid for meeting the goals.

The reward system (merit rating, bonuses, etc.) not only serves its basic purpose of rewarding human performance; it also serves to inform all concerned of the upper managers' priorities.

Approaches based solely on exhortation are doomed to failure because they lack the substantive content needed to compete with the existing order.

Whether the upper managers should take the company into SQM is a unique decision for each company.

TASKS FOR UPPER MANAGERS

If the needed quality councils are not already in existence, the upper manages must create them.

Upper management should take steps to assure that the quality-policy statements are updated.

Upper managers should serve as a source of nominations for strategic quality goals.

Goals for cases of chronically high cost of poor quality should be based on planned breakthroughs using the quality-improvement process.

In deploying goals that involve macroprocesses, the upper managers should squarely face the question, Deployment to whom?

Upper managers should place on the agenda of the quality council the question: What quality control subjects warrant upper management's personal attention?

Upper managers' roles in SQM include

1. Serving on the quality council
2. Participating in policy formation

3. Participating in goal setting and deployment
4. Providing the needed resources
5. Establishing the organizational infrastructure
6. Reviewing progress
7. Giving recognition
8. Revising the reward system

] 7 [

Operational Quality Management

The purpose of this chapter is to provide a structured approach to managing for quality at those levels of the company hierarchy that are intermediate between the nonsupervisory work force and upper management. More specifically, the purpose is to show how the trilogy of managerial processes (planning, control, and improvement) can be applied to managing for quality at these organizational levels.

WHAT IS AN OPERATIONAL DEPARTMENT?

As used here, the word *department* refers to any organizational unit that is intermediate between a division (for example, a profit center) and the nonsupervisory work force. Figure 7-1 shows this relationship in graphic form.

As depicted in Figure 7-1, a department includes (a) any functional organization, such as finance, marketing, human relations, manufacture, and product development; and (b) any subordinate unit, such as payroll, advertising, employment, assembly, and electronic design. (The terminology has not been standardized. "Departments" may also be called sections or units. The leaders may have the title of manager, director, or supervisor.)

There is much variation in the mission of departments. Some have responsibilities that are limited to carrying out one step (operation, task, and so forth)—for example, key punching, or gear cutting. Other departments have broad responsibility for multiple steps.

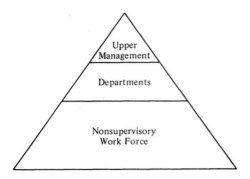

FIGURE 7–1 Location of the department in the organizational hierarchy

MACROPROCESSES AND MICROPROCESSES

All companies employ major systems that are inherently multifunctional in nature. We shall call these macroprocesses. Some of these macroprocesses are directly involved in producing the company's sales income, for example, processing customers' orders or buying input materials from suppliers. Others are the numerous business processes that are auxiliary to producing income, such as billing and recruiting employees. Often these business processes are internal monopolies.

A macroprocess consists of multiple segments that we shall call microprocesses. Each microprocess is typically carried out within a single functional organizational unit, often presided over by a first-line supervisor. The activity of a microprocess consists of operations (steps, tasks, and so forth), such as opening the mail or assembling gear boxes.

The "anatomy" of the macroprocess is often a "procession" of sequential processes such as is depicted in Figure 7–2.

An example of a sizable procession is the approach used by one large company for producing its credit cards.

The procession consisted of twenty-two separate operations (steps) that took place within the domains of five different vice presidents. The process was slow; it took several weeks to issue a credit card. The process was also error prone. For every one hundred applications that entered the process, only eighty-five emerged; the rest were lost or got stuck somewhere. Some applicants received multiple credit cards.

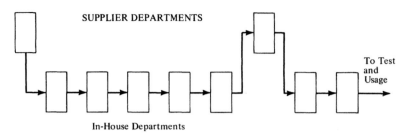

FIGURE 7–2   A macroprocess as a procession

Another major form of macroprocess is the "assembly tree," shown in Figure 7–3.

In this form the output from numerous microprocesses converges into an assembly department that assembles the final product.

Relation to Functional Organizations

Macroprocesses and functional organizations are seldom coextensive. Most macroprocesses move into and out of multiple major functional organizations. (For example, the process for launching

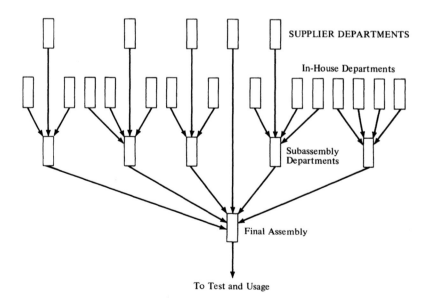

FIGURE 7–3   A macroprocess as an assembly tree

] *221* [

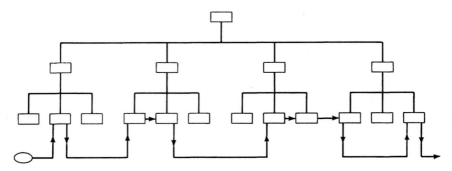

FIGURE 7–4 A macroprocess conducted in multiple functional organizations

new products progresses through virtually all major functional organizations.) Figure 7–4 shows a macroprocess superimposed on a conventional organization chart.

The macroprocess works its way through the domains of multiple major functions. There is no obvious answer to the question: Who should be made responsible for quality management of the macroprocess?

The Concept of "Ownership"

Management practice in the United States has a long tradition of favoring individual responsibility. The term often used to denote such responsibility is "ownership"—for example, "He owns the process." In keeping with this tradition some companies look for ways to assign the quality management of macroprocesses to individual owners despite the multidepartmental and even multifunctional anatomy of the macroprocess. These assignments are usually made to either of two categories: (1) an assumed owner or (2) a designated owner.

The Assumed Owner

It is often assumed that a manager from the dominant function owns the entire macroprocess. This assumption is not rigid; it is known that multiple functions are involved. Nevertheless, the assumption is often acted on. Such action can readily take place by default: Lacking a clear intended assignment, the result is a vacuum. It then becomes logical for the dominant function to be drawn into that vacuum.

It may seem reasonable for the dominant functional department to do the quality planning. However, the risk is that the planning priorities will focus on that department's mission rather than on an optimum for the company. To illustrate, here are several macroprocesses along with the associated dominant function and a major focus of that function:

MACROPROCESS	DOMINANT FUNCTION	MAJOR FOCUS
Purchase orders	Purchasing	Purchase price
Sales contracts	Marketing	Sales volume
New products	Product development	Field performance

What is really at issue here is whether quality planning for macroprocesses can safely be left to any individual function or to any individual. The answer appears to be no: a multifunctional approach is needed—some kind of team.

The Designated Owner

Some companies are experimenting with the idea of designating owners for macroprocesses. For example, in one major company a large marketing organization has designated owners for key macroprocesses, for example, selling, installing, billing, and collecting. Each owner is given responsibility for "process management," which is defined by the nine steps depicted in Figure 7–5. The owner is also made responsible for

- Defining the subprocesses
- Ensuring the line-manager subprocess ownership is assigned and agreed upon
- Identifying critical success factors and key dependencies in order to meet the needs of the business during the tactical and strategic time frame
- Ensuring that information integrity exists throughout the process, including integrity of measurements at all levels
- Resolving or escalating cross-functional issues.

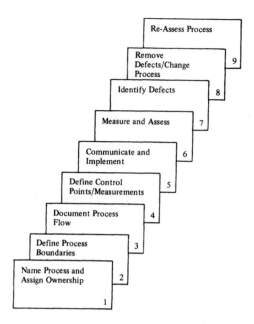

FIGURE 7–5 One definition of the responsibilities of an owner of a macroprocess

In this same company the assigned owner is made "responsible and accountable" for activities that seem to include all the processes of the Juran Trilogy.

> An owner is selected and is responsible and accountable for the operational quality of the process. An owner must be at a level high enough in the organization to identify the impact on the process of new business direction, to monitor effectiveness (does the process produce the required effect?) and efficiency (does the process do it without waste?), to influence change in practices/procedures affecting the process, and to make a commitment to a plan and implement change for process improvement.

(For further elaboration see Nickell and McNeil 1987.)

Individual or Team Ownership?

Applied to macroprocesses, the concept of individual ownership is risky. In most cases it is illusory as well. To arrive at the optimum requires participation by the affected departments in the form of data inputs, challenges to theories, trade-offs to arrive at the optimum, and agreements to take action. Note that for the process depicted in Figure 7–4, the decisions on action rest primarily with the hierarchical structure (the chain of command) and only secondarily with the owner of the macroprocess.

In practice the individual owner must provide for some degree of participation by the departments, even if this is limited to providing data inputs. The result is an informal team structure with some built-in deficiencies:

1. An informal team lacks legitimacy in the organizational hierarchy.

2. The owner's formal departmental responsibilities can bias the informal ownership role.

3. The major factors in securing results are the skills, training, and persuasiveness of the owners. Since these vary widely, the results will vary widely.

QUALITY MANAGEMENT OF MACROPROCESSES: A LOOK BACK

Quality management of macroprocesses has in the past suffered from various deficiencies. Most of these deficiencies had their origin in (1) vague responsibility for ownership, or (2) quality planning done by experienced amateurs, as discussed in chapter 4, the section Who Has Been Doing Quality Planning?

Figure 7–6 sets out some of the principal deficiencies along with the corresponding remedies. The material that follows focuses on how to apply the needed remedies to management of macroprocesses.

QUALITY PLANNING FOR MACROPROCESSES

Organization

Companies have invented numerous kinds of organizational structure for the quality-planning of macroprocesses. The more usual forms include the following:

Owner plus informal participation. The merits and limitations of this approach were previously discussed in the sections The Assumed Owner and The Designated Owner.

DEFICIENCIES OF THE PAST	NEEDED REMEDIES
Quality planning emphasized the needs of the functional departments	Plan so as to meet the needs of all customers
Available coordination structures seldom emphasized managing for quality	Provide for emphasis on managing for quality
Planners lacked expertise in the methodology and tools of planning for quality	Provide the planners with expertise
Quality control of macroprocesses was handicapped as a result of vague responsibility for ownership	Establish clear responsibility for ownership
Effectiveness of quality control was handicapped by underutilization of the tools of data collection and analysis	Provide for utilization of the tools of data collection and analysis
Responsibility for quality improvement of microprocesses was vague, and on a voluntary basis	Establish clear responsibility for improvement Make improvement mandatory
There was no organized provision for quality improvement of macroprocesses	Establish an organized approach for quality improvement of macroprocesses

FIGURE 7–6   Past deficiencies and remedies

Planner plus formal design review. Under this approach formal design-review committees are established to enable affected departments to review the plans and to provide early warning, that is, "If you plan it this way, here will be the effect in my area."

Joint planning. This approach eliminates the "handoff" in which the results of each planning phase are transferred to the persons who are to carry out the next planning phase. Instead one team of planners carries out all the planning, phase after phase. This approach probably provides the most thorough planning. It is also the most demanding in terms of hours spent in planning and in terms of the calendar time.

Matrix organization. This is a form of team structure superimposed on a functional hierarchy. In some companies it has been quite useful for coordinating the functions associated with specific products or markets. It has also been used for fire fighting: for dealing with sporadic problems that cut across functional lines. The use of matrix organizations as quality-planning teams has not been widely documented. However, some experience indicates that even within a matrix organization, the best vehicles for successful planning are focused joint planning teams.

Responsibilities of the Planning Team

These responsibilities are essentially alike no matter what kind of team is created. The responsibilities include the following:

1. *Defining the mission of the macroprocess.* Every team is created for some specific purpose. One of the first steps is to clarify that purpose. In effect the team should finish the sentence: "This plan has been completed when. . . ."

2. *Following the quality-planning road map.* This road map is the step-by-step planning process set out in some detail in chapter 4. The major headings include

Identify the customers, external and internal.

Determine the needs of the customers.

Develop products whose features are able to meet customer needs.

Develop processes that are able to produce the product features.

3. *Defining the microprocesses.* It is quite common to delegate planning for microprocesses to local departmental teams. Such an arrangement requires a clear definition of each such delegated microprocess, along with criteria for the interfaces. We shall shortly have a look at quality planning for microprocesses.

4. *Coordinating the planning.* Planning for a macroprocess always includes some planning done by sources that are not on the team, for example, planners of microprocesses, external customers, outside suppliers, and various forces of society.

The planning team has the responsibility of coordinating all this so as to arrive at the optimum.

Expertise for Quality Planning

A widespread deficiency of the past has been the phenomenon of planning without expertise in quality—the phenomenon of quality planning by experienced amateurs. The need is to provide the missing expertise. The major options for doing this have been

1. *Appointing quality specialists to the planning teams.* This option has been favored by companies in the United States.

2. *Training the planners in the needed expertise.* This option has been favored by major companies in Japan.

Each of these options has been widely tested. Extensive feedback is available regarding the respective results. Based on this feedback it appears that option 2—training the planners in the needed expertise—has significantly outperformed option 1 and should therefore be adopted for the future.

The job of training the planners in the needed expertise has recently been made easier by the development of new training materials and courses specially oriented to quality planning. Chapter 5 went extensively into some of the most fundamental planning tools: the quality-planning road map, the flow diagram, and the spreadsheet. We shall shortly look at another such fundamental tool: the triple role diagram. (For additional discussion, see chapter 10, "Training for Quality.")

QUALITY CONTROL
FOR MACROPROCESSES

Virtually all quality controls are built around the feedback loop, which is shown in Figure 7–7.

A critical element of effective quality control is clear responsibility for closing the feedback loop. This means clear responsibility for comparing actual performance to goals and taking action on the differences.

For many macroprocesses, this responsibility is vague, that is, no one owns the macroprocess. Often the problem is more fundamental than that. The original planning does not establish quality goals or provision for evaluating performance. In effect, the con-

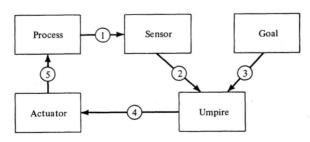

FIGURE 7–7 The feedback loop

cept of process capability is applied to the microprocesses but not to the macroprocess. All too often it has been assumed that if provision is made for quality control of the microprocesses, the end result will also include a well-controlled macroprocess. All too often the end results have shown otherwise. Such deficiencies in the macroprocesses should not go on and on.

Note that we are talking about macroprocesses. These are processes whose anatomy does not match that of the organization chart (see Figure 7–4). To deal with deficiencies in macroprocesses requires action by upper managers. Such action consists essentially of the following:

1. Identify the key macroprocesses.

2. For each key macroprocess, establish clear responsibility for reviewing the state of quality control and for filling in any gaps in the system of information and responsibility required to close the feedback loop. (The nature of quality control and the elements of the feedback loop are elaborated in chapter 5.)

3. For each macroprocess that is discovered to exhibit significant deficiencies in results, undertake a quality-improvement project to get rid of the deficiencies. (The conduct of quality-improvement projects is described in chapter 3.)

The Quality Instrument Panel

Most companies evolve a report package—an instrument panel—that summarizes for upper managers performance with respect to such key parameters as sales, expenses, profit, schedule, and productivity. In many companies this report system includes performance with respect to quality. In such companies there is a striking difference in emphasis with respect to control subjects: The major emphasis is on those performances that relate to product salability and to customer dissatisfaction with respect to the products sold. There is much less emphasis on performances of business processes despite the fact that these have significant impacts relative to the company's quality image and to the cost of poor quality. (For further elaboration, see chapter 6, the section Quality Control at Upper-Management Levels.)

This imbalance should not continue. Some researches have indicated that the business processes are quite as influential in terms of customer reaction as the processes that produce the products for sale.

The existing quality instrument panels are usually the result of gradual evolution. Over the years control subjects have been added at the initiative of specific managers, or as a reaction to some crisis: "Let's set up an early warning system so that that doesn't happen again."

It is of course feasible to leave it to future years of evolution to eliminate the imbalance in reporting. But the upper managers would do better not to wait for that lengthy evolutionary process. Instead upper managers should *take positive action to bring performance of macroprocesses into the system of upper-management reports.* The end result of such action is to provide upper managers with measures such as the following:

CONTROL SUBJECT	UNIT OF MEASURE
Promptness of service	Average time elapsed; percent of promises met
Avoidable changes in engineering drawings, purchase orders, etc.	Avoidable changes as a percent of all drawings, purchase orders, etc.; cost of avoidable changes
Document quality	Percent of pages requiring revision
Software quality	Errors per 1000 lines of code; cost to correct errors
Invoicing errors	Percent of invoices in error; cost of correction

QUALITY IMPROVEMENT FOR MACROPROCESSES

The project-by-project approach for quality improvement (described in chapter 3) is readily applicable to macroprocesses.

NOMINATIONS FOR PROJECTS. Some of these become evident from the flow diagram. For example, many flow diagrams exhibit rework loops, as shown in Figure 7–8.

The existence of such a loop is evidence that work is being redone. Generally, the head of the associated microprocess has been

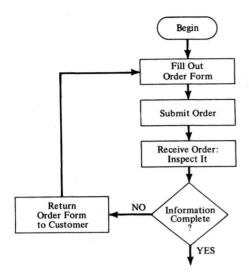

FIGURE 7–8   Flow diagram exhibiting a rework loop

unable to get rid of the loop because the problem is inherently interdepartmental in nature.

Still other nominations may be evident from the flow diagram; for example, some products are found to have no known customers.

The evaluations of performance of macroprocesses may also provide nominations for improvement, for example:

Customer needs are not being met.

Products are not competitive.

Excess costs are being incurred.

PROJECT TEAMS. Selection of teams follows the approach set out in chapter 3, the section The Project Team. The designated team then becomes the owner so far as quality improvement is concerned. The project then progresses as described in chapter 3.

UPPER MANAGEMENT AUDITING OF MACROPROCESSES

The most important macroprocesses are carried out by a series of microprocesses that are under the command of multiple major company functions. Such macroprocesses, once in place, are difficult to revise because they do involve multiple major company functions. Yet many of these important macroprocesses do need revision because they exhibit poor performance and many deficiencies. So there is a deadlock. The customers of the macroprocess may be unhappy with the results. Yet they see no way to change things because no one is in charge—there is no owner. One way to break up such deadlocks is through upper-management auditing.

The case of the macroprocess for producing credit cards involved twenty-two microprocesses progressing through the domains of five vice presidents. Results were poor: the overall cycle time was lengthy; 15 percent of the applicants failed to receive credit cards; and some applicants received multiple credit cards. Yet there was a deadlock that could be broken only by some form of upper-management intervention. One form of such upper-management intervention is the quality audit.

A Quality Audit Can Be a Lot of Work

To conduct a quality audit of a macroprocess is usually a lot of work, consisting of

1. *Identifying the questions to which answers are needed.* Frequent key questions are,

Who are the key customers?
What are their needs?
How well are those needs being served?
How does this service compare with competition?

2. *Securing the answers.* Some of these answers involve evaluation of the performance of the macroprocess and those of its competitors. Other answers must come from understanding the way in which the process is carried out, for example, by means of a flow diagram.

3. *Conclusions, recommendations, and revisions.* These elements vary from case to case. In some cases the need is to change the basic anatomy of the macroprocess. For example, in the credit

card case the need may be to establish a separate organizational entity to produce credit cards, and to reduce the number of "hand-offs" as well. In other cases the remedy may require better definition of the microprocesses and the interfaces. In still other cases the need may be to improve the conformance of the micro-processes to their respective goals.

Much Can Be Delegated

Most of the aforementioned work consists of "securing the answers." This work can largely be delegated to subordinate levels. It consists in part of securing data on performance and deficiencies. The work also includes preparing flow diagrams, spreadsheets, exhibits, and so forth, to make it easy for upper managers to understand the macroprocess.

The remaining elements (identifying the questions to which answers are needed; conclusions, recommendations, and revisions) are normally not delegable.

Which Macroprocesses to Audit

The list will differ from company to company, so the quality council will need to establish priorities based on the feedback it receives. By way of example we can look at two key macroprocesses (product development and supplier relations) from the standpoint of what are the questions to which answers are needed.

AUDITING OF PRODUCT DEVELOPMENT

Our definition for product development was set out in chapter 4 as follows: product development is the activity of determining the product features that respond to customer needs.

Product development is of course a part of the broader macroprocess of bringing new products to market—"concept to customer." In the case of manufactured goods, this broader macroprocess follows the sequence of the familiar "spiral of progress in quality," reproduced in Figure 7-9. (A similar spiral is used for bringing new services to market, although the functions around the spiral may have different names.)

In the interest of brevity, we will refer to the broad macro-

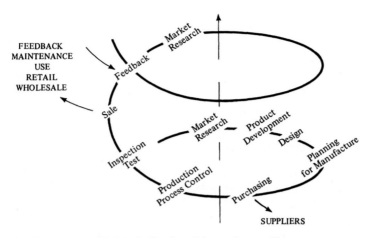

FIGURE 7-9 The spiral of progress in quality

process of concept to customer as a journey around the spiral, or just the spiral.

The Impacts

Product development takes place early in the spiral. It has major impacts on all other macroprocesses, and these impacts are magnified as events progress around the spiral. The potential for damage is considerable. The major way to head off such damage is to provide an early-warning system that can identify potential problems long before the crisis stage is reached. During the upper-management audit, the most critical focus should be on the adequacy of the early-warning system.

The Key Questions

When quality councils do undertake to audit the product-development process, the questions to which answers are needed include most of the following:

1. What has been the previous record of product developments? What has been the proportion of successes, failures, near misses?

2. What are now the measures we use for judging the performance of our product-development area? For our kinds of prod-

ucts, what would be appropriate measures for judging such performance?

3. What is now our system of early warning for detecting problems that new product developments will create during later stages of the spiral? How effective has this system been?

4. What is the cost of poor quality due to the product development process? That is, if there were no backtracking to rectify design problems, what would be the resulting reduction in time interval and in costs throughout the spiral?

Note that the traditional "categories" of "quality costs" have not included certain costs associated with new product launches. The case of the failed product launch involved costs as follows:

	$(MILLIONS)
Market research	0.5
Product design	6.0
Manufacture	36.0
Sales promotion	2.0
Total	44.5

(For further elaboration, see chapter 3, the section Project Nomination.)

5. What policy questions in the product-development area require decisions by upper management (for example, design for intended use versus actual use)?

6. What has been the training of our designers in the quality disciplines? What changes are needed?

7. To what extent are failure-prone features of old designs embodied into new designs? Who makes the decision on allocation of design effort to new features of new products versus remedies for failure-prone features of old designs?

Answers to such questions are best provided after reviewing the history of prior cycles of new product launches. Such a review should be done in depth, using a methodology such as the Santayana review, described in chapter 4. A superficial review will result in superficial answers. Failure to conduct such reviews in depth can result in overlooking the major opportunities for improvement. To illustrate:

In one electronics company the vice president for product development was actively trying to reduce the prevailing thirty-month new-product launch cycle time. To this end he made two investments of about three million dollars each:

1. He acquired facilities to perform, in-house, an operation that had previously been contracted out.

2. He acquired a computer capability to do electronically certain tasks previously done manually.

Each of these investments enabled the vice president to reduce the cycle time by several weeks. What was not done was to look for ways to reduce the amount of redoing of prior work.

This redoing was estimated to consume about a third of all the effort. To reduce the amount of such redoing would have required identifying the areas of concentration, discovering the causes, and providing remedies. The cost of such analysis might have run to one or two hundred thousand dollars. The reduction in time cycle might have come to several months, along with considerable cost reduction.

Note that the above example exhibits two forms of behavior to which upper managers should be alert:

Suboptimizing. The vice president for product development gave priority to those areas of the product-development cycle that were under his command. He did not give priority to other areas (internal customers) that endured much redoing due to work done within the the product-development department.

Preference of capital expenditures. In some companies projects involving a capital expenditure carry a higher "social status" than projects that are not capital intensive. Such matters of status are not discussed openly, but they are a reality. Upper managers should be alert to assure that, when the opportunities are similar, the priority should go to projects that are not capital intensive.

AUDITING OF SUPPLIER RELATIONS

Goods and services purchased from suppliers are often a sizable part of operating costs. The quality of these purchased products then becomes influential with respect to the buyer's product quality and the associated cost of poor quality.

Adversary to Teamwork

In the United States the traditional approach to supplier relations has been adversarial, involving,

1. Multiple sources of supply
2. Pre-award surveys, samples, etc.
3. Competitive bids and awards
4. Incoming inspections; on-site surveillance
5. Performance rating of suppliers
6. Allocation of share of market based on performance

During the 1980s, there emerged a trend to adopting a teamwork relationship with suppliers. In companies that adopted this change, the effects have been somewhat as shown in Figure 7–10.

Criteria for Supplier Survival

The trend to fewer suppliers becomes an opportunity for the survivors. This opportunity takes such forms as higher market share, longer contracts, and a more predictable basis for business planning. However, to survive they must meet the emerging criteria for survival. This involves willingness to

1. Participate in the team concept: mutual visits, the sharing of information, and joint planning.

Supplier Relations Practice Under:

ELEMENT	ADVERSARY CONCEPT	TEAMWORK CONCEPT
Number of suppliers	Multiple; often many	Few; often single source
Duration of supply contracts	Annual	Three years or more
Criteria for quality	Conformance to specifications	Fitness for use
Emphasis of surveys is on:	Procedures, data systems	Process capability; quality improvement
Quality planning	Separate	Joint
Pattern of collaboration	Arms length; secrecy; mutual suspicion	Mutual visits; disclosures; assistance

FIGURE   7–10   Trends in supplier relations

2. Establish adequate process capability: technology, and training

3. Adopt modern methods of and tools for managing for quality

4. Establish annual quality improvement

5. Provide "full service" in such forms as product development and process development

The Key Questions

Understanding of the foregoing trends is a useful basis for identifying the key questions to be answered by an upper-management audit of supplier relations:

What has been our policy of supplier relations within the spectrum of adversary to teamwork?

How do we evaluate suppliers' performance with respect to quality?

What has been the performance of suppliers with whom we have an adversary relationship?

What has been the performance of suppliers with whom we have a teamwork relationship?

To what extent are our quality problems with our customers traceable to products purchased from suppliers?

How much of our cost of poor quality is traceable to suppliers?

What are our criteria for qualifying a new supplier with respect to quality? For terminating a supplier with respect to quality?

Here again (as in the audit of the product development macroprocess) to provide in-depth answers requires in-depth analysis. A major part of that analysis should consist of review of prior performances of suppliers, both "good" and "poor," so as to discover the causes behind the differences.

AN INITIATIVE FOR UPPER MANAGERS

The foregoing two macroprocesses are only examples. There are additional macroprocesses that make vital contributions to the company's quality performance, and that should therefore undergo quality audits by upper management. Upper management should *identify the macroprocesses that require high-level quality audits and should take steps to organize such audits.*

QUALITY MANAGEMENT FOR MICROPROCESSES

Compared with macroprocesses, microprocesses are much more numerous and much narrower in function. There are also profound differences in organizational form and in relationship to the hierarchy, as set out in Figure 7–11.

It is not feasible for upper managers to become involved with the microprocesses individually. However, upper managers can and should become involved with the microprocesses *collectively.* One way to do this is to establish clear responsibility for managing the macroprocesses, as already discussed in this chapter in the section Quality Management for Macroprocesses.

Supervisory Analysis of Microprocesses

There is a second form of upper-management involvement with the microprocesses collectively. It consists of designing a broad methodology intended to help supervisors analyze their own microprocesses with a view to improving performance. This methodology usually extends across all the processes of the Juran Trilogy.

	MACROPROCESS	MICROPROCESS
Usual scope	Multidepartmental; often multifunctional	Tasks or operations within a single department
Relation to hierarchical organization	Seldom closely related	Usually closely related
Ownership of macroprocess	No natural owner	Departmental supervisor is natural owner
Responsibility for quality planning	Requires multidepartmental team	Often can be delegated to local departmental personnel
Relationship of planners to operating personnel	Seldom identical	Often identical

FIGURE 7–11   Contrast: Quality management for macroprocesses versus microprocesses

It often also gets into parameters other than quality, for example, productivity and value added.

The broad methodologies designed by various companies, while differing in detail, have exhibited much similarity in their conceptual approach. The material that now follows looks at the essential elements of this conceptual approach and offers a critique of the applications made by the companies.

QUALITY PLANNING FOR MICROPROCESSES

Quality planning has been the main focus of the company approaches. However, those same approaches have not limited their scope to quality alone. More usually they have included some planning for other parameters such as productivity and value added. In keeping with our basic subject matter, we shall limit this critique to the quality parameter.

The TRIPROL Diagram

The TRIPROL diagram (reproduced in Figure 7–12) is the basic model used for explaining the quality-planning process.

The model is readily applicable to microprocesses and has in fact been used in some of the company approaches.

The three roles of the TRIPROL diagram are carried out by a "processor team," which we defined in chapter 5 as follows: a processor team is any organizational unit (of one or more persons)

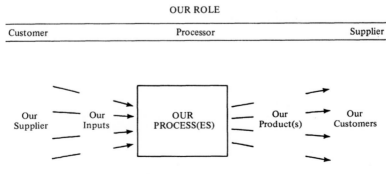

FIGURE 7–12 The TRIPROL diagram

that carries out a prescribed process. The definitions of the three roles were also set out in chapter 5 and are repeated here:

1. *Customer.* The processor team acquires various kinds of inputs that are used in carrying out the process. The processor team is a customer of those who provide the inputs.

2. *Processor.* The processor team carries out various managerial and technological activities to produce its products.

3. *Supplier.* The processor team supplies its products to its customers.

Some company training materials have been quite lucid in explaining this basic and useful concept.

The Flow Diagram

A logical starting point for the quality planning or replanning of a microprocess is to prepare a flow diagram of the present process. This diagram should show the activities (steps, tasks, operations, decisions, actions, etc.) and the sequence in which they take place. It is a good idea to number the activities for easy reference during subsequent discussion. It is also a good idea to make use of the standard symbols for flow diagrams as set out in Figure 7-13.

The use of standard symbols makes it easier for a supervisor to identify the customers and to explain the microprocess to other processor teams who are affected. The training needed to construct a flow diagram is minimal. Nevertheless most companies have not required construction of flow diagrams during programs aimed at replanning microprocesses.

Who Are the Customers?

This question is raised universally in the company approaches. Usually the supervisors are provided with printed forms for recording the list of customers. Some approaches include applying the Pareto principle, that is, identifying the key customers.

Generally the supervisors are readily able to identify the immediate customers: the neighboring processor teams to whom products are delivered. They are not so readily able to identify distant neighbors, some of whom may be significantly impacted. This in-

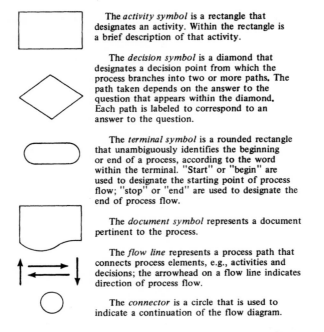

The *activity symbol* is a rectangle that designates an activity. Within the rectangle is a brief description of that activity.

The *decision symbol* is a diamond that designates a decision point from which the process branches into two or more paths. The path taken depends on the answer to the question that appears within the diamond. Each path is labeled to correspond to an answer to the question.

The *terminal symbol* is a rounded rectangle that unambiguously identifies the beginning or end of a process, according to the word within the terminal. "Start" or "begin" are used to designate the starting point of process flow; "stop" or "end" are used to designate the end of process flow.

The *document symbol* represents a document pertinent to the process.

The *flow line* represents a process path that connects process elements, e.g., activities and decisions; the arrowhead on a flow line indicates direction of process flow.

The *connector* is a circle that is used to indicate a continuation of the flow diagram.

FIGURE 7–13   Standard symbols for flow diagrams

ability is an inherent risk in any approach that relies on an individual rather than on a team.

The companies generally have accepted the concept that "customers" include internal customers. This same concept is usually built into the approaches for replanning microprocesses. However, in some respects the means for identifying customers are incomplete. The incomplete areas include

1. Customers who are overlooked because some products have been overlooked (for example, the operating data that are delivered to internal customers such as accounting or human relations)

2. Suppliers (they are customers for feedback)

3. "Distant neighbors"

Such deficiencies (and others we shall see shortly) make it clear that an effort to do quality replanning on a broad scale should be preceded by training in how to plan for quality. The central feature of such training should be a project of replanning a real microprocess.

What Are the Customers' Needs?

Here the company approaches have varied. In some companies the approach assumes that customer needs are already known and are represented by the procedures and specifications. The question then raised is, Are the standards being met? Other companies correctly urge contacts with customers to discuss needs and whether the needs are being met.

None of these company approaches have gotten into the subtle varieties of customer needs (stated, real, perceived, cultural, and so forth) as described in chapter 4, the section Customers' Needs. Neither have they gotten into the problem of translation—bridging the differences in dialect. For some microprocesses these differences are important.

Some approaches do raise the question of competitiveness in meeting customer needs. This, however, is limited to matters of product salability. It should also be raised with respect to monopolies in serving internal customers.

The Products

The company approaches provide for identifying the outputs: What are the products of the microprocess? To whom are they delivered? Generally this identification is limited to those products that are central to the entire sequence of microprocesses. The products that are omitted are generally associated with customers who have been overlooked.

Questions often raised are whether the products meet customers' requirements and whether the products have value. Questions seldom raised relate to whether the products are competitive.

Product development as such is understandably not stressed in these analyses. However, it is made clear that if customers' needs are not being met, steps should be taken to secure remedial action. These steps will sometimes lead to action in the form of product development.

The Process

The company approaches usually include some form of activity analysis:

What activities are being conducted?
What are the inputs to each activity?
What is the value added?

The adequacy of the inputs to the process is questioned. The ability of the process to meet requirements is questioned. In the case of manufacturing processes, there is an expectation that process capability should be quantified.

Process development is not brought up. However, there is an expectation that the supervisor can come up with ideas that will lead to improvement, whether locally within the microprocess or externally through process development.

A usual omission is competitive analysis of the process, especially in the case of internal monopolies. In some cases it is quite useful to look at what the offerings of outside services are. If the internal monopolies seem to not be competitive, it becomes easier to improve the internal service or to consider contracting out.

Another usual omission is the matter of adequacy of feedback to suppliers. In some cases this is a significant omission.

CRITIQUE OF QUALITY PLANNING FOR MICROPROCESSES

The Objectives

Companies which have gone into supervisory analysis of microprocesses have done so for reasons that are entirely constructive. The objectives have been to

1. Improve the microprocesses through replanning

2. Utilize the experience and creativity of the supervisors and the work force

3. Provide the supervisors with greater participation and with a greater sense of ownership

4. Broaden the supervisors' understanding of their roles

5. Take some steps toward converting experienced amateurs into professional quality planners

The Methodologies

To meet these objectives, the companies have generally prepared a formal methodology, including forms to be filled out, and training in how to go at the replanning. Collectively these methodologies have exhibited strengths and weaknesses. The strengths have included

1. A focus on supervisory ownership of the microprocesses

2. Adoption of much of the quality-planning road map (see Figure 4–2)

3. Provision of a structured, understandable procedure, including forms to help in the data preparation (see, for example, the forms shown in Figure 7–14)

4. Provision of training that is focused on real problems

The weaknesses have included

1. Addressing multiple parameters, and thereby reducing the focus on quality

2. Addressing segments of each of the processes of the Juran Trilogy, with resulting confusion as to the objective

3. Concentration on microprocesses without provision for coordination with other elements of the macroprocess

4. Incomplete use of the quality-planning road map

5. Individual responsibility for a quality-planning activity that inherently requires extensive teamwork

6. Overly complex paperwork in some cases

A Common Illusion

Managers should be alert to a common illusion relative to the replanning of microprocesses. Such replanning seldom solves the

DEPARTMENT ACTIVITY ANALYSIS

Function Name	
Production Control	

Department Name		Dept. No.
Receiving, Administration, Back orders		

GENERAL DESCRIPTION OF WORK PERFORMED WITHIN THIS DEPARTMENT (LISTING MAJOR OR ALL ACTIVITIES):

Keypunch

Transaction screening

Receiving buy/pay parts

Credit req. activity

Daily activities report

Fill back orders

Type letters

Drop shipping

R.O.M. control

Receiving/Distribution

Z/A Relations

Plus and minus transfer

Manager's Signature	Date	Extension

FIGURE 7–14   Quality planning for microprocesses sample form
From "Department Activity Analysis: Management and Employees Working Together," Kenneth T. Parker, Information Products Division (IBM Corporation, Charlotte, NC), 1984 IAQC Conference *Proceedings*. (IAQC has now changed its name to Association for Quality and Participation.)

DEPARTMENT ACTIVITY ANALYSIS

Function Name	
Production Control	

Department Name		Dept. No.
Receiving, Administration, Back orders		

Activity:	Date:	Prepared By:
Keypunch		

INPUT

What:	Unassigned Inventory: bulk fill reqs., (+) (−) delta adj. scrap transactions, new vendor P/N's & bal. changes, credit reqs. planned reqs. R.O.M., non-consumptive, header and program cards, count cards,
	loc. changes, grey stripes, + & − transfers, stock receipts

From:	
	Kitting, sequence area, coordinators, receiving, finished cards, zones

VALUE ADD—WORK ACCOMPLISHED IN DEPT

Why Do:	System is updated by the input of keypunched cards. It updates
	our inventory and vendor inventories

Value Added:	The proper punches in the proper fields of each card—necessary
	to update system

Impact If Not Done:	Loss of control: physical inventory, unassigned inventories

OUTPUT

What:	Decks of transactions sorted by the header and loader cards
	submitted daily through screening

To:	
	Receiving, kitting

FIGURE 7–14 *(continued)*

macroplanning problems. In the credit card example the major need is to reexamine the macroplan, for example:

Should such a process involve the hierarchies of five different vice presidents?

Can the number of steps be reduced dramatically?

An example of a successful reduction in the number of steps in a process is that of the telephone directories:

Every telephone company produces numerous telephone directories, one for each city served. In one telephone company

DEPARTMENT ACTIVITY ANALYSIS page 3

Function Name		
Production Control		
Department Name		Dept. No.
Receiving, Administration, Back orders		

Activity:	Date:	Prepared By:
Keypunch		

What are the input requirements that you and your supplier have agreed to?
Correct cards used for various types of activities
All input fields correctly filled out (zero defects)
No missing information
All schedules for data input strictly adhered to

What are the output requirements that you and your customer have agreed to?
All transactions punched with zero errors
All schedules for data output strictly adhered to
All transactions have proper TX codes

What are the quality measurements that will show if your output meets requirements?
Tracking of. . . Schedule misses
Defective keypunches
Transaction errors
Turnaround time

How many hours/week are spent on this activity? _____35_____ Hrs/Wk

COQ can be further classified into prevention, appraisal, and failure. What are they?

Prevention	_____	Hrs/Wk
Appraisal	_____	Hrs/Wk
Failure	_____	Hrs/Wk
Total COQ	_____	Hrs/Wk

FIGURE 7–14 *(continued)*

the directories were prepared for publication using a procession of twenty-one clerical steps, each step being performed by a separate employee. (Some steps required more than one person's full time, so the total department consisted of thirty-three employees.) The reorganization gave each employee the job of preparing a complete telepone directory, that is, each person performed all the twenty-one clerical steps needed to do the job. The results of the change were stunning:

	BEFORE	AFTER
Annual turnover of employees	28	0
Absenteeism rate	2.8%	0.6%
Errors per 1000 lines	3.9	1.1

In our dialect, the anatomy of the process was changed from a procession to an autonomous unit.

Conclusions on Company Efforts to Help Supervisors Analyze Their Microprocesses

The efforts to date have been few in number and of recent origin. Collectively they must be regarded as experimental. It is too early to be able to say with confidence that these efforts have been proven to lead to a good direction (or disproven).

The concept of bringing the supervisor and work force into the planning of the microprocess seems inherently sound. However, the methods tried out during the 1980s did not result in establishing a widely accepted approach. We are still in the experimental stage.

QUALITY CONTROL FOR MICROPROCESSES

Company efforts to increase supervisory participation in managing for quality have included some activities of a quality-control nature. Generally these efforts have missed the opportunity to use the feedback loop as a basis for developing the approach to quality control. In addition, because the programs have consisted of a mixture of elements from each process of the Juran Trilogy, the quality-control process has not been clearly identified. It should be.

Chapter 5 went into planning for quality control and also into quality control itself: carrying out the plan. In view of that, what we shall do now is to discuss the application to microprocesses. In doing so we shall follow the feedback loop as our guide.

Designing for Delegation of Quality Control

Note at the outset that *planning* for quality control is best done in a participative way. In contrast, *execution* of the plan is best assigned to individuals. In microprocesses that assignment must be mainly to the work force. The challenge to the planners and supervisors is to (a) design a quality-control process that is delegable, and (b) qualify the work force to be able to accept that delegation. The program for review of the microprocesses should provide for meeting both of these challenges.

Control Subjects

Control subjects for microprocesses include the numerous product features, process features, and input features. In addition there are features associated with maintaining the facilities. (Maintenance of facilities has grown in importance as a result of the trend to automated processes.)

The supervisory training should include use of the spreadsheet. Applied to planning for control, this spreadsheet lists the control features in the left-hand column. The remaining vertical columns are then filled in to show such things as units of measure, sensors, quality goals, and frequency of measurement (see Figure 5–3 for an example).

Measurement

Filling in the spreadsheets makes it easy to identify those features for which provisions for measurement are incomplete. The supervisor's experience can identify other cases in which measurement has been a problem. Feedback from the work force is helpful throughout.

Certain aspects of measurement (for example, how often to measure, what data to record, and what charts to prepare) are greatly dependent on local conditions. The supervisors should undergo enough training in basic statistical tools to qualify them to plan this aspect of the quality-control system.

A special problem in measurement is evaluation of the performance of the overall microprocess. The supervisor should, in collaboration with the customers, propose units of measure and sensors for this purpose. The resulting reports can then be published, critiqued, and revised based on experience.

Human Error During Measurement and Operations

At the microprocess level there is extensive use of human beings as sensors. This human sensing is subject to a whole array of sources of error. The most common of these types of errors, along with the associated remedies, are set out in Figure 5-4.

Human error is also a continuing problem during operations. At the microprocess level, work is often highly repetitive and thereby subject to lapses in human attention, that is, inadvertent errors. A major form of remedy is to try to eliminate the possibility of error, or "foolproof" the process, that is, redesign the process so it is not possible to make the error. The work force is an excellent source of ideas on error proofing.

Responsibilities for Quality Control

The question Who is responsible for quality? is unanswerable. The question must be broken down into responsibilities for specific actions and decisions, as illustrated by the special spreadsheet shown in Figure 5-5.

Ideally the work force should be placed in a state of self-control. This requires meeting the criteria set out in chapter 5, pages 147–150. Also, the analysis of the microprocess should ideally include determining whether these criteria have been met for all control subjects. Each exception then becomes a problem waiting to be solved.

In some microprocesses there is superimposed an independent checking or inspection that evaluates the final product and determines disposition. This is a form of cost of poor quality—a waste. To eliminate this waste requires meeting the criteria for self-inspection (see chapter 5, the section Determining Product Conformance: Self-Inspection).

Decision making based solely on facts can be delegated to the work force once the criteria for self-control and self-inspection have been met. Decisions involving judgment can also be delegated to the work force, provided that the criteria for decision making have been established and met (see, for example, Figure 5-7 and the associated discussion).

Although the great majority of control must be delegated to the work force, certain vital-few decisions should be reserved for the supervisor. These should be specifically identified and spelled out in the procedures.

QUALITY IMPROVEMENT
FOR MICROPROCESSES

The most important potential quality improvements are multifunctional or multidepartmental in nature. Such problems are not soluble by the supervisor of this or that microprocess. They require multidepartmental teams, as discussed in detail in chapter 3.

However, there remain a very large number of potential quality improvements that are *intra*departmental in nature, that is, within a microprocess. Such problems are often soluble by the departmental personnel, provided they are given the responsibility, training, and motivation.

Symptoms and Opportunities

Many symptoms of quality problems become evident from analysis of the quality-control plan and from the operating feedbacks. The evidence takes such forms as

1. Loops in the flow diagrams show that work is being redone.

2. Excess facilities have been provided as backups against service failures.

3. The list of customers is not fully known.

4. The vital-few customers have not been fully identified.

5. Some customer needs are not fully known or understood.

6. Some customer needs are not being met.

7. The list of products has not been fully identified.

8. Some products are not competitive.

9. The relation of product cost to value is inadequate.

10. Some products serve no useful purpose.

Each of such symptoms (and others) points to an opportunity for improvement. Collectively these are so numerous that it becomes necessary to establish priorities: which problems are to be tackled and which must wait.

The Infrastructure

The effort to improve quality at the microprocess level should be a part of the overall quality-improvement approach of the company. The infrastructure discussed in chapter 3 can be extended to include quality improvement for the microprocesses.

In some companies the review of microprocesses has been tackled without first (or simultaneously) undertaking quality improvement for the major quality problems. (This approach is not favored by the author.) In such cases the infrastructure is established at the lower levels of the company. Typical features include a structured procedure, a training package, and a facilitator-trainer who also coordinates the effort.

The Improvement Process

This is discussed in detail in chapter 3. Applied to projects within microprocesses, the project team consists of the supervisor or, alternatively, a group of work-force members, for example, a QC circle. However, the improvement process does not differ from that used for macroprocesses. The team is trained to

1. Study the symptoms
2. Theorize as to causes
3. Test the theories
4. Find the cause or causes
5. Stimulate a remedy
6. Establish controls to hold the gains

(The approach to training will be discussed in chapter 10, "Training for Quality.")

Resources

It is all too common for upper managers to launch quality-improvement undertakings without adequate attention to the resources needed. This has been a problem for the microprocesses as well. One of the critical resources needed is the time required to carry out the improvement process. To tackle an improvement project likely adds about 10 percent to the workload of the supervisor. The supervisor may nevertheless find ways to work it out, but the "system" has not made it easy. (For elaboraion, see the section that follows.)

Analysis of the Microprocess: By Whom?

This analysis involves some time-consuming tasks, such as preparing the flow diagrams and spreadsheets, contacting those who are affected, summing up the available data, and tracking down other needed data. Various options are available for getting this work done. These options consist mainly of the following:

1. *The full-time analyst.* In this approach a full-time analyst (systems analyst, quality engineer, procedures analyst, industrial engineer, and so forth) is assigned to conduct the analysis. He or she "makes the rounds," interviewing the cognizant people (managers, supervisors, the work force) and observing the activities. Based on these inputs he or she prepares the flow diagrams, spreadsheets, and so forth. He or she then prepares a report and makes recommendations for revisions.

For the supervisor, use of a full-time analyst helps to solve the problem of finding the time to do the analysis. However, this approach has deficiencies that some companies are no longer willing to accept:

The approach retains much of the concept of separating planning from execution. This concept is inherently divisive, especially at departmental levels.

The analysts exhibit the biases inherent in *their* culture. These biases then enter their recommendations.

Use of full-time analysts tends to confer "ownership" of the process on the analysts. Companies are increasingly moving in the direction of shifting this sense of ownership to the line personnel.

Line managers whose jobs are affected by recommendations prepared by someone else tend to feel that there has been a lack of full participation. This feeling reduces their willingness to support the resulting recommendations.

Giving line managers greater responsibility for quality planning requires that the line managers acquire proficiency in the use of the tools of analysis. This acquisition is delayed if full-time analysts continue to do the analysis.

2. *The departmental supervisor.* In this approach each supervisor is given the responsibility of getting the analysis done, either on a do-it-yourself basis or by enlisting the help of others. The supervisors are provided with a structured plan for analysis (procedures plus forms to fill out). They are also given training in how to carry out the structured plan.

3. *Managerial teams* (of supervisors, analysts, and so forth). Under this concept the supervisor of a microprocess and selected customers and suppliers are assigned, as a team, to do the analysis and replanning. This assignment is preceded by training in how to plan for quality.

Generally, use of these managerial teams has met such objectives as

a. Arming the supervisors with the tools and skills of quality planning

b. Increasing the supervisors' sense of participation in quality planning

c. Shifting the function of quality planning to the line supervisors

d. Increasing the line supervisors' sense of "ownership" of the process

e. Minimizing the effect of biases of full-time planners

f. Increasing the willingness of line supervisors to support the recommendations of the analysis

The big disadvantage of using managerial teams is the time it takes. Multiple people (teams) must do what could be done by one trained individual. In addition, this added work is superimposed on the time of people who already are carrying a full-time load.

We do know that as the line supervisors acquire experience in the use of the quality-planning tools they become more proficient. But to reach a state of proficiency does require finding the time to participate in the work of the teams.

4. *The work force.* The urge to increase work-force participation in quality planning is part of a broader movement to involve workers in decisions that affect their jobs. The premises are that

a. All workers have contributions to make, owing to their intimate knowledge of job conditions.

b. These contributions can include ideas for improvement as well as identification of problems.

c. Many workers want to contribute.

d. Such contributions increase worker morale, provide a sense of ownership, and improve management-worker relations generally

To date, organized methods to provide for worker participation have consisted largely of (a) provison for *individual* contribution in forms such as suggestion systems, or (b) provision for group contribution by *teams* of workers in forms such as QC circles.

In the case of planning for quality, worker participation appears to require yet another form: teams consisting of a mixture of supervisors and work-force members. The reason is the mixture of inputs needed. The workers have much expertise on the details of "their" operations. However, the effects of those operations usually extend well beyond departmental boundaries.

As yet we have no clear picture of the effectiveness of such teams. The experiments have been few and the results have been inconsistent: "the jury is still out."

In many Japanese companies QC circles successfully carry out much replanning for quality. What has made this possible is their training and experience derived from carrying out huge numbers of quality-improvement projects. For most of these projects, the remedy has consisted of replanning the processes.

THE END RESULT OF THE ANALYSIS

When done systematically, the end result of the analysis is an information package consisting of

1. The conclusions reached by the analysis

2. Proposals (recommendations) relative to products, processes, inputs, and so forth

3. Supporting information (flow diagrams, spreadsheets, data, and so forth)

The proposals are generally presented in the standard formats used in the company for describing products, processes, and procedures.

Some of the proposals concern matters over which the microprocess itself has full jurisdiction. In such cases the departmental supervisor can adopt them forthwith.

Other proposals require the concurrence of, or action from, other departments. Such proposals then require follow-up until (a) the recommended action is taken or (b) there is a decision by cognizant authorities not to adopt the proposals.

UPPER MANAGEMENT'S ROLE IN THE QUALITY MANAGEMENT OF MICROPROCESSES

With respect to the quality management of microprocesses, there is no practical way for upper management to contribute to these processes *individually*. The microprocesses are numerous. Many involve technology and details that are unfamiliar to upper managers. However, it is feasible for upper management to make a useful contribution to the microprocesses *collectively*.

What upper management can and should do is to *mandate a self-auditing of microprocesses,* to be conducted by the supervisors in charge, aided by their customers and suppliers. Such a mandate must be specially designed to fit the needs of each company, and this special design requires a team approach. To this end upper management should *create a project team whose mission is to design an appropriate system for the self-auditing of microprocesses by the respective supervisors.*

MOTIVATION FOR QUALITY IN OPERATIONAL MANAGEMENT

Our main discussion of motivation will be in chapter 9, "Motivation for Quality." However, it is useful at this point to notice a special aspect of motivation for quality improvement as applied to macroprocesses and microprocesses.

A successful quality improvement within a microprocess often improves the departmental performance of the supervisor who carried out the project. This feature of personal benefit has stimulated many supervisors of microprocesses to undertake quality improvement on a voluntary basis, that is, even in the absence of an upper-management mandate to improve quality.

In the case of macroprocesses, the motivational situation is quite different. Now the process is multidepartmental in nature; therefore a multidepartmental team is needed to carry out a quality-improvement project. If the project is successful, there is a benefit to the company but not necessarily to the departmental performance of any team member. This feature of absence of personal benefit is an obstacle to securing quality improvement of macroprocesses on a voluntary basis. Instead such improvement must be mandated by upper management. In addition, the necessary infrastructure must be established, as set out in chapter 3.

TRAINING FOR OPERATIONAL QUALITY MANAGEMENT

Training for quality (and the associated tools) is the subject of chapter 10, "Training for Quality." What is pertinent at this point is that there is extensive commonality that is applicable to operational quality management.

At the microprocess level the commonalities include

1. *The TRIPROL concept* (supplier, processor, customer). It applies to every processor team.

2. *The flow diagram.* It is a universal aid in identifying the customers.

3. *The spreadsheet.* It is a universal aid in the orderly arrangement of masses of detail.

4. *The responsibility matrix.* It lists the decisions and actions to be taken, and identifies who does what.

5. *The feedback loop.* It is basic to all quality control.

For macroprocesses, there are additional commonalities, including:

1. *The quality-planning road map.* It generalizes the approach to meeting customers' needs.

2. *The spiral.* It sets out the sequence of "concept to customer" new-product activities.

3. *The breakthrough sequence.* It is basic to all quality improvement.

These and yet other commonalities make it clear that much of the training in managing for quality can be built around a few basic concepts and tools.

HIGH POINTS OF CHAPTER 7

Planning for macroprocesses requires some form of team approach.

Planners who are trained in quality-oriented expertise have outperformed planners who must secure the needed expertise from quality specialists.

For many macroprocesses, responsibility for quality control is vague, that is, no one owns the macroprocess.

Upper managers should not wait for an evolutionary process to develop performance reports for macroprocesses.

Upper-management auditing is one way to break up deadlocks with respect to poor performance of macroprocesses.

During upper-management auditing of the product-development process, the most critical focus should be on the adequacy of the early-warning system.

Failure to conduct Santayana reviews in depth can result in overlooking the major opportunities for improvement.

Upper managers should be alert to assure that, when the opportunities are similar, the priority should go to projects that are not capital intensive.

A major part of the analysis of supplier relations should consist of review of prior performances of suppliers, both "good" and "poor," so as to discover the causes behind the differences.

It is not feasible for upper managers to become involved with the microprocesses individually. However, upper managers can and should become involved with the microprocesses *collectively.*

An effort to replan microprocesses on a broad scale should be preceded by training in how to plan for quality.

Managers should be alert to a common illusion relative to replanning of micrprocesses. Such replanning seldom solves the macroplanning problems.

In microprocesses the responsibility for execution of the plan of quality control must be delegated mainly to the work force.

The vital few decisions which are reserved to be made by supervisors should be specifically identified and spelled out in the procedures.

TASKS FOR UPPER MANAGERS

To deal with deficiencies in macroprocesses requires action by upper managers.

Upper managers should take positive steps to bring performance of macroprocesses into the system of upper management reports.

Upper management should identify the macroprocesses which require high level quality audits, and should take steps to organize such audits.

Upper management can make a useful contribution to the microprocesses collectively by mandating a self-audit of microprocesses, to be conducted by the supervisors in charge, aided by their customers and suppliers.

Upper management should create a project team whose mission is to design an appropriate system for self-audit of microprocesses by the respective supervisors.

] *8* [

The Work Force and Quality

The purpose of this chapter is to

1. Identify the potential contributions of the work force to managing for quality
2. Show how to establish the infrastructure and conditions that are necessary to realize this potential

Who Is the Work Force?

As used here, the term *work force* applies to all employees except the managerial hierarchy and the "professional" specialists. (The dividing line is not precise, and there are borderline cases.)

Division of the Subject Matter

The overall relationship of the work force to quality goes beyond potential contributions and necessary infrastructure. It also includes (a) the motivation to make the contributions, and (b) the training required to be able to make the contributions. This subject matter is divided up as follows:

SUBJECT MATTER	CHAPTER DISCUSSED IN
Potential contributions of the work force, and the necessary infrastructure	8, "The Work Force and Quality"
Motivation to make the contributions	9, "Motivation for Quality"
Training to be able to make the contributions	10, "Training for Quality"

With respect to the three processes of the Juran Trilogy, we shall use the following sequence:

1. *Quality control.* This comes first because it has for decades been the dominant form of quality-related responsibility assigned to the work force.

2. *Quality improvement.* This comes next in view of recent activity to bring the work force into the quality-improvement process.

3. *Quality planning.* This is the least developed area of work-force involvement but one that will undergo expansion in the years ahead.

The Need to Be Specific

Any effort to introduce change into work-force practice requires providing each work-force member with a clear answer to the question, What should I do that is different from what I have been doing? Applied to efforts to increase work-force participation in quality-related matters, the answer to that logical question must be in specific job-related terms:

What are the quality-related actions and decisions involved in the worker's process?

In what way can the worker participate in those actions and decisions?

THE CONTROL CONCEPT: THE FEEDBACK LOOP

In chapter 5 we looked at the concepts behind the quality-control process and at how that process is built around the feedback loop. In this chapter we shall examine the application of that concept to work-force activities. For the sake of convenience, we shall occasionally repeat some material out of chapter 5.

We define quality control as a managerial process during which we

1. Evaluate actual performance

2. Compare actual performance with goals

3. Take action on the differences

The concept of control is one of "holding the status quo," that is, keeping a planned process in its planned state so that it remains able to meet the operating goals.

The Feedback Loop

The control process takes place by use of the feedback loop. The basic elements of the feedback loop and their interrelations are reproduced in Figure 8–1.

The flow of events progresses as follows:

1. The sensor (which is "plugged into the process") evaluates actual performance.

2. The sensor reports this performance to an umpire.

3. The umpire also receives information on what the goal or standard is.

4. The umpire compares actual performance to the goal. If the difference warrants action the umpire energizes an actuator.

5. The actuator makes the changes needed to bring performance into line with goals.

The Control Pyramid

Any company has a huge number of things to control: the myriad features of the various products and the myriad features of the various processes. There is no possibility for the managers and professional specialists to do all that control work. Instead the company designs a plan of delegation somewhat as depicted in Figure 8–2.

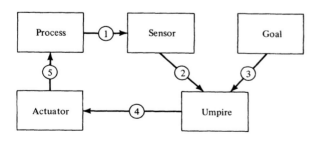

FIGURE 8–1 The feedback loop

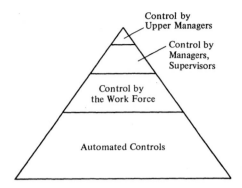

FIGURE 8–2 The pyramid of control

In this chapter we are concerned with the two lower levels of the control pyramid.

THE IDEAL: MAXIMUM DELEGATION TO THE WORK FORCE

Ideally quality control should be delegated to the work force to the maximum extent possible. Under such an ideal arrangement, the work force carries out all the repetitive roles within the feedback loop: sensor, umpire, and actuator. Such delegation provides benefits for managers as well as work-force members:

1. A shorter feedback loop and thereby an earlier response to quality problems

2. A greater sense of participation and ownership by the work force

3. Liberation of managers from much delegable work

Before making such delegation it is essential to meet certain criteria—criteria for self-control and self-checking. We shall shortly return to these criteria.

DELEGATION TO ARTISANS

The ideal of maximum delegation to the work force is largely attained in the case of the artisan. We define the term *artisan* as someone qualified to carry out a skilled occupation (craft, etc.) requiring special training and experience.

The popular image of an artisan is someone who undergoes an apprenticeship and thereby becomes qualified to practice a skilled trade as an independent craftsman, for example, carpenter or shoemaker. Such independent craftsmen still abound. However, many artisans are employed within the work force of organizations, large and small. Their occupations have names such as computer programmer, maintenance mechanic, field service representative, and tool maker.

As related to quality, what distinguishes the artisan from other work-force members is the high degree of self-sufficiency. This self-sufficiency extends to many aspects of quality planning and quality control.

Product Design

In many cases the artisan has direct access to customers, external and internal, and thereby to customer needs. Some of these needs repeat over and over again, so that product design can be standardized. Other needs vary from customer to customer or from time to time. To meet such varying needs requires special designs. Hence the term "tailored to fit."

Process Design

The artisan's skills are based on knowledge of a process—a combination of certain information, materials, facilities, and tools. This process is dedicated to a certain class of product features. However, in many cases the artisan must vary (tailor) the process to be able to produce the needed product.

Quality Control

Artisans also conduct operations: they execute their own plans by running the processes and producing the products. In doing so they are largely in a state of self-control: the criteria for self-control have been met. In addition, artisans often are in a state of self-inspection: they make the decision of whether their products meet customer needs.

The Artisan Concept as a Model

Most managers have been searching for ways to provide the work force with greater participation in job-related matters. Those same managers have also been looking for ways to delegate more responsibility to the work force. It is evident that the concept of the artisan is a major aid in reaching those goals. To the extent that jobs can be redesigned to enable the job holders to become artisans, to that extent it becomes easier for managers to reach those goals. Upper managers should look closely at the way in which the concept of the artisan *enables workers to participate widely in quality-related matters and to accept a broader delegation of responsibility.*

DELEGATION TO OTHER WORKERS

The bulk of the work force lacks, in varying degrees, the special skills that make possible a self-sufficiency in product design, process design, and quality control. This lack of special skills imposes limits on the ability of the managers to delegate responsibility to the work force. In consequence, a great deal of activity is carried out by separating planning from execution. In particular, product design and process design are largely assigned to specialists, as discussed in chapter 4.

One of the by-products of separating planning from execution is that the work force becomes insulated from knowledge of fitness for use—from knowledge of the impact of their product on various customers. Lacking this knowledge, the work force would be doomed to produce and control blindly *unless* they were provided with some form of knowledge that can serve as a substitute for knowledge of fitness for use. That substitute consists of specifications, standards, and procedures. Collectively this array of substitute knowledge provides the work force with the means of understanding what their responsibility is and with some of the essentials of self-control.

The separation of planning from execution also creates a division of responsibility and thereby a breeding ground for confusion. Managers have learned that the way to minimize such confusion is through defining clearly who is to be responsible for what.

THE WORK FORCE AND QUALITY

The Specifics: Decisions and Actions

Managers have spent untold hours in futile efforts to answer the question: Who is responsible for quality? There can be no satisfactory answer to that question because it is not phrased in terms of decisions and actions. For work-force activities that repeat themselves many times annually, it is necessary to identify, with precision, those decisions and actions that are inherent in the worker's job. Then and only then does it become possible to be specific with respect to responsibility.

In like manner, to give maximum delegation to the work force requires being specific about which decisions and actions are to be delegated. The delegation must be made item by item—specific decisions and specific actions. Each such item has its own criteria to be met before the delegation can be made. (See the section Who Does What? which follows in this chapter.)

Work Stations, Control Stations, and Spreadsheets

At the work-force level, work is organized by (1) work stations that carry out the prescribed operations of running the processes and producing the product features, and (2) control stations that are quality-oriented and that carry out the steps within the feedback loop.

In the ideal situation the control station is identical with the work station, that is, the workers who conduct operations also carry out the quality controls. Whether this ideal is reached or not, the functions of operation and control are different. The difference can be seen by comparing the respective spreadsheets. A generic spreadsheet for operations (sometimes called a route sheet) is shown in Figure 8–3.

In Figure 8–3 the horizontal rows show the operational steps (tasks, etc.) to be performed and the sequence to be followed. The vertical columns contain information pertaining to the performance of the operations: specifications to be met; procedures to follow; and equipment, tools, and instruments to use.

A generic spreadsheet for quality control is shown in Figure 8–4.

] 267 [

Sequence of Operations	Product Specification	Process Specification	Procedures, Cautions	Equipment, Facilities	Tools	Instruments	Data Requirements	Decision Criteria
1.								
2.								
3.								
4.								
5.								
6.								

FIGURE 8-3   Spreadsheet for the planning of operations

In Figure 8-4 the horizontal rows are "control subjects," that is, various product and process features for which quality goals have been set. The vertical columns contain information relative to elements of the feedback loop, such as the quality goals, the units of measure, the means for sensing, the measurement plan (for example, size of sample, frequency of sampling, data to be recorded and analyzed), and the criteria for judging conformance. (For a specific example, see Figure 8-5.)

Control Subjects	Quality Goals	Units of Measure	Sensors	Sample Size	Frequency of Sample	Data Requirements	Decision Criteria
1.							
2.							
3.							
4.							
5.							
6.							

FIGURE 8-4   Generic spreadsheet for quality control

] 268 [

Control Subject \ Process Control Features	Unit of Measure	Type of Sensor	Goal	Frequency of Measurement	Sample Size	Criteria for Decision Making	Responsibility for Decision Making	...
Wave solder conditions:								
Solder temperature	Degree F	Thermo-couple	505 Deg.F	Continuous	N/A	510 Deg.F reduce heat 500 Deg.F increase heat	Operator	...
Conveyor speed	Feet per minute (fpm)	fpm meter	4.5 fpm	1/hour	N/A	5 fpm reduce speed 4 fpm increase speed	Operator	...
Alloy purity	% Total contam-inants	Lab chemical analysis	1.5% max.	1/month	15 grams	At 1.5%, drain bath, replace solder	Process engineer	..
.	.	.	.	.	.	.	.	
.		.	.	.			.	

FIGURE 8–5   The process-control spreadsheet

Decisions and Actions: The Commonalities

In terms of the technology used, virtually no two spreadsheets are alike. However, in terms of the decisions and actions taken on the work floor, the operations and controls are alike; they exhibit a high degree of commonality despite wide differences in the technology. This commonality shows up in the form of a universal series of decisions and actions as follows:

1. *Set up.* This action consists of assembling the information, materials, and equipment needed to commence operations and organizing them into a state of readiness to produce.

2. *Verify setup.* This action is control oriented. It consists of determining (evaluating) whether the process, if started, will produce good work. The evaluation may be done directly on the process (check list, count down, etc.). Alternatively the evaluation may be done on the product (for example, the printer's page proof): the product "tells on the process."

3. *Start up or not?* This decision is based on the evaluation made to verify the setup. The evaluation is largely factual: Is there conformance to the criteria or not?

4. *Produce.* This is the familiar central action of conducting operations: running the process and producing the product.

5. *Reverify.* This control-oriented action is taken periodically to assure that the process remains in a state of readiness to produce in accordance with the quality goals.

6. *Continue to run, or stop?* This decision is based on the results of reverification. Some of the criteria are identical with those of the "start up or not" decision. For mass production processes, this cycle of reverification and decision making is repeated over and over again.

7. *Product conformance or not?* Until now, the series of decisions and actions are all related to the process. This step relates to the product produced by the process. At the work-force level, the question arises, Does the resulting product conform to the quality goals or not? This is yet another decision to be made, over and over again.

8. *Disposition of the product.* The usual rule is that products that conform to established standards are sent on to the next destination. Disposition of nonconforming products is more complex and requires a more detailed definition of responsibility. (See the section Self-Inspection, which follows in this chapter.)

Note that this list interlaces with the planned activities set out in the spreadsheets for operations and quality control (Figures 8–3 and 8–4).

Who Does What?

Responsibility for quality should be clear, but it is never made clear by pronouncements such as "Quality is everybody's job." Responsibility at the work-force level becomes clear through the process of identifying the decisions and actions that are critical to quality and then assigning clear responsibility for each. A proven methodology is to prepare a spreadsheet such as Figure 8–6.

In Figure 8–6 the critical decisions and actions are shown in the horizontal rows. The vertical columns list the persons who may be candidates for making the decisions and taking the actions: the workers who run the processes (clerks, assemblers, and so forth), setup specialists, equipment-maintenance personnel, inspectors, engineers, and supervisors of all of the foregoing people.

Reaching a Consensus

Once such a spreadsheet has been created, the problem is to arrive at a consensus on who should make which decisions, and who

	PRODUCTION			INSPECTION		
DECISIONS, ACTIONS	Setup man	Worker	Supervisor	Bench	Patrol	Other
Process Decisions						
setup						
setup verification						
run						
running verification						
Product Decisions						
conformance						
fitness for use						

FIGURE 8–6   Spreadsheet for who does what

should take which actions. The process for arriving at a consensus is as follows:

1. Convene those who have an interest in "who does what."

2. Through discussion, identify which are the key decisions and actions needed to attain quality for the product and process under discussion.

3. Identify also who is available to make these decisions and take these actions.

4. Enter the information of steps 2 and 3 into the rows and columns of the spreadsheet (Figure 8–6).

5. Give each person a copy of the resulting spreadsheet.

6. Ask each person to fill out the spreadsheet based on "Who in your opinion should make which decisions and take which actions?"

7. Collect all the spreadsheets; tally up all individual opinions so as to create one spreadsheet that summarizes all opinions. It will be found that with respect to some matters, there is unanimity; with respect to other matters there are differences of opinion.

8. Discuss the differences so as to arrive at a consensus.

THE WORK FORCE
AND THE FEEDBACK LOOP

A second source of commonality relative to quality control on the work floor has its origin in the universal feedback loop (Figure 5-1). The steps within that loop are common to all forms of control. It is useful to examine those steps as they apply to quality control on the work floor, with special attention to those steps that have been undergoing substantial change.

Control Subjects

The center around which the feedback loop is built is the *control subject.*

At the outset control subjects consist of the product and process features evolved during product design and process design. Then, as operating experience is acquired, additional control features evolve for reasons related to improvements made, conditions that have changed, and lessons learned.

Each control subject then requires its own feedback loop, resulting in a great many combinations of control subjects and elements of the feedback loop. To keep track of all these combinations, it is useful to adopt a structured approach in the form of the quality-control spreadsheet, as set out in Figure 8-4 and the associated explanation.

Quality Goals

Most quality goals are established during the product-design and process-design phases of quality planning. In organizations where planning is widely separated from operations, these goals are typically stated in the form of specifications to be met, or procedures to be followed. Of course, such goals are substitutes for the real thing; the real goals are to meet customer needs.

It is now widely accepted that quality is better served if the work force understands the purposes behind the goals—the "why." Ingenious ways have been evolved to provide such understanding to work-force members: moving pictures of how the product is used, exhibits of quality problems encountered by customers, visits by customers, work-force visits to customers' premises. These and still other methods are beneficial to quality in two very different ways:

1. They provide the work force with a deeper understanding of how their work relates to that of other persons, and thereby with a better base for decision making.

2. They provide a subtle form of motivation. Awareness of how one's actions impact other human beings is a stronger motivator than lifeless specifications and procedures.

Sensing and Decision Making

The sensors (technological and human) evaluate the product and process. The resulting data provide the umpire with the basis for decision making.

Decision making on the work floor can be aided greatly by providing the work force with well-designed data inputs such as summaries and trends. Some of these are discussed in the section Statistical Tools: Aids in Decision Making, which follows later in this chapter.

Decisions on the process (run or stop) have traditionally been delegated to the work force, subject to established criteria. (The role of umpire is assigned to the work force.) Such delegation carries a risk of producing poor quality unless the worker is in a state of self-control. (See the section Self-Control at the Work-Force Level, which follows in this chapter.)

Decisions on the product (conformance or not) have in the United States often been delegated to an "independent" umpire, that is, an inspector or checker. This arrangement is outwardly protective of quality but it creates some unwelcome side effects; for example, human relations are adversely affected, and quality problems are "solved" by detection rather than by elimination.

It is feasible to delegate decisions on the product to the work force, but only under certain conditions. (See the section Self-Inspection, which follows in this chapter.)

Corrective Action

A finding of nonconformance by an umpire signals a need for corrective action. Some of these nonconformances have their origin in process features that are controllable by the work force. In such cases the work force can take corrective action through process readjustments: new instructions are keyboarded into the computer; dials are reset; valves are opened or shut.

In other cases the origin of the nonconformance lies elsewhere, or is unclear. For such cases, corrective action is often beyond the capacity of the work force. For elaboration of the approach, see chapter 5, the section Corrective Action.

SELF-CONTROL AT THE WORK-FORCE LEVEL

The basic concept of self-control is set out in chapter 5, in the section Self-Control. The concept applies fully at the work-force level. Ideally the work force should be in a state of full mastery with respect to quality: they should be provided with all the essentials required to produce products that meet the quality goals. These essentials consist of the following, which become the criteria to be met:

1. The means of knowing what are the quality goals. This criterion is met by providing the work force with specifications and procedures.

2. The means of knowing what is the actual performance. This criterion is met by providing the work force with a system of measurement.

3. The means of changing the performance in the event of nonconformance. This criterion is met by providing the work force with a process that (a) is inherently capable of meeting the quality goals, and (b) is provided with features that enable the work force to readjust the process as needed to bring it into conformance.

If all the above criteria have been met, the work force is in a state of self-control. Any resulting nonconformances are said to be worker controllable. If any of the criteria have not been met, the management's planning has been incomplete, and the resulting nonconformances are said to be management controllable.

Obstacles to Self-control

The advantages of putting the work force into a state of self-control are obvious and important. To this end, upper managers are well advised to establish improvement projects with a mission of *identifying past obstacles to self-control so that they will not be carried over into new plans.* Traditionally, the more usual obstacles have included the following:

LACK OF REAL-TIME MEASUREMENT. For some processes, the work force is unable to secure real-time information: the measurement system is designed to evaluate the final product but not the intermediate stages; the means for measurement are not made available on the work floor; for example, a sample must be sent to some laboratory. When such problems are specifically addressed, often enough some simple solutions emerge.

For many processes, certain essential tests have required sending samples to a nearby (or distant) laboratory for evaluation. In some cases the associated waiting times are risky. In some of these processes, simple tests have been designed to be conducted on the work floor by the work force. Comparison of test results establishes that there is high correlation. The work force is then trained to do the testing locally, on a real-time basis. Thereafter the decisions are based on the local tests, while the laboratory maintains an audit.

LACK OF DATA ANALYSIS. Certain processes produce their products on a unit-by-unit basis: one document after another, one gear wheel after another. In many such cases knowledge of whether individual units of product conform to quality goals is only a part of a complete approach to quality control. Often such processes are essentially continuous and harbor certain inherent trends—for example, the ink gets progressively more faint; the tools wear; the temperature rises. Knowledge of such trends can help the work force to secure early warning of quality problems ahead. Similarly, the products collectively can drift in their relation to the goals, or their dispersion can change. Knowledge of such trends can likewise warn the work force of quality problems ahead.

Traditional control systems made only minimal provision to bring such information to the work force; the emphasis was on detection of nonconforming products. The recent trend is strongly in the direction of providing information on process trends and on the relation of process conditions to product results. To provide this new information has required radical changes in the systems for measurement, data collection, and data analysis.

LACK OF ADJUSTMENT CAPABILITY. Ideally the work force should be able to "dial in" the instructions to the process at the time of start-up and also as needed for periodic readjustment. Some processes are so equipped; others are not. The ideal criteria to be met by the planners are well known:

1. Each product feature should be linked to a single process variable.

2. Means should be provided for convenient adjustment of the process setting for that variable.

3. There should be a predictable, precise relationship between the amount of change in the process setting and the amount of effect on the product feature.

Before these criteria can be met, the planners themselves must learn a good deal about the relationships between process variables and product results.

Self-control and Motivation

The foregoing discussion of the criteria for worker self-control is pertinent also to the subject of worker motivation for quality. A lot of damage can be done (and has been done) by efforts to motivate the work force to do good work despite the fact that many are not in a state of self-control.

Before embarking on any plan of motivating the work force to do good work, upper management should determine *the extent to which the workers are in a state of self-control.*

SELF-INSPECTION

The concept of self-inspection is quite different from that of self-control. Self-control relates to the worker's role in running the process and producing the product. Self-inspection relates to the worker's role in making the product-conformance decision, that is, judging whether the product conforms to product goals. This is a critical decision because of the widespread management policy that products that conform to quality goals are presumed to be fit for delivery to the next destination. Under such a policy a worker who makes product-conformance decisions also decides whether products should be sent on to the next destination.

In most companies the product-conformance decision has traditionally *not* been delegated to the work force. A major reason has been that the system of judging worker performance did not give top priority to quality. Hence, it was risky to delegate the product conformance decision to the work force. Instead the decision was (usually) delegated to "independent" inspectors and checkers.

Ideally the operating forces at the lowest levels of organization *should* make the product conformance decision. However some prerequisite criteria must be met first:

1. *Quality is number one.* Quality must have undoubted top priority.

2. *Mutual confidence.* The managers must trust the work force enough to be willing to make the delegation, and the work force must have enough confidence in the managers to be willing to accept the responsibility.

3. *Self-control.* The conditions for self-control should be in place so that the work force has all the means necessary to do good work.

4. *Training.* The workers should be trained to make the product conformance decisions and should also be tested to assure that they make good decisions.

In connection with self-inspection, it is well to keep in mind that the human component of sensing and decision making is subject to considerable error. The principal error types and their remedies are tabulated in Figure 5–4. (For further elaboration see Juran 1988.)

STATISTICAL TOOLS: AIDS
IN DECISION MAKING

The 1980s ushered in a surge of interest and training in statistical tools, especially at the supervisory and work-force levels. This interest and training is pertinent to the subject of quality control by the work force.

Statistical Tools: What and Why

As used here, the term *statistical tools* refers to the tools employed for data collection and analysis.

In thinking about statistical tools, it is important not to confuse the means with the end. The end purpose is to improve decision making. Decisions based on fact have always outperformed decisions based on hunch or empirical judgment.

Craftsmen produced high quality products long before statistical tools were evolved. They did so by close attention to such things as the properties of materials and the effects of processes. The proliferation of measuring instruments then provided facts of higher and higher precision. In the offices accountants evolved systems of data collection and analysis without calling them statistical tools. The contribution of statistical tools to this march of events has been to *systematize* data collection and analysis. This systematic approach provides helpful guidelines in how to collect, analyze, and interpret data.

Statistical tools are being increasingly applied to improve decision making on the work floor. The major areas of application involve two types of decisions that must be made on the work floor, over and over again:

1. Should the process run or stop?
2. Does the product conform to the quality goals?

Decisions on the Process

To make the decisions on the process, the work force periodically selects and evaluates samples from the process. The resulting data are then compared with the process goals to see if the process is well aimed. In addition, the data are examined for trends to see whether the process is undergoing change—that is, whether the present data differ from the preceding evaluations, and by how much. Any observed differences then raise a further question: whether the difference is due to (a) a real change in the process, or (b) an apparent change arising from chance variation.

An ingenious statistical tool helps to answer this question—to distinguish between real changes and false alarms. That tool is the Shewhart control chart. (For elaboration, see chapter 5, Figure

5-5, and the associated explanation in the section Interpretation: Statistical Significance.)

Decisions on the Product: Individual Units

Decisions on the product consist of decisions at two levels:

1. Units of product individually
2. Units of product collectively

At the *individual* level, the product goal is set out in a specification, for example, the instructions for filling out some document, or an engineering drawing. That specification applies to each and every unit of product. For any unit of product, the decision to be made is whether or not it conforms to specification. This is a factual determination. It is made by comparing the results of evaluation with the specification. The decision then takes the form of (a) the unit conforms fully with the specification, or (b) the unit is nonconforming with respect to one or more of the goals set out in the specification.

It is feasible to delegate this decision to the work force provided the criteria for self-inspection have been met.

Decisions on the Product: Units Collectively

At the level of the products collectively, an additional decision arises. Many products are made in such large numbers that 100-percent evaluation is not economic—for example, the cost of test is high, the test is destructive, or the process is very uniform. In such cases testing is done on only a sample of the units. The test results are then used to make a decision on whether the batch conforms.

Note that in such cases the criteria for deciding batch conformance are not spelled out in a specification issued by a product-development department. Instead the criteria are set out in a sampling plan issued (usually) by the quality department. These criteria consist of goals such as the minimum for mean time to failure, tolerance limits on the average of the evaluations, the maximum limit on the dispersion of the evaluations, and the maximum on the number of nonconformances in the sample.

It is feasible to delegate such conformance decisions to the work force as well. However, these decisions on the units collectively are at a higher level of sophistication, and at the same time, there is more at stake. Not only must the criteria for self-inspection be met; the training in the underlying statistical methodology must be more extensive as well.

DELEGATION TO UNATTENDED (NONHUMAN) PROCESSES

At the base of the control pyramid (Figure 5–2) delegation of control is to unattended processes, such as automated processes, robots, numerically controlled machines, and computer-aided processes. These processes may be dedicated to a very narrow list of tasks. Alternatively they may be programmable for a variety of tasks.

Quality planning for these nonhuman processes makes use of the same concepts as are used for processes employing human workers. An unattended process may be a work station, a control station, or both. The same spreadsheets (Figure 8–3 and 8–4) are applicable.

The principal concepts for quality control consist of one of the following:

1. *A high degree of built-in stability.* An example is the hardened steel die that can stamp out tens of thousands of pieces at a high level of uniformity before it requires resharpening.

2. *The feedback loop in the form of a servomechanism.* A simple example is the thermostat used to regulate temperature, in which all the steps within the feedback loop are carried out by nonhuman means.

Despite being unattended, nonhuman processes require attention in the form of *maintenance*. The measuring elements require maintenance of their accuracy and precision; the operating elements require maintenance of their process capability.

The methodology for such maintenance is well known. It consists of:

1. A schedule for frequency of check
2. A countdown of what to do during a check

3. The necessary facilities and procedures for recalibrating and resetting

The weakest link in this maintenance chain is adherence to schedule. For unattended processes, the need to adhere to scheduled maintenance is at its highest. The popular maxim "If it ain't broke, don't fix it" has no place here.

THE WORK FORCE AND QUALITY IMPROVEMENT

The term *quality improvement* is used here in the same sense as in chapter 3. The definitions are unchanged: organized creation of beneficial change; attainment of unprecedented levels of performance. The relation to managing for quality remains as shown on the Juran Trilogy diagram, Figure 2–3.

The Prior Cycles

Most companies periodically undertake efforts (programs, drives, etc.) to make improvements in various directions, such as productivity, safety, and human relations. Each such effort goes through a cycle of launch, scale up, maturity, decay, and phase out. Often these efforts are directed at the work force as well as the managerial levels. In any case the work-force members are interested spectators. From their perceptions, they draw conclusions as to the merits and detriments of the prior cycles. These conclusions are then used to judge the likely effect of new initiatives taken by the company, including an effort to secure improvement in quality.

These prior perceptions will obviously influence the reception that the work force will give to a new initiative. Managers should take *soundings to understand the work force's perceptions and to use those perceptions as an input to the proposed quality-improvement effort.*

Potential Roles

The work force has the potential to assist in the quality-improvement process. The extent of this assistance varies, depending on (a) the specific steps in the improvement process and (b) whether the project is interdepartmental or intradepartmental. Figure

Extent of Contribution to Quality –
Improvement Projects:

NATURE OF CONTRIBUTION	DEPARTMENTAL	INTERDEPARTMENTAL
Identify problems	++	++
Describe symptoms	++	++
Theorize as to causes	++	+
Test theories by data collection and analysis	+	
Identify cause	+	
Propose remedy	++	+
Design remedy	+	
Install remedy	+	
Test remedy	+	+
Establish controls	++	+

Legend:
Strong ++
Moderate +

FIGURE 8–7   Work-force contribution to quality-improvement projects

8–7 lists some of the steps of the quality-improvement process, along with the usual potential contribution by the work force.

The Improvement Processes

Over the years companies have tested out numerous ways to secure quality improvement from the work force. Most of these can be classified into the categories that follow.

Rewards and penalties. Under this approach the worker's pay is directly affected, up or down, by the quality of the work produced. Early in the century this method was used in some factories as an adjunct to piece-work pay systems. The method aroused criticism on the ground that many defects were outside of the control of the workers. Following passage of the National (Wagner) Labor Relations Act, such methods of rewards and penalties were essentially abolished and have not been reinstated. (Meanwhile, numerous forms of group rewards have emerged, such as profit sharing and gain sharing. These are seldom keyed to the quality performance of workers.)

Drives and exhortations. These approaches were widely used in recent decades in an effort to induce the work force to produce higher quality. A major underlying premise was that the workers were in a state of self-control. Where this premise was invalid (as it often was), the drive could lead to an atmosphere of unwarranted blame. The recent trend has been toward approaches based on factual analysis.

Job enlargement. See the section The Work Force and Quality Planning, Job Redesign as an Option, which follows later in this chapter.

Suggestion systems. In this well-known approach, workers are urged to propose improvements of all sorts, including quality improvements. The systems always provide for recognition and rewards. The resulting suggestions range widely as to economic significance. A few involve substantial effects; most involve minor effects. The depth of the suggestions also ranges widely, all the way from mere problem identification to thorough diagnosis and proposing of remedy.

It takes a good deal of work to administer a suggestion system, and many have been abandoned as not being cost-effective. However, in some companies these systems continue to thrive. Proponents contend that suggestion systems have intrinsic merit because they provide workers with an opportunity to participate in creative activity. Proponents also contend that the systems are cost-effective if well managed.

Project-by-project improvement. This improvement process has outperformed all others, by a wide margin. The methodology at managerial levels is described in chapter 3. At the work-force level, project-by-project improvement has primarily taken the form of QC circles.

QC CIRCLES

The Concept

A QC circle is a volunteer group of work-force members who have undergone training for the purpose of solving work-related problems. (The terminology varies. Japanese publications in the English language use the term QC circle. Organizations in the United States and Great Britain use quality circle, quality-control circle, and employee circle, among others. We shall use the term QC circle.)

The dominant reasons for going into QC circles have been

1. To help solve the company's quality problems

2. To provide the work force with an opportunity to participate creatively in matters relating to their own jobs

To solve work-related problems, the QC circles employ the same project-by-project approach as is used by managerial project teams. However, there are important differences, and these are summarized in Figure 8–8.

The Contrast: Japan and the United States

Figures 8–9a and 8–9b show the growth pattern of QC circles in Japan and in the United States. The patterns exhibit striking differences, and much can be learned from the reasons behind these differences.

In Japan the QC circles started in 1962 and have been growing ever since in numbers of circles, work-force members, and projects completed. In the United States, QC circles started in the late 1970s, underwent an explosive growth, and then declined precipitously. These differences appear to be traceable to three major factors (Juran 1987):

FEATURE	QC CIRCLES	PROJECT TEAMS
Primary mission	To improve human relations	To improve quality
Secondary mission	To improve quality	To improve participation
Scope of project	Within a single department	Multidepartmental
Size of project	One of the useful many	One of the vital few
Membership	From a single department	From multiple departments
Basis of membership	Voluntary	Mandatory
Hierarchical status of members	Typically in the work force	Typically managerial or professional
Continuity	Circle remains intact, project after project	Team is ad hoc, disbands after project is completed

FIGURE 8–8 Contrast: QC circles and project teams

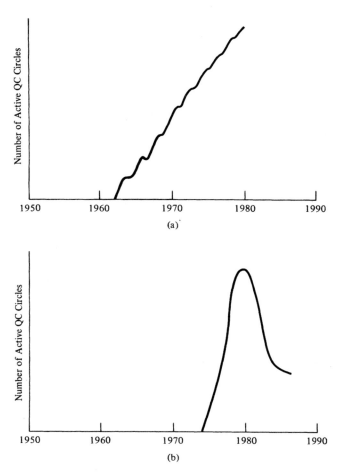

FIGURE 8–9   QC circles: (a) Trend in Japan; (b) Trend in United States

1. *The conceptual approach.* In Japan the QC-circle concept was viewed as an extension of the earlier efforts to improve quality by managerial means. These means had included sending teams abroad to learn from other countries, translating foreign litera-ture into Japanese, inviting foreign lecturers, training managers and supervisors in how to manage for quality, and the use of man-agement teams to carry out numerous quality-improvement proj-ects. By 1962 it seemed logical to extend QC training to the work force, and to use teams of workers to achieve further improve-

ment, as well as to broaden the extent of worker participation in the affairs of the company.

In the United States the QC-circle concept was not viewed as an extension of prior managerial activity. Instead, it was viewed as a separate entity with its own purposes: (a) to improve human relations by providing a new form of worker participation, and (b) to solve the companies' quality problems. (In those days many upper managers believed that the prime cause of poor quality was the work force.)

The participation feature proved to be attractive to the media. They gave much publicity to the QC-circle concept, and this publicity then stimulated a rapid growth rate.

2. *Prior training of managers.* The Japanese quality crisis became evident in the late 1940s. There followed more than a decade of massive training of the Japanese management hierarchy in how to manage for quality. By 1962, when the QC-circle movement was launched, the Japanese managers and supervisors were qualified to direct the QC circles into productive channels. They did not delegate this direction to "facilitators" or to outsiders.

In contrast, most United States companies were not faced with a quality crisis until the middle 1970s. At that time the United States managers had not yet undergone extensive training in managing for quality. Lacking such training, they were unsure of how to respond. The QC-circle concept seemed attractive, so it was tested out. Since the managers and supervisors lacked the necessary training, the direction was delegated to facilitators and consultants. This delegation bypassed the supervisory structure, leading to much confusion and resentment.

3. *Coordination and guidance.* In Japan the QC-circle movement has been coordinated by the Japanese Union of Scientists and Engineers (JUSE). It was JUSE that prepared the training materials, provided the seed training courses, provided consulting assistance, organized conferences, published the leading papers, and set up the award system. These supporting activities provided by JUSE contributed greatly to coordinating and guiding the movement into useful directions.

In the United States there has been little of such central coordination and guidance. The recognized professional QC societies largely ignored the movement during its formative years. The resulting vacuum was then filled by company enthusiasts, consultants, and journalists. Such a mixture of interests was unable to provide broad coordination and guidance to the QC-circle movement. The absence of such coordination and guidance no doubt contributed to the decline of the movement.

Training and Methodology

Training courses for work-force members are widely available. Most of them are derivatives of the materials evolved in Japan. (See Ishikawa 1972.) Numerous consultants, inside and outside, are also available to conduct training and to assist in getting started. Much has been learned about how to proceed:

1. Worker participation in QC circles should be voluntary. (There are some exceptions.)

2. Training and project work must be carried out on company time. (Whether it is during regular hours or overtime depends on local conditions.)

3. Training in problem solving must accompany project work.

4. Training must be provided for the supervisors and QC-circle leadership as well as for QC-circle members.

5. Nominations for projects may come either from workers or managers.

6. Projects should be closely related to the regular jobs of the QC-circle members. (The worker is regarded as an expert on his job.)

7. Choice of projects is a matter of agreement between the QC circle and management.

8. Final recommendations of the QC circle must be acceptable to management before they are made effective.

Vested Interests

Much has also been learned about the major vested interests:

1. *Managers* are concerned about losing "prerogatives"; also about the relative value of employee time spent on projects versus time spent producing.

2. *Staff specialists* face competition in planning and analysis—a near monopoly to date.

3. *Workers* are concerned with the effects of improvements on their job security; also with extra rewards for project work.

4. *Unions* are wary of shifting employee loyalty from the union to the company.

Prognosis

The present trend is clearly to train all managers in how to manage for quality. It will take at least a decade for the managers in the company hierarchies to acquire this training and then to acquire experience in its use. As all this proceeds it is quite likely that there will emerge a revival of interest in QC circles.

THE WORK FORCE AND QUALITY PLANNING

The broad approach to quality planning is set out in chapter 5. At the work-force level, participation in quality planning necessarily concentrates on microprocesses.

The TRIPROL Diagram and Work-Force Perceptions

At this same work-force level, the basic quality planning model is the TRIPROL diagram, reproduced in Figure 8–10.

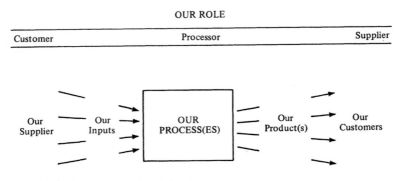

FIGURE 8–10   The TRIPROL diagram

The work force plays all the roles of the TRIPROL model: customer, processor, and supplier. However, in many job situations the workers have not thought of their jobs as consisting of these three roles.

An internal survey conducted by one public utility found that only 25 percent of the work force recognized the fact that they had customers.

Similar findings are to be expected in all situations where planning has been clearly separated from operations. It is common in such cases for the work force to perceive their role as one of following procedures and meeting the goals. Under that perception it is understandable if workers conclude that

1. The inputs (procedures, goals, facilities, data, materials) are determined and fixed during the planning.

2. The role of the worker is to process the inputs (data and materials) so as to conform to procedures and specified goals.

3. The apparent product is "conformance."

4. The apparent customer is the supervisor or company.

If we redraw the TRIPROL diagram to conform to these perceptions, the result is something like Figure 8–11.

Figure 8–11 shows that the planners are perceived as the prime suppliers for the start-up inputs consisting of specifications, procedures, and quality goals. These same start-up inputs are regarded

SUPPLIERS	INPUTS	PROCESS	OUTPUTS	CUSTOMERS	
				Visible	*Other*
Planners	Goals Procedures Specifications		Conformance to goals, procedures, specifications	Supervisor	
		Worker			
Other suppliers	Facilities Materials Etc.			Company	

FIGURE 8–11 TRIPROL diagram as perceived by some workers

as rigid and sacred: only the planners may change them. Other suppliers provide subsequent and continuing inputs—the data, materials, and so forth—that become the grist for the processing mill. These inputs do vary, and the work force has a degree of responsibility to cope with these variations as well as with variations inherent in the processing facility.

Turning to the output side of Figure 8–11, the product is perceived as consisting of "conformance" to specifications, procedures, and quality goals. The customer is perceived as the supervisor or the company rather than as some subsequent user.

The Feedback Paths

It is also useful to look at the path followed by customer feedback in these same cases of strict separation of planning from operations. Figure 8–12 shows this path superimposed on the TRIPROL diagram.

Figure 8–12 points out that feedback from the "real" customers does not go directly to the work force. Instead the feedback goes to the supervisor. If the problem appears to be traceable to the planning, the path of the feedback in due course leads to the planners. The revised plans then become a revised input to the worker, who lives in a world of conformance.

A similar situation prevails with respect to feedback from the work force to suppliers. The feedback path does not run directly;

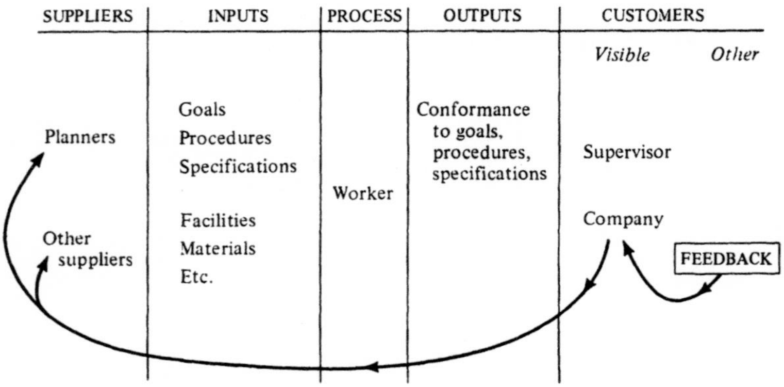

FIGURE 8–12   Customer feedback superimposed on the TRIPROL diagram

it goes through the supervisor (who may run it through some intermediate function before it reaches the supplier).

In effect, the work force (other than for the artisan category) is out of the mainstream of the feedback flow. This is a fatal obstacle to successful participation in quality planning.

Participation Requires a Methodology

For workers to participate in quality planning requires creation of a methodology as well as an opportunity. Such has been the pattern in the other processes of the Juran Trilogy:

1. In the case of quality control, the statistical process control (SPC) movement has trained many workers in how to apply basic statistical tools to strengthen quality controls.

2. In the case of quality improvement, the QC-circle concept has enabled many teams of workers to make improvements on job-related matters.

Job Redesign as an Option

The artisan is solidly involved in quality planning through (a) direct exposure to the needs of various customers and (b) adapting his inputs and process to meet those needs. It follows that one approach to worker participation in quality planning is to redesign jobs in ways that bring the worker closer to the status of artisan. More fundamentally, the purpose of job redesign is to replace the obsolete features of the Taylor system (the separation of planning from execution). A major premise of the Taylor system was the low level of education of the work force. The subsequent rise in educational levels has made that premise obsolete. It is now feasible to increase the delegation to the work force, provided that the jobs are redesigned so as to make it possible for the work force to accept the delegation.

How to redesign the jobs has turned out to be complicated. In most cases it is not feasible to go to a fully artisanal concept; the damage to such parameters as cost and productivity is too great. So there is much groping and some experimentation. The job designs tested have included the following:

1. *Job enlargement—horizontal.* Under this concept jobs of a repetitive short-cycle content are converted into jobs of broader

scope. A factory assembly line is redesigned to enable each worker to perform multiple tasks—even to assemble units of product completely. Similar job enlargements are feasible in the office. Preparation of telephone directories, previously done as a procession of twenty-one different short-cycle jobs becomes a job to be done in its entirety by one worker. In such job redesigns the worker becomes his or her own customer, over and over again, leading to easier identification of quality-planning deficiencies.

2. *Job enlargement—vertical.* In this approach the worker is assigned multiple *functions.* For example, a production worker may be made responsible for his or her job-related material supply, tool maintenance, and judgment of product conformance. Such job designs bring the worker into quality planning of a multifunctional nature.

3. *Self-supervising teams.* This is a form of job enlargement both horizontal and vertical. An added, significant feature is that the teams are largely self-supervising. The team decides which workers are to perform which operations. The team also takes on multiple functions (material supply, tool maintenance, product test, record keeping, etc.). The need for quality planning is extensive, and the team participates actively in such planning. (The supervisor becomes a key customer whose needs must be discovered and met.)

Job Analysis as an Option

Methods and tools for systematic analysis (of quality planning for microprocesses) are now available. (See chapter 7, the section Quality Planning for Microprocesses.) However, the concept of conducting such analyses has not met with widespread acceptance. As of the late 1980s, few companies had field tested the concept. Their approaches must be regarded as experimental.

The concept of bringing the work force into the quality-planning process must also be regarded as still undergoing field tests. The major area of experience has been with QC circles, some of which have tackled projects of replanning departmental processes. These projects have demonstrated that most workers have the education, job knowledge, and creativity to be able to contribute to quality planning if the opportunity is provided.

Obstacles

The obstacles to bringing workers actively into the quality-planning process are similar to those described previously in the section QC Circles, Vested Interests. Overcoming these obstacles is not done simply by logical reasoning. What is decisive is the results achieved during field tests of the concept of worker participation in quality planning.

Options for Upper Managers

Many upper managers have been in a quandary over whether and how to bring the work force into the quality-planning process. This quandary is traceable to their desire for "action now" despite lack of depth of knowledge concerning the consequences. A widespread example of "action now" was the rush into QC circles without meeting some essential prerequisites.

The range of choice is not limited to the two alternatives of (1) action now or (2) inaction. A third option is to conduct a pilot test of the contemplated "action now." A fourth option is to acquire the depth of knowledge needed to choose a course of action. This seems to be the best option. It involves creating a multifunctional project team to examine the pros and cons of quality planning by the work force and to recommend a course of action. To this end, upper management should create a multifunctional team whose mission is to examine *the feasibility of extending the role of the work force in quality planning, and to recommend a course of action.* (The team's mission statement should require that the team secure inputs from the work force.)

WORK-FORCE PARTICIPATION IS ESSENTIAL

It has long been known that under the Taylor system the experience and creativity of the work force were major underemployed assets of the companies. More recently it has become evident that work-force participation can also add significantly to companies' quality performance. However, certain prerequisites must be met if the participation concept is to become effective on a continuing basis:

1. Upper management must undergo the training needed to understand and support the objectives of the participation concept: to develop people by using their education, experience, and creativity to improve company operations.

2. Other members of the management team (managers, supervisors, and staff specialists) must accept the concept of participation, realizing that in doing so they will be delegating to the work force some activities that have in the past been regarded as "management prerogatives."

3. These same members must undergo sufficient training in quality matters to be able to understand what is being offered to the work force. In addition, the first line of supervision must undergo minimally the same training program as will be offered to the work force.

4. Management must face up to the work force's apprehension as discussed in chapter 3, in the section Face Up to Employee Apprehensions.

HIGH POINTS OF CHAPTER 8

Any effort to introduce change into work-force practice requires providing each work-force member with a clear answer to the question, What should I do that is different from what I have been doing?

To give maximum delegation to the work force requires being specific about which decisions and actions are to be delegated.

It is now widely accepted that quality is better served if the work force understands the purposes behind the goals—the "why."

The recent trend is strongly in the direction of providing the work force with information on process trends and on the relation of process conditions to product results.

The work-force members are interested observers of any management drive for improvement, whether directed at the work force or not.

A fatal obstacle to successful participation in quality planning is exclusion from the mainstream of the feedback flow.

For workers to participate in quality planning requires creation of a methodology as well as an opportunity.

Work-force participation can add significantly to companies' quality performance.

TASKS FOR UPPER MANAGERS

Upper managers should look closely at the way in which the concept of the artisan enables workers to participate widely in quality-related matters and to accept a broader delegation of responsibility.

The advantages of putting the work force into a state of self-control are obvious and important. To this end, upper managers are well advised to establish improvement projects with a mission of identifying past obstacles to self-control so that they will not be carried over into new plans.

Before embarking on any plan of motivating the work force to do good work, upper management should determine the extent to which the workers are in a state of self-control.

Managers should take soundings to understand the work force's perceptions and to use those perceptions as an input to the proposed quality-improvement effort.

Upper management should create a multifunctional team whose mission is to examine the feasibility of extending the role of the work force in quality planning, and to recommend a course of action.

Certain prerequisites must be met if work-force participation is to become effective on a continuing basis:

1. Upper management must undergo the training needed to understand and support the objectives of the participation concept.

2. Other members of the management team (managers, supervisors, and staff specialists) must accept the concept of participation, realizing that in doing so they will be delegating to the work force some activities that have in the past been regarded as "management prerogatives."

3. These same members must undergo sufficient training in quality matters to be able to understand what is being offered to the work force.

4. Management must face up to the work force's apprehension.

Motivation for Quality

The purpose of this chapter is to

1. Identify the human behavioral forces that are related to managing for quality

2. Examine how these forces hinder or promote the attainment of high quality

3. Set out the managerial actions needed to guide these behavioral forces into constructive directions

WHY TALK ABOUT MOTIVATION?

A lively beginning to a lecture on quality is to ask, Who in the room is against quality? No hands are raised. Everyone is "for" quality. No one is "against" quality. No one—not managers, supervisors, specialists, the work force, the union. No one.

Do we then need to talk about motivation for quality? We do, but not in the sense of convincing people that quality is desirable. Instead the need for motivation arises because there are some very real obstacles to achieving quality and because getting rid of some of those obstacles does involve motivation.

The Obstacles

The obstacles that are removable by motivation include

1. *Unawareness.* People are not aware that they are creating quality problems.

2. *Competition in priorities.* People are unable to achieve quality because other goals that have higher priority get in the way.

3. *Suboptimization.* The achievement of quality locally gets in the way of overall quality.

4. *Cultural myths.* People hold certain sincere beliefs that are related to quality but that are not based on fact. These "myths" can be an obstacle to constructive efforts to achieve quality leadership.

In most companies these obstacles have their origin in prior managerial practices. It is therefore important to avoid any atmosphere of blame. The emphasis should be on what to do differently, and on the methods for making the needed changes.

REMEDIES FOR UNAWARENESS

The prime remedy is education to provide information on how one's work affects customers.

In the higher levels of organization this requires multifunctional teams to reexamine the major processes. In such major processes each step is thoroughly understood by its "owner." However, these owners seldom thoroughly understand the overall process. The overall process has no owner.

The approach is quite similar to that used for quality planning as discussed in chapter 4. Such reexaminations can and do turn up specific instances in which unawareness in one step causes damage at other steps. The remedies take such forms as (1) the provision of new feedback to prior steps, (2) the combining of previously separated steps, and (3) the revision of sequences.

At departmental levels it is feasible to deal with unawareness as part of the process of departmental managing for quality. (See, in this connection, chapter 7, the section Quality Planning for Microprocesses.)

At the supervisory and worker levels, awareness is usually raised by

1. *Increasing the visibility of the subject.* For example, exhibits are prepared to show how the product is used, and the impact on customers. Stress is put on the concept that "the next process is your customer."

2. *Establishing self-interest.* For example, posters are displayed pointing out that "quality makes sales; sales make jobs."

CHANGING THE PRIORITIES

Quality has always been one of the criteria to be met by managers. The job descriptions have said so and the reward systems have said so. However, quality has by no means had top priority. Other criteria, notably delivery dates, have usually had top priority.

Not a Simple Change

Managers have learned that to move quality to the level of top priority is not a simple change. Certainly it is not just a matter of hoisting banners that proclaim that quality has top priority. Instead it has turned out to be a profound change. It is quite important for upper managers to understand why.

The basic reason is that priorities are rooted in specific managerial practices. Until these managerial practices are changed the priorities will not change. So it is necessary to identify these underlying managerial practices.

Managerial Practices That Determine Priorities

As viewed by the middle and lower levels in many companies, the prevailing managerial practices do *not* add up to giving quality top priority. Figure 9–1 sets out some of the prevailing perceptions, and the associated needs for revision in managerial practices.

Each of these revisions in managerial practice affects the priority given to quality relative to other parameters. In addition, each revision sends a message to the lower levels—each is an unmistakable expression of upper-management priorities.

REMEDIES FOR SUBOPTIMIZATION

The basic remedy is to plan for quality in ways that optimize overall performance in the first place. The methods for doing this involve participation in quality planning by the affected customers, external and internal. In some situations joint planning is better yet.

The methodology is described in chapter 4, the section Optimizing Product Designs.

Some practitioners feel that many reward systems are inherently designed for suboptimization because they emphasize de-

PERCEPTIONS	NEEDS FOR REVISION
Numerous chronic wastes go on and on, and there is no clear responsibility for putting an end to them.	The company should undertake a broad approach to abolish these wastes through annual quality improvement.
The quality-planning process continues to create new wastes and new quality crises.	Planners should be trained in how to plan for quality so as to put an end to the practice of quality planning by experienced amateurs.
Competing parameters such as delivery dates derive high priority through structured systems of goals, measurement of performance, managerial review and rewards.	A parallel system should be provided for quality.
For top priority parameters upper managers personally participate in establishing goals, reviewing performance, etc.	Upper managers should similarly participate personally in establishing quality goals, reviewing performance, etc.

FIGURE 9–1   Perceptions of managerial practices and needs for revisions

partmental performance rather than overall goals. There is merit in this contention, and it follows that those who design reward systems should take a look at the side effects of departmental performance on overall performance.

HUMAN BEHAVIOR, CULTURAL PATTERNS, AND MYTHS

Motivation is concerned with human behavior. The chief distinguishing feature of managerial activity is its employment of the forces of human behavior to achieve results. Applied to our subject of managing for quality, a good starting point for upper managers is to acquire an understanding of what are the actual motivators of human behavior in the company relative to attainment of quality. We shall refer to these motivators as the *cultural pattern.*

Every company is also a human society. The cultural pattern is a body of beliefs, habits, and practices that the human population has evolved to deal with perceived problems. In large companies there are multiple societies, that is, various functions, levels in the hierarchy, and professional disciplines. These societies differ in their perceptions and therefore evolve cultural patterns that differ one from another.

Each cultural pattern is a logical response to the respective perceptions. Each resulting pattern has much value to the society of origin. In consequence the patterns are perpetuated: each society requires new members to adapt to the pattern. Of course, people take action based on their perceptions. And of course, if the perceptions are in error, the actions will likely be in error as well.

Managerial Myths

These errors in perception have been extensive, and it is useful to clear ground by listing some of the widespread errors in perception (myths, misconceptions) that have led many managers astray.

1. *The work force is mainly responsible for the company's quality problems.* This perception by upper management is often due to biases in the flow of information. The chronic quality problems (which were planned that way and which do the bulk of the damage) do not easily come to upper management's attention; the effects are hidden in the overheads. Reports on sporadic errors made by managers and supervisors tend to acquire more protective coloration than reports on errors made by the work force. Objective researches have regularly shown that about 80 to 90 percent of the damage done by poor quality is traceable to managerial actions.

2. *Workers could do good quality work but they lack the motivation to do so.* The realities are that many workers are not in a state of self-control and therefore cannot produce good work; they can only avoid making bad work. In addition many workers are supervised by managers whose top priority is not quality but something else.

3. *Quality will get top priority if upper management so decrees.* The reality is that nothing of the sort will happen unless management follows through with some fundamental changes: goal setting, planning to meet goals, provision of resources, measures of quality, progress reviews, and revision of rewards.

4. *To change people's behavior, it is first necessary to change their attitudes.* There is some validity to this, but mostly it is the other way around: if we first change people's behavior, that will change their attitudes. For example, managers who have been required to serve on quality-improvement teams (a mandated

change in behavior) exhibit greater receptivity to participation in quality improvement than managers who have merely been urged to change their attitude.

Managers whose beliefs include such myths are not aware that their perceptions are in error. Their beliefs are sincere, and they take action accordingly. That is why the 1980s witnessed such an outpouring of efforts to solve company quality problems solely by motivational programs, decrees, and efforts to change attitudes.

Work-Force Myths

The work force also accumulates beliefs based on perceptions. Some of these beliefs are well grounded; others are myths. Especially troublesome to managers has been the work-force belief that job security can be achieved by establishing monopolistic rights to certain tasks—in effect, job ownership. This belief was enforced by events in the United States, where many labor unions for decades were able to establish just such monopolies, along with associated restrictive work rules. (Ever since the 1930s, the labor unions have been exempt from the antitrust laws.) Management efforts to avoid the resulting high costs then contributed to an adversary relationship. Many of these accumulated monopolies have since been broken by a flood of imported goods. What had seemed to be a well-founded belief turned out to be a myth.

A Role for Upper Managers

Before going into an extensive effort of motivation for quality, upper managers should commission a survey *to determine the state of the cultural pattern and its impact on quality.* This survey should extend to the upper managers as well as to other societies: middle managers, supervisors, specialists, and the work force.

The questions to be addressed by such surveys should be tailored to the special needs of each company. Typical questions have been

1. What is your perception of the company's quality compared with that of competitors: superior? the same? inferior? don't know?

2. Whom do you regard as your customer: the company's cli-

ents? the next department? the boss? someone else? no customer? don't know?

3. How do you rate the quality of the product you are turning out: high? adequate? low? don't know?

4. If you rate the quality of your product as low, what do you feel are the obstacles that stand between you and producing high-quality product? List up to three obstacles.

5. When your supervisor judges your performance, which element of performance receives the greatest weight: meeting the budget? meeting the cost standard? productivity? quality? safety? meeting schedules? other?

Summary of Motivational Means to Deal with Obstacles

Figure 9-2 summarizes the motivational means for dealing with the aforementioned obstacles to achieving quality.

THE NEW CULTURE: INGREDIENTS AND RESPONSES

The 1980s have ushered in some revolutionary changes in managing for quality, such as quality goals at top priority and in the business plan, and mandated quality improvement. These changes

OBSTACLES	MOTIVATIONAL TOOLS
Unawareness	Education; communication; establishment of self-interest
Lack of top priority	Establish annual quality improvement; provide planners with training; provide goals, measures, reviews, rewards; upper managers personally participate in goal setting, reviews, etc.
Suboptimization	Participation; joint planning
Cultural patterns and myths	Conduct surveys to identify the nature of the cultural pattern and myths; use the "Rules of the Road" for dealing with cultural resistance.

FIGURE 9-2 Motivational means for dealing with obstacles to achieving quality

have met with considerable cultural resistance, from managers and work force alike. To deal with this cultural resistance requires an understanding, in depth, of the inherent cause-and-effect relationships. To develop this understanding in depth, the subject matter that follows is organized based on specific major changes. Each such major change is described, along with an explanation of

1. Its impact on the cultural pattern

2. The response of the members of the respective societies

3. The motivational steps that are being tested out as aids in effecting the changes

Finally, the general problem of how to deal with cultural resistance will be discussed in the section Dealing with Cultural Resistance.

QUALITY HAS TOP PRIORITY

A declaration that "quality has top priority" (or similar wording) has been a feature of virtually every upper-management initiative for improving quality. In many companies this declaration was not accompanied by an action plan, so that nothing changed—the prior goals, measures, and rewards all remained unchanged. In other companies an accompanying action plan demonstrated that the new priority was to be taken seriously. Such cases usually encountered cultural resistance, and sometimes this was significant.

Effect on Operating Managers

An important source of cultural resistance came from those operating managers who were the experts at meeting the former top priority. To illustrate, in many companies the top priority had been meeting the schedules.

Supervisors who mastered the art of on-time delivery were rewarded by promotions. They also became the recognized experts at the game of meeting schedules. Establishment of quality as the top priority suddenly changed the game being played. The experts had been champions at playing the old game. Would they also be champions at the new game? They could not be sure; it was safer to continue playing the old game.

Effect on Functional Heads
and Staff Specialists

Another source of cultural resistance came from the functional heads and the staff specialists who had vested interests in the former top priority, whether it was productivity, costs, or schedule. Their new lower priority would mean greater difficulty in securing such essentials as budgets and support from line managers. Also significant was the loss of status—being pushed off center stage. In some cases there emerged a subtle contest over jurisdiction: those who presided over the previous top priority tried to take jurisdiction over the new top parameter.

Effect on the Work Force

At the work-force level, the effect of giving top priority to quality can be extensive. Here are some of the areas that may require changes:

1. Policy on job design, e.g., whether to make jobs inherently interesting, and whether to establish a state of self-control (strict separation of planning from execution, that is, the Taylor system, is inherently a poor motivator for quality)

2. Recruitment practices that include consideration of ability and willingness of prospective employees to meet quality standards

3. Induction procedure on a basis that gives adequate emphasis to quality

4. Training that explains the why as well as the how of doing quality work

5. Supervision on a basis that sets a good example in emphasizing quality

6. Communication to keep workers informed of decisions and actions taken by management relative to those products and processes in which the workers have an interest

7. Special provisions such as certification (for critical operations) or opportunities for participation

To enable workers to give top priority to quality also requires increasing the communication of information on quality. The higher priority requires managers to

1. Provide positive means for workers to communicate their views and ideas

2. Provide information about worker performance on quality in ways comparable to those provided on other parameters

3. Provide communication to workers to explain those management actions that, on their face, are antagonistic to quality

If communication is incomplete, it is easy for upper managers and the work force to draw different conclusions from the same basic facts. Here are two examples:

1. A process is producing nonconforming product because the equipment needs repair. The managers decide not to repair the equipment because a new machine is on order. However, this information has not been communicated to the work force. Conclusion by the work force: management is not willing to provide the resources needed to produce quality.

2. Some nonconforming product has been produced. The managers discuss the facts with the client who agrees to accept the product as being fit for use. However, this information has not been communicated to the work force. Conclusion by the work force: management does not regard the specification as important.

A further need is to improve the climate in those cases where the prevailing atmosphere is one of blame. The new emphasis must be on analysis for causes rather than looking for someone to blame—on providing answers to the question, What should I do that is different from what I have been doing?

A Lesson Learned

"Quality has top priority" may seem to be a simple announcement. Yet in fact, there are many consequences. Some of these can be anticipated only by examining the likely impact on the cultural patterns of the various societies in the company. For example, a study of the reward system can provide information about where the existing priorities are. An internal survey can bring out views concerning which functions are regarded as being of "high caste." Similarly it is feasible to identify which kinds of failures result in the sharpest criticism. It is most helpful if such examinations are made *before* announcing a major change in priorities.

MANDATED QUALITY IMPROVEMENT

The introduction of mandated quality improvement is probably the most beneficial single change that a company can make regarding quality. It also probably has a greater impact on the cultural pattern of the managerial hierarchy than any other change.

Here Comes Another One

We can first dispose of those "mandates" that are empty; they lack the essential substance as discussed in chapter 3 in the section The Illusion of Delegation. The lessons learned from prior cycles of such empty mandates are stored in the memory bank of the culture. Based on this memory bank, the members of the culture are able to judge the extent to which the new mandate possesses or lacks substance. If it is empty, they know that they can safely give it lip service without disturbing the cultural pattern.

Adding a New Function

Whenever mandated quality improvement is in fact backed up by substance, the impact on the cultural pattern is profound. The operating managers are required to undertake a new, time-consuming responsibility: annual quality improvement on an unprecedented scale. The time consumed is substantial. It takes time to become trained, attend meetings (quality councils, project teams), do the associated "homework," and conduct progress reviews. The likely order of magnitude is about 10 percent of the work load. In the case of operating managers, the job content changes somewhat as follows:

	PERCENT OF TIME DEVOTED TO:	
	CONTROL	IMPROVE-MENT
Before going into annual quality improvement	99	1
After going into annual quality improvement	90	10

A natural cultural reaction to such a change is: "This will interfere with my 'regular' job." In other words, the regular job is perceived as consisting of control (which in fact has been the case). However, the intention of the change is different. Quality improvement is not intended to become an *addition* to the regular job; it is intended to become a *part* of the regular job. This change in job content is a step away from the familiar and into the unknown. Most members of the culture prefer the familiar.

Use of a Test Site

A proven approach for introducing annual quality improvement has been to create a test site. The test site may consist of a specific segment of the organization whose leadership welcomes the opportunity to try out the concept of annual quality improvement. Alternatively the test site may consist of selected projects that are assigned to teams for the specific purpose of testing out the merits of project-by-project improvement.

Either way a favorable climate is created for getting good results: the team members are limited to willing volunteers. The results are then publicized to stimulate interest and action by others, as well as to recognize the achievements of the successful teams. (See the extract from the Bethlehem Record, in chapter 3.)

Additional stimuli are provided by the methods set out in chapter 3, such as personal leadership by upper managers, provision of resources, reviews of progress, and revision of the reward system. (For a case example of recognition in a large company (Caterpillar), see Scanlon 1986. In general see the proceedings of Juran Institute's Annual Conference on Quality Improvement (IMPRO).)

There are also some well known rules of the road for dealing with cultural resistance. We shall have a look at them later in this chapter, in the section Cultural Resistance: Rules of the Road.

Work-Force Reactions

Work-force participation in quality improvement is voluntary, not mandatory. (Some companies make exceptions to this rule.) The final step in a quality-improvement project consists of establishing the controls needed to hold the gains. Maintaining such controls usually becomes a mandated responsibility of the work force. There are also cases in which management launches drives urging the work force to improve quality. Some of these drives are poorly conceived, that is, the bulk of the problems are management controllable but the implication is otherwise. In such an atmosphere of unwarranted blame, the management loses credibility. The drive is classified as "here comes another one" and is disposed of through lip service.

A more direct involvement of the work force in quality improvement takes place through the QC-circle concept. (For a detailed discussion see chapter 8, the section QC Circles.)

Probably the most serious obstacle to work-force participation in quality improvement is apprehensions relative to job security. This obstacle is present no matter who is to make the improvement, whether teams of managers or QC circles. A usual by-product (or even purpose) of quality improvement is elimination of the redoing of prior work. As viewed by management, such a result leads to better service and lower costs. As viewed by the work force, such a result eliminates jobs.

Faced with such apprehensions, the work force looks for protective shields. One possible source of such protection is the management. (For elaboration, see chapter 3, the sections The Roles of Upper Management and Face Up to Employee Apprehensions.) Workers who feel that the protection provided by upper management is inadequate will look to other sources: the union, political leaders, the community, and the public.

A Role for Upper Management

Chapter 3 sets out the roles to be played by upper managers during the introduction of mandated quality improvement. Some of those roles are pertinent to motivation for quality.

STRUCTURED QUALITY PLANNING

With respect to quality planning, the major ingredient of the new culture is a structured approach. One such approach is set out in chapter 4 in the section The Quality-Planning Road Map, and in Figure 4-2. That same chapter points out that

1. Chronic quality problems were usually planned that way.

2. Much quality planning is done by experienced amateurs.

3. The planning process is a dual hatchery: in addition to hatching out new plans, it hatches out new chronic quality problems.

4. Avoiding new chronic quality problems requires a structured approach and much participation by customers, internal as well as external.

The foregoing list identifies some of the major changes inherent in a structured approach:

ASPECT OF QUALITY PLANNING	TRADITIONAL	NEW
Extent of structure	Largely unstructured	Largely structured
Participation by customers	Limited; especially as to internal customers	Extensive; applies to all customers
Quality expertise of planners	Limited; "experienced amateurs"	Extensive; trained as professionals

These are sharp breaks with tradition; therefore they stimulate extensive cultural resistance. The material that follows examines several key features of that cultural resistance and the associated reasons, some stated, some unstated.

Reaction to Adoption of Structure

The typical reaction is negative, for reasons such as the following:

1. *It takes longer to plan under a structured approach.* The planning process is in fact slowed up. It takes time to acquire the information needed by the spreadsheets and additional time to fill out the spreadsheets. Much of the information turns out to be of minor importance.

2. *The structured approach reduces the status of experienced planners.* Such planners have acquired useful knowledge from their work on previous planning cycles. This knowledge confers a status that is not possessed by inexperienced planners. The structured approach puts the emphasis on data collection and analysis. As a result, the highest status tends to shift to those who excel at data collection and analysis.

The experienced planners can in theory become trained in the new ways and thereby maintain their advantage over their younger colleagues. However, such a course creates other negative reactions. Younger personnel seem to learn the structured methodology more readily. There is also an unstated resentment about the unfairness of any situation in which younger people are able to bypass a status earned through years of experience.

Reaction to Increased Participation

This reaction is likewise negative, again for stated and unstated reasons:

1. *Participation delays the planning process.* The facts support this reaction. The review meetings consume time. It also takes time to respond to the comments that emerge from the review meetings. "Time" here includes person-hours devoted to planning activity as well as the overall calendar length of the planning cycle.

2. *Participation infringes on prior monopolies.* These monopolies are a source of status, and they may for that reason be fiercely defended. For example, one of these monopolies is choice of inputs to decision making. This monopoly is seldom intentional; more usually it is the result of gradual unnoticed encroachment. Abolishing such monopolies is a benefit to the company, but the monopolist may resist such action anyway, since it appears to result in loss of status. (For further elaboration, see chapter 5, the sections Product Design and Internal Monopolies.)

Reactions to Mandated Training in Quality Planning

These reactions have largely been negative, on multiple grounds:

1. *Not essential.* For virtually all professional categories (e.g., engineers), the special methodology and tools of quality planning are not a part of the official curriculum that results in degrees and licenses. Being extracurricular, they tend to be regarded as not essential.

2. *Implication of prior illiteracy.* The planners raise no objection if the training is placed on a voluntary basis. However, putting it on a mandatory basis carries an implication of illiteracy in an essential area. This implication is resented, especially by older planners who feel that they have acquired their literacy through long experience.

3. *"Don't tell me how to produce it."* For centuries craftsmen and professionals have said to their customers, "Tell me what result you want, but don't tell me how to produce it." This reaction is understandable but is valid only if the professional is up-to-date in methodology and tools. In competitive situations the customer has the option of looking for another supplier. In monopoly situations, especially internal monopolies, mandated training is a valid alternative but can still be offensive to the monopolist.

The Work Force and Structured Quality Planning

At the work-force level, structured quality planning has minimal impact. A potential role of the work force is as a source of inputs to those who have the responsibility for quality planning of departmental processes. Another potential role consists of membership in QC circles. Such membership is voluntary and does involve training as a prerequisite to tackling projects.

A Role for Upper Management

The roles of upper management with respect to structured quality planning are elaborated in chapter 4.

SELF-CONTROL AS THE IDEAL QUALITY CONTROL

With respect to quality control, the major thrust of the new culture is self-control. The criteria for self-control were set out in chapter 5, in the section Self-Control. It was also noted there that self-control is a necessary prerequisite to motivation.

No culture rejects the concept of self-control. Such a state provides full mastery with respect to quality control. This does not mean that quality control will be complete. Other goals can compete with quality goals; sporadic problems can interfere. But self-control does make life more predictable and increases the range of options available.

Managers' Motivation for Quality Control

Managers at every level have goals to meet, including quality goals. In this sense control is a never-ending activity for managers. Quite early in their managerial career they learn to accept responsibility for control as a way of life. The obstacle to quality control is not lack of managerial motivation. The obstacles are traceable to such matters as

1. The existence of multiple and competing goals
2. Changes due to the market and other major forces
3. Deficiencies in the control process itself (such as failure to meet the criteria for self-control)

Those who suspect some operating manager of a lack of quality-mindedness are well advised to pose the question, If I traded jobs with that manager, would I be able to reform that department? Or would the prevailing forces reform me?

Work-Force Motivation for Quality Control

Workers are strongly "for" quality. They are of course consumers, and they want good quality in the products they buy. They are generally aware that their work influences the quality of what customers buy and they want those customers to receive good quality as well.

This general motivation for quality does not assure that at the work-force level quality control will be well conducted. The prime responsibility of the work force is conformance to standards, not meeting the needs of customers. (That is quite different from the situation of the village craftsman, whose very livelihood required meeting the needs of customers.)

There is merit in explaining to workers how their job fits into the overall scheme of meeting customer needs. Such explanations make use of the principle of depersonalizing the order (see the following section, Work-Force Conscious Errors). Other promising alternatives are the various forms of job redesign as discussed in chapter 8, in the sections The Work Force and Quality Planning, and Job Redesign as an Option.

Work-Force Conscious Errors

Work-force errors are of multiple varieties: inadvertent, lack of technique, conscious, and still others. Conscious errors are especially troublesome to managers. The workers are *knowingly* failing to conform to standards!

The reality is that many, perhaps most of these conscious errors are management-initiated. Management priorities (e.g., we must ship on schedule) force the workers to adopt the same priorities. Management's neglect (e.g., poor machine maintenance) may lead workers to question management's sincerity. An atmosphere of blame may foster hostility.

Many other conscious errors are worker originated, and these range from innocent and well meaning to deliberate and vicious. The root causes for such conscious errors are often beyond us; the journey from symptom to cause leads into the jungles of the behavioral sciences. Instead practical managers try to go direct from symptom to remedy. There are in fact some broad-spectrum remedies available:

1. *Depersonalize the orders.* There are many situations in which knowledge of *why* is a better motivator than the specification or the orders of the boss. Workers may depart from specification because they don't like the boss. However, once they learn that such departure is creating trouble for workers in the next department or for consumers, this knowledge usually becomes a decisive motivator.

2. *Establish accountability.* In all species of error, a prime need is to know who the worker is. If we don't know who did which work, we are handicapped both in diagnosing for causes and in securing remedial action. To illustrate:

In one company the final product was packaged in bulky bales that were transported by conventional forklift trucks. Periodically a prong of a fork would pierce a bale and do a lot of damage. But there was no way of knowing which trucker moved which bale. When the company introduced a simple means of identifying which trucker moved which bale, the amount of damage dropped dramatically.

3. *Establish measurement.* The worker discovers the company's priority from the boss's behavior pattern—the boss's instructions, decisions, and actions. In addition, the worker looks to see what forces are pushing the boss around. A common source of evidence is the system of *departmental scoreboards.* If there are departmental scoreboards on productivity and delivery rates but not on quality, the workers can draw their own conclusions. Similarly, if

the company keeps *individual* score on worker productivity but not on quality, the workers can draw their own conclusions. (Such an unbalance in scorekeeping is also a form of unbalance in accountability.)

4. *Conduct quality audits.* Quality audits can be designed to provide, on a sampling basis, information of an accountability and scorekeeping nature. The sample of work actually studied during the audit is small relative to the unaudited residue. However, the very fact of exposure to possible auditing is itself a form of deterrent.

5. *Provide assistance to workers.* A major form of such assistance is through discovery of the knack possessed by superior workers. This discovered knack can then be supplied to the remaining workers through retraining (or through change in technology) so that all workers are brought up to the level of the best.

6. *Improve communications.* Most companies do a good job of communicating essential quality information to workers on matters such as specifications, standards, procedures, and methods. This information, although necessary, is not sufficient with respect to willful errors. We should also (a) provide means for workers to communicate their views and ideas, and (b) explain to workers those management actions that on their face are antagonistic to quality.

7. *Create competition, incentives.* These devices have potential value provided that they are not misused. Workers and unions resent bitterly any approach that pits workers against each other. Hence competitions among workers and teams must be designed to be in good humor and on a friendly level, such as prevails among the interdepartmental sports competitions.

Financial incentives are deceptively attractive. They look good while pay is going up—during that part of the cycle they are "bonuses" for good work. It all changes when the work turns poor and the removal of bonuses results in lower pay. Now it is no longer an incentive system; it has become a system of "penalties" with all the accompanying argument about who is responsible.

Nonfinancial incentives avoid the pitfall of bonuses becoming penalties, but must be kept above the gimmickry level.

8. *Errorproof (foolproof) the operation.* The concept of foolproofing is applicable to all types of worker error. For some mod-

ern products, errors are no longer tolerable. T
quality in such cases requires the use of nonhuman

9. *Reassign the work.* An option usually available t
is selective assignment, that is, assign the most deman
to the workers with the best quality record. Application
remedy may require the redesign of jobs: separation of c
work from the rest so that selective assignment becomes feasib
In cases involving workers who are prone to errors the easies
solution may be to go from symptom directly to remedy by finding
less critical jobs for such workers.

STRATEGIC QUALITY MANAGEMENT

Strategic quality management (SQM) as set out in chapter 6 represents the new culture at the highest levels of organization. To introduce SQM requires an initiative by upper managers, along with
extensive personal participation thereafter.

The motivation for such an initiative can come from various
sources, principally,

1. A perceived *opportunity* to increase sales and reduce costs
through better quality

2. Early warning of a *threat* that can be headed off

3. A current *crisis* that requires getting back to fundamentals
as well as putting out the fire

The upper managers are then faced with motivating the subordinate managers to accept SQM as a way of life—a new culture.
Chapter 6 describes the principal ways for doing this:

1. Establish strategic managing for quality on a basis that parallels strategic business management: goals, plans, resources,
measures, progress reviews, recognition, and rewards. Minimize cultural resistance by attaching all this to the business
plan. Avoid portraying SQM as something new. Instead emphasize that SQM is an enlargement of something old and familiar:
the strategic business plan.

2. Provide participation for managers through deployment of
goals (and so forth, as discussed in chapter 6).

3. Enforce conformance to goals by revising the system of recognition and rewards (see the following section).

] *315* [

AND REWARDS

ion relates to public acknowledg-
ormance. *Rewards* consist of sal-
tions that are conferred (usually
st goals generally. Both are es-
quality.
arking on SQM require corre-
recognition and rewards. One
n of annual quality improve-
...recognition and rewards are dis-
..., in the sections Recognition, and Rewards for
...ty and Quality Improvement, respectively.

In the case of adoption of structured quality planning, the role
of motivation includes the following:

1. *Inducing the managers and specialists to undergo the prerequisite training.* This training can in effect be mandated by making it a prerequisite to qualification for assignment to leading
roles.

2. *Inducing these same personnel to use the structured planning
process.* This can be enforced by requiring that the evidence of
such use (spreadsheets, etc.) be produced to support the proposals of the planners.

In the case of quality control, the major change is in the priority
given to quality relative to other parameters. This requires no
change in the basic system of control but may require a considerable change in the weight given to the quality parameter.

DEALING WITH CULTURAL RESISTANCE

Any intended technological or managerial change actually consists
of two changes:

1. *The intended change.*

2. *The social consequence.* This is a sort of uninvited guest that
rides in on the back of the intended change.

The Clash Between Cultures

The social consequence is the troublemaker. The trouble arises
from a clash of two cultures: (1) that of the advocates of the change

and (2) that of the recipient society. The recipient society always examines the proposed change from the standpoint, What threats does this change pose to the cultural pattern of this society? To the recipient society, this question is important indeed. Their cultural pattern includes such vital matters as status, beliefs, and habits. Often enough, these matters take precedence over company rules.

The advocates of change focus their attention on the technological and managerial benefits of the intended change. Often the advocates fail to consider the impact of the change on the cultural pattern. Some advocates are not aware of the importance or even the existence of the cultural pattern.

We can illustrate the differences in viewpoint by looking back at several of the major changes we have discussed:

	THE INTENDED CHANGE AS VIEWED BY:	
THE INTENDED CHANGE	THE ADVOCATES	SOME MEMBERS OF THE RECIPIENT SOCIETY
Mandated quality improvement	An essential part of remaining competitive	An added work load without added resources
Elimination of chronic waste	A benefit: better service; lower costs	A disaster: loss of jobs
Structured quality planning	A way of avoiding future chronic problems	A blow to the status of experienced planners

From these and other examples, we can summarize the clash between cultures somewhat as follows:

1. Advocates of change are mainly interested in the effect on operating results.

2. They are generally unaware that their proposals pose a threat to specific values in the recipient culture.

3. They are therefore baffled by the mysterious resistances offered to their logical proposals.

Even when the advocates do address the question, they must be on the alert for differences in value systems between their own culture and that of the recipient society. Those threats must be examined from the viewpoint of the recipient society. Failure of the advocates to address the question—What threats does this change pose to the cultural pattern of the society?—will at the least slow down the execution of the change. At the worst such failure will block the change completely.

Rules of the Road

Behavioral scientists have provided some specific "rules of the road" for dealing with cultural resistance:

1. *Provide participation to the recipient society,* during both the planning and the execution of the change. Such participation establishes a communication link between the cultures and facilitates creating a sense of ownership by the recipient society.

2. *Avoid surprises.* A major benefit of the cultural pattern is predictability. A surprise is a disturber of the peace. (Providing participation is one way to minimize surprises.)

3. *Provide enough time for the recipient society* to (a) evaluate the merits of the change versus the threat to their values, and (b) find an accommodation with the advocates.

4. *Start small and keep it fluid.* A proposal for an experiment arouses fewer apprehensions. The use of a test site reduces the risks for the advocates as well as for the recipient society and implies provision for midcourse correction.

5. *Create a favorable social climate.* If upper managers set an example by serving on quality-improvement teams, that sends a signal to subordinate managers. Changes in the system of recognition and rewards similarly affect the social climate.

6. *Weave the change into an existing, acceptable part of the cultural pattern.* An example is making strategic quality management a part of the long-standing business plan.

7. *Provide a quid pro quo* (something for something). A proposal to mandate certain training for professionals may include a provision to make the training optional for persons with extensive experience.

8. *Respond positively.* Positive responses to problems raised by the recipient society contribute to a constructive atmosphere.

9. *Work with the recognized leadership of the culture.* The cul-

ture is best understood by its members. They have their own leadership and this is often informal. Convincing the leadership is a significant step in getting the change accepted.

10. *Treat the people with dignity.* The classic example is that of the relay assemblers in the "Hawthorne experiments." Their productivity kept rising, under good illumination or poor, because in the "laboratory" they were being treated with dignity.

11. *Keep it constructive.* Proposals for change should emphasize benefits and solutions, not prior deficiencies or blame. An atmosphere of blame is fatal to essential communications.

(For further elaboration on the subject of dealing with cultural resistance, see Juran 1964. The major seminal work is Mead 1951.)

HIGH POINTS OF CHAPTER 9

The need for motivation arises because there are some very real obstacles to achieving quality and because getting rid of some of those obstacles does involve motivation.

In most companies the obstacles that can be removed by motivation have their origin in prior managerial practices.

As viewed by the middle and lower levels in many companies, the prevailing managerial practices do *not* add up to giving quality top priority.

Those who design reward systems should assure that emphasis on departmental performance is not a detriment to overall performance.

Managerial myths have been extensive.

Work-force myths have also been extensive.

To deal with cultural resistance requires an understanding, in depth, of the inherent cause-and-effect relationships.

Before announcing a major change in priorities, it is most helpful to examine the likely effect on the affected cultures.

There are some broad-spectrum remedies available to deal with conscious errors:

1. Depersonalize the orders.
2. Establish accountability.

3. Establish measurement.
4. Conduct quality audits.
5. Provide assistance to workers.
6. Improve communications.
7. Create competition, incentives.
8. Errorproof the operation.
9. Reassign the work.

Any technological or managerial change actually consists of two changes: (1) the intended change and (2) the social consequence.

The social consequence is the troublemaker.

Behavioral scientists have provided some specific "rules of the road" for dealing with cultural resistance.

TASKS FOR UPPER MANAGERS

Before going into an extensive effort at motivation for quality, upper managers should commission a survey to determine the state of the cultural pattern and its impact on quality.

Provide participation to the recipient society, during both the planning and the execution of the change.

Avoid surprises: a major benefit of the cultural pattern is predictability.

Provide enough time for the recipient society to (1) evaluate the merits of the change versus the threat to their values, and (2) find an accommodation with the advocates.

Start small and keep it fluid.

Create a favorable social climate.

Weave the change into an existing, acceptable part of the cultural pattern.

Provide a quid pro quo (something for something).

Respond positively.

Work with the recognized leadership of the culture.

Treat the people with dignity.

Keep it constructive.

] *10* [

Training for Quality

The purpose of this chapter is to

1. Explain the nature and extent of the training required to make quality happen
2. Evaluate the actions recently taken by companies with respect to training for quality
3. Identify the options available to upper management
4. Identify the likely consequences of choosing specific options

THE BASIC PREMISES

There are several basic premises that underly the need for extensive training in how to make quality happen.

The Change in Culture

The preceding chapters have made clear that managing for quality demands some sharp breaks with tradition—virtually a change of culture. So extensive an array of changes requires some corresponding changes in the area of training—training in how to make quality happen.

The All-pervasive Needs

In the United States the tradition has been to concentrate training for quality within the quality department. The new need is to extend such training to the entire management team—all functions and all levels. This need becomes more obvious if we use an analogy from training in finance.

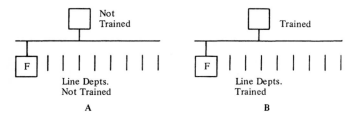

FIGURE 10-1 Training in finance

Consider two companies, A and B, as shown in Figure 10-1.

In company A the finance department is well trained in matters of finance, such as budgets, controls, and reports. However, no one else has such training—not the line managers nor the upper managers.

In company B, not only does the finance department have such training; so do the line managers and so do the upper managers.

Which company will get the better financial results?

Now turning back to quality, consider two companies C and D, as shown in Figure 10-2.

In company C the quality department is well trained in matters of quality. However, no one else has such training—not the line managers nor the upper managers.

In company D, not only does the quality department have such training; so do the line managers and so do the upper managers.

Which company will get the better quality results?

It is pertinent in this connection to note that companies in the United States have generally followed the pattern of company C, whereas the major companies in Japan have followed the pattern of company D.

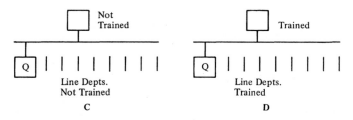

FIGURE 10-2 Training in quality

A Coherent Body of Knowledge

A third basic premise is that there is in existence a coherent body of quality-related knowledge that can serve as the basis for the needed training. There is in fact a wide body of such knowledge in existence, and it is adequate to meet the training needs of companies.

SOME CRITICAL DECISIONS

All-pervasive or Not?

The problem of training to make quality happen presents some specific questions that require decisions at upper-management levels. The most fundamental question is whether to break with tradition and extend training in managing for quality to the entire management hierarchy. In this regard, experience seems to indicate that upper management should take steps to extend training in managing for quality *to the entire management team—all functions and all levels.*

Additional critical questions include

1. Should training be mandatory or voluntary?
2. In what sequence should training be done?
3. What should be the subject matter?
4. Should training include doing?

MANDATED OR VOLUNTARY?

Opportunities for managers and specialists to acquire training in managing for quality became widely available during the 1980s. As the decade progressed, companies increasingly began to urge their management personnel to undergo such training. In some cases this urging grew into mandates. Where these mandates encountered strong cultural resistance, the companies adopted alternative strategies. For example, possession of certain training was made a prerequisite to job progress (e.g., assignment to higher grade work), much like a license to practice.

Once it is determined that universal training in managing for quality is essential to meeting the company's quality goals, such training should *not* be put on a voluntary basis. Instead, training in managing for quality should be *mandated by upper management*.

Applied to the work force, acquisition of training in managing for quality has always been on a voluntary basis. However, various inducements were offered in such forms as opportunity for participation in projects and qualification for higher grades.

IN WHAT SEQUENCE?

Companies have tested out various sequences in their approach to all-pervasive training. Feedback from their experiences points to a "lesson learned": Upper managers should be the first to acquire the new training. The reasons are quite persuasive:

1. By being first, upper managers become better qualified to review proposals made for training the rest of the organization.

2. By setting an example, the upper managers change an element of the corporate culture, that is, for lower levels to take the new training is to do what has been done in respected circles.

For some purposes the upper managers themselves should serve as trainers. To do so requires prerequisite training. To illustrate:

During the 1980s numerous companies tried to carry out accelerated quality improvement with the aid of the videocassette series Juran on Quality Improvement (Juran Institute 1981). One of the more successful of these companies was Texas Instruments. Under Texas Instruments' approach each division general manager became the trainer for his subordinates. Those subordinates in turn became the trainers for their subordinates. This top-down approach continued throughout.

TRAINING IN WHAT SUBJECT MATTER?

The subject matter of managing for quality is quite extensive and multidimensional. One dimension is concerned with fundamental concepts, such as the definition of quality and the role of quality in the business mission. A second dimension is the processes of the Juran Trilogy: quality planning, control, and improvement. A third dimension is the hierarchical level of the trainees. Still another dimension is the various organizational functions, such as finance, marketing, and product development. A further dimension is the numerous tools and techniques.

In the face of this multidimensional content, the company must establish a training curriculum. This curriculum is a list of training courses (modules, packages, etc.) that collectively can meet the training needs for all those dimensions. The designing of such a curriculum is done keeping in mind the training needs of the various categories of company personnel. The end result of planning the curriculum should be a matrix that shows the list of courses along with which categories of personnel are to take which courses. An example of such a matrix is shown in Figure 10–3 (Nickell 1985).

A critical decision for upper managers is, Who should determine

COURSES		PROGRAM MANAGERS OF QUALITY	EXECUTIVE MANAGEMENT	MIDDLE AND FIRST-LINE MANAGEMENT	NON-MANAGEMENT EMPLOYEES
Quality Management System II • Concepts of quality management • Concepts of cost of quality • Managerial breakthrough • Elementary statistics	(1)	X	X		
Upper Management & Quality	(2)	X	X		
Quality Awareness Training	(3)		X	X	X
Quality Implementation Training • Concepts of quality management • Department/task analysis workshop • Problem analysis workshop • Elementary statistics • Vital issue selection	(3)		X	X	Selected
Data Handling Statistics	(1)	X			
Basic Statistics	(3)			Planned	Planned
Juran on Quality Improvement • Video program	(2)	X			

Note: Classes/sessions taught by:
    (1) IBM Quality Institute
    (2) Juran Institute, Inc.
    (3) IBM/NMD Program Managers of Quality

FIGURE 10–3   An example of a matrix for training in quality

the curriculum? There are various options, and they have been widely field tested. The principal options are set out below.

Determination by Upper Management

In many companies the general manager has personally chosen the training curriculum. Sometimes this was done based on the recommendation of an internal specialist, for example, the quality manager. In other cases the general manager responded to the recommendation of an outsider—an author or a consultant. In most cases this option has yielded only minor benefits. However, the price paid has been a delay of two or three years in tackling the major quality problems. This is because the general manager was at the time not sufficiently knowledgeable about the subject to be able to judge whether the recommendations were responsive to the needs of the company.

In an appreciable number of cases, the general manager first listened to various "gurus" and then selected a "religion" to be adopted by the company. This provided the general managers with a broader range of choice. Despite this the general managers lacked the training needed to select the "right" religion. In fact, for many companies, it is a mistake to adopt a prefabricated religion designed by this or that advocate. For such companies, the need is to design a tailor-made company religion that may well include features chosen from the offerings of various advocates.

In one company the chief executive officer and his immediate staff underwent a comprehensive four-day training course in managing for quality. This experience enabled them to make useful decisions about what should be the training subject matter for the respective departmental managers and specialists.

Delegation to Specialists

A second popular option for determining the curriculum has been to delegate the job to some specialist. Internal specialists have included quality engineers and training specialists. Outside consultants have included statisticians and behavioral scientists. Not surprisingly, the specialists tend to exhibit a bias in favor of their specialty.

The most extensive form of this bias took place in the area of statistical methodology. A widely viewed telecast, "If Japan Can,

Why Can't We," had focused attention on the use of statistical methodology. The resulting publicity stimulated many upper managers to turn to statisticians as a source of consulting advice relative to quality. A sizable cottage industry then sprang up to fill the demand for training in "statistical process control."

This option of delegation to specialists is in effect a form of choice of remedy before knowing what the major quality problems were. In those cases where the chosen specialty can be responsive to the company's major needs, the results can be substantial. Otherwise, the results can only be minor; the major problems will remain.

Delegation to a Broad-based Task Force

Under this concept upper management creates a task force (project team, etc.) whose mission is to develop a plan for training in managing for quality. The task-force membership is made up of high-level managers. They include the quality manager and the training manager, as well as representatives from the major operating and staff departments.

More specifically, the task force mission is to

1. Identify the company's needs for training in managing for quality

2. Propose a curriculum of courses that can meet these needs

3. Identify which categories of personnel should take which bodies of training

4. Identify the sources of needed training materials, whether self-developed or acquired from suppliers

5. Identify the need for leaders, i.e., trainers and facilitators

6. Propose a time table

7. Estimate the budget

Experience has shown the training plans developed by such task forces to be decidedly superior to those developed through the other options. The planning usually takes longer but the resulting approach is much more responsive to the company's needs. This experience suggests that upper management should establish *a broad-based task force to plan the company's approach to training in managing for quality.*

POLICY GUIDELINES

In making a delegation to a broad-based task force, upper management should provide some policy guidelines. The potential guidelines include the following:

Corporate plan or not? The practice varies. Some very large companies have left it to each division to work up its own plan of approach, with only limited coordination by corporate headquarters. Smaller companies tend to do the planning on a corporate basis, with participation by the divisions (or plants).

Where broad corporate planning is used, it tends to concentrate on broad matters:

1. Coordination with other active programs (e.g., productivity improvement, participative management)

2. Training for upper managers

3. Development of training materials that are applicable to multiple divisions

4. Development of leaders for the seed courses

Self-sufficiency or not? Large companies tend to become self-sufficient with respect to training. Employee turnover creates a continuing need for training. So does growth. So does creation of new products and new processes. An internal resource can conduct training with knowledge of the company culture while being cost-effective as well. Such a training resource extends to instructors as well as to training materials. (Even when training materials are purchased, they undergo revision to adapt them to the culture.)

The policy question posed is whether to extend the concept of self-sufficiency to training for quality.

Tailor-made or off-the-shelf? A related question is the extent to which the training materials should be tailored to the specific culture of the company. Some companies buy training materials from suppliers but then adapt them to the company's dialects and culture. They revise certain parts of the language. They introduce local case examples. Such adaptation simplifies the job of the instructors. It also makes it easier for the participants to relate to the training.

Orientation of training. It has been a widespread practice to carry out training in quality purely as an educational process. For example, many managers have been trained in a quality-improvement process but without carrying out a quality-improvement project. Similarly many supervisors and work-force members have undergone training in basic statistical tools but have not applied the tools to actual job situations.

Such practice misplaces the emphasis. The basic purpose of the training should be to secure *a change in behavior:* to carry out an improvement project, to replan some existing plan, or to evaluate process capability for some ongoing operation. The purpose of the training should be to assist the participants in making the change in behavior. It is usually feasible to design the training in ways that provide the participants with the means of applying the training to actual job situations. In light of this, upper management should mandate that quality-related training *require trainees to apply the new knowledge to their own jobs.*

The needed expertise. There is a subtle yet critical distinction to be made relative to the expertise possessed by instructors. This expertise is actually a combination of expertise in (1) the subject matter and (2) the skills of how to train. The importance of these two kinds of expertise varies depending on (1) what the subject matter is and (2) who the trainees are.

To illustrate, in teaching simple subjects (reading, writing, arithmetic) to children, the prime qualification for the teacher is possession of the skills of teaching. In contrast, for teaching advanced subjects at the postgraduate level, the prime qualification of the teacher is mastery of the subject matter—the ability to answer the questions. This same principle is applicable to training in various quality-related subjects:

1. To train the work force in basic statistical tools, the prime qualification of instructors is knowledge of how to teach. They acquire this knowledge by being specially trained in how to teach the subject and by being supplied with instructors' guides that have been designed by experts in the teaching process.

2. To train engineers in the use of advanced statistical methodology, the prime qualification of instructors is expertise in the subject matter. The crises arise when the trainees raise questions that the instructor is unable to answer. (If the instructor is also a good teacher, so much the better.)

3. To train managers in how to enlarge strategic business plan-

ning to include strategic quality management, the prime qualification of the instructor is expertise in the subject matter. The instructor should be able to answer the questions of the managers.

These requirements for expertise are important enough to engage the attention of upper management. When reviewing proposals for quality-oriented training, upper managers should assure that the planned sources of instructors *meet the criteria for teaching skills as well as for the needed expertise in the subject matter.*

Training for nonemployees. Some companies have extended their quality-oriented training to nonemployees. The most common of these extensions has been to suppliers. For example, early in the 1980s various major original-equipment manufacturers (OEMs) undertook large-scale training of their supervisors and work-force members in basic statistical tools, or statistical process control (SPC). Some of these OEMs then extended this training to their suppliers. In part this was done by offering training courses that suppliers could attend without charge. In part it was done by imposing new criteria to be met by suppliers, that is, a mandated use of SQC during conduct of their operations.

Of course a company should first test out among its own employees any training it proposes to extend to nonemployees. Once it finds that such training has merit, there arises a policy question: Should the company take steps to extend the training to nonemployees? Whether to do so by persuasion or by mandate is a separate question.

UPPER-MANAGEMENT INVOLVEMENT IN TRAINING

Training in making quality happen should include the entire company hierarchy, starting at the top. Until the 1980s such a proposal was seldom welcomed by upper managers in the United States. Their instinctive belief was that upper managers already knew what needed to be done, and that training was for others—the middle managers, the engineers, the work force. The quality crisis of the 1980s then forced a reexamination of these beliefs.

Events in Japan followed a different scenario. The Japanese quality crisis emerged soon after World War II, and it was more severe than the subsequent crisis in the West. The Japanese crisis forced the upper managers to take training in managing for quality, starting in the 1950s. (The seed courses were given by the author, in 1954.) As of the mid-1980s, the outline for the Top Management Training Course (sponsored by the Japanese Union of Scientists and Engineers) consisted of the following topics:

TOPIC	HOURS
Role of top management in implementing QC	1.5
QC in new-product development	2.0
Statistical methods	3.5
Management of QC	3.5
QC in manufacture	3.5
QC in purchasing and sales	3.5
Quality assurance	3.5
QC in Japan and in the world	3.5
Group discussions on promoting QC in the companies	3.0
Reports of group discussions	3.0
TOTAL	30.5

Upper Managers as Trainees

The section In What Sequence? earlier in this chapter sets out some reasons for conducting training by starting at the top. Experience in conducting numerous training courses for upper managers in the United States and Europe has evolved a body of subject matter somewhat as follows:

1. *Some basics:* the key definitions; big Q and little Q; the Juran Trilogy.

2. *Strategic quality management:* developing a quality strategy; the quality council; quality policies, goals; deployment; resources; measures; rewards.

3. *Quality planning:* The training should focus on planning or replanning some product or process with the aid of the quality-planning road map.

4. *Quality improvement:* the infrastructure; cost of poor quality; return on investment; the project-by-project concept. The train-

ing should include carrying out a quality-improvement project using the universal sequence for quality improvement.

5. *Quality control:* measures of quality at upper-management levels; establishment of the upper-management quality report package; quality audits by upper managers. The training should include the application of the feedback loop to a selected control subject.

Some Realities

A look back at many case examples of training for upper managers points to some commonalities in their behavior. Upper managers

1. prefer to sit in training meetings that are attended exclusively by upper managers

2. are reluctant to accept training from their subordinates

3. are willing to be trained by outsiders who have earned a public status through expertise

4. are eager listeners to the experience of upper managers from well-managed companies, especially the chief executive officers of such companies

5. prefer a training site away from the office, for example, a "meeting in the woods"

6. are willing to visit companies that have earned recognition through their quality

This behavior pattern offers guidelines to those who have the responsibility to plan meetings in which upper managers will be the trainees.

Other Sources of Training

Upper managers can secure much training from sources outside of formal training courses. Such sources include the following:

1. *Audits.* Upper managers can learn a great deal about their own company's approach to quality by taking a "walk around the spiral" and by reviewing the coordination used to optimize companywide performance.

2. *Projects.* Upper managers are well advised to participate in

projects to plan for quality or to carry out quality improvements. Such projects are the means of applying training on the job.

3. *Study of company practices.* It is enlightening to visit companies that are in the forefront with respect to quality. Such visits, and especially visits to cultures different from one's own, are a stimulus to new, imaginative thinking.

Upper Managers as Trainers

Upper managers should participate in the training of subordinate levels in managing for quality. In this role of trainer, the upper managers should concentrate on those areas in which they have the widest experience and are the most authoritative sources. With respect to such areas, upper managers can bring to the trainees

1. An explanation of what the company is trying to accomplish, and why

2. Information on policies, goals, results, competitive status, and the prognosis of what lies ahead

3. Answers to troublesome questions

It is clearly desirable for the trainees to receive such information at first hand from the most authoritative source. In the Texas Instruments case (see the section In What Sequence? earlier in this chapter) the upper managers chose to carry out a policy of top-down training in quality improvement, with gratifying results.

Upper managers who become trainers should keep in mind that to subordinates the trainer is also the boss. It is all too easy for the two roles to become confused, by the trainees and by the trainer as well.

THE TRAINING CURRICULUM

Upper managers generally lack the time to become involved in the details of the training curriculum. For most courses, the upper managers also lack the needed expertise. But upper managers can and should *establish the criteria to be followed* in design of the curriculum. In addition the upper managers should *review the planned curriculum to assure that the criteria have been met.* Criteria that are common to most companies include

1. The team that plans the training curriculum should be broad based; it should include the customers for the training as well as the suppliers.

2. The training courses should be jobs- and results-oriented, to best secure changes in behavior.

3. The choice of training materials should be preceded by a review of offerings from multiple sources.

Specific Design of Training Courses

It is possible to design the training courses based on any combination of dimensions of the subject matter, including basic concepts, the processes of the Juran Trilogy, hierarchical level, organizational function, tools and techniques, and still others. The actual practice has varied. Many companies have opted to focus narrowly on training in statistical tools or on "awareness." In such companies it has been usual to make distinctions based on levels in the hierarchy as well as distinctions based on the education and experience levels of the participants. At the work-force and supervisory levels, the courses were rather brief and limited to simple tools and concepts. At higher levels the courses were longer and in greater depth. Companies that opted for broader training also made distinctions based on hierarchical levels, both in terms of hours devoted and depth of subject matter.

The basic division of the subject matter is best done, however, in accordance with the processes of the Juran Trilogy: quality planning, quality control, and quality improvement. Following this basic division, it is preferable to vary the training content based on the positions in the hierarchy. The usual categories of positions consist of upper managers, middle managers, supervisors, professional specialists, and the work force. Following this allocation, the tools and techniques are regarded as a "shopping list" from which selection is made as appropriate. (In the lists that follow, some course contents necessarily overlap the "tools and techniques.")

The lists that follow set out some specific designs for training courses as conducted in various companies, but with some editing done by the author. Generally the details of these designs do not require participation by upper managers. They are included for information and for completeness.

Course Content for Quality Planning

Course content relates mainly to the content of chapter 4, "Quality Planning," but with some supplements from other chapters. The elements of subject matter include

1. Strategic quality management
2. Quality policies
3. Strategic quality goals; deployment of strategic goals
4. The Juran Trilogy
5. Big Q and little Q
6. The triple-role concept
7. The quality-planning road map
8. Customers: external and internal
9. Identifying customers; the flow diagram
10. Discovering customer needs
11. The planning of macroprocesses
12. The planning of microprocesses
13. Product design; the product-design spreadsheet
14. Process design; process capability; the process-design spreadsheet
15. Planning for process control; the feedback loop; the process-control spreadsheet
16. Transfer to operations
17. Lessons learned; the Santayana review
18. Tools for planners

Course Content for Quality Control

The list that follows largely reflects the content of chapter 5, "Quality Control." It may come as a surprise to some that the list is not dominated by statistical tools and methodology. This content is not due to some deliberate deemphasis of the usefulness of the statistical tools. It is the other way around: in many companies the training in quality control has seriously underemphasized the importance of the managerial aspects of quality control. This unbalance is traceable to the widely viewed NBC videocast "If Japan

Can, Why Can't We?" That videocast focused narrowly on the use of statistical methodology to the virtual exclusion of all else. The subsequent growth of "statistical process control" then retained this imbalance.

1. Strategic quality management
2. The control concept; the feedback loop
3. Self-control; controllability
4. Planning for control, for macroprocesses and for microprocesses
5. Control subjects
6. Responsibility for control
7. Evaluation of performance; units of measure; sensors; control reports
8. Interpretation; statistical significance; economic significance
9. Decision making
10. Corrective action
11. Motivation for control
12. Audits for quality assurance
13. Tools for control

Course Content for Quality Improvement

This content has been well established by an extensive body of experience:

1. Strategic quality management
2. The Juran Trilogy
3. The quality council; responsibilities
4. Estimate of cost of poor quality
5. The project-by-project concept
6. Return-on-investment estimate
7. The infrastructure for quality improvement
8. Project nomination, screening, and selection
9. Projects to improve macroprocesses

10. The diagnostic journey
11. The remedial journey
12. Progress review
13. Motivation for improvement; recognition and reward
14. Tools and techniques

Course Content for Product Development

In some industries (e.g., electronics) the key to sales growth is bringing new, superior products to market. The competition in new-product development is intense, both for providing new product features and for shortening the cycle time required to bring new products to market. This same competition has in turn stimulated a growth in training courses for those managers and engineers who are active in the product-development process.

The subject matter for these courses usually includes a selection from the following:

1. Definitions: quality, customer, etc.

2. The trilogy of managerial processes: quality planning, quality control, and quality improvement

3. Measures of quality

4. Product development: the phases

5. Product design for reliability, producibility, and maintainability

6. Basic statistical tools

7. Reliability engineering

8. The designing of experiments

Some of these courses focus on the research-and-development portion of the new-product cycle, so the emphasis is on engineering, that is, product design, reliability engineering, qualification testing, and so forth. Other courses focus on a structured planning approach, that is, the quality-planning road map, spreadsheets, and so forth (Sullivan 1986).

Note that such courses on product development relate to "product" in the little-Q sense, that is, development of salable goods. In chapter 4 the terms *product* and *product development* are used in the big-Q sense. While there is much similarity in the respective quality-planning road maps, there are significant differences in the tools and methodology.

Course Content: Other

Training courses have long been available for such categories of personnel as quality engineers and reliability engineers. The most widely used text has been Juran and Gryna 1980.

During the 1980s, there emerged a dramatic growth of training in basic statistical methodology for first-line supervisors and for the work force. The principal text materials have consisted of derivations from the popular Japanese training manual (Ishikawa 1972).

With growth in the volume of training, there will emerge a proliferation of specialized courses. Such has been the history in Japan under the sponsorship of the Japanese Union of Scientists and Engineers (JUSE). Their first course was established in 1949. By the early 1980s they were offering over forty types of courses. However, five of these courses account for over 70 percent of the registrations.

TRAINERS

The diversity of the subject matter and of the audiences has required a corresponding diversity of trainers. During the expansion of the 1980s, many approaches were tried. The feedback from these trials is reflected in the comments that follow.

For Upper Managers

Upper managers have exhibited some distinct preferences relative to training in managing for quality:

1. They regard themselves as business managers. Hence the training should establish a clear linkage to business goals.

2. They are results-oriented; they are measured by business results. Hence the training should be directed toward results, not techniques.

3. They are usually aware that they themselves may be a part of the problem. Hence they look for answers to the question, What should I be doing that is different from what I am doing now?

4. They strongly prefer to be in training meetings with other upper managers. They feel that no one else understands the problems faced by upper managers.

As a consequence of the foregoing, upper managers are reluctant to accept insiders or subordinates as leaders. Instead their preference is to listen to outsiders. These outsiders may be upper managers from other companies. Alternatively the outsiders may be consultants who appear to be

1. Knowledgeable in quality-oriented matters

2. Able to convey this knowledge in ways that relate squarely to the business realities faced by upper managers

3. Able to provide answers to the question, What should I do which differs from what I am doing now?

For Middle Managers

Middle managers are also results-oriented. However, middle managers have departmental responsibilities. In large companies these departmental responsibilities can dominate the attention of middle managers, that is, they are judged based on measures of departmental performance. This same domination has its effect on such wide-spectrum training programs as annual quality improvement. In such programs these middle managers show a clear preference for case examples in their specialty and for improvement projects in their specialty.

Middle managers have not resisted training by insiders or even by subordinates provided the trainers possess expertise in the subject matter and have the needed teaching skills.

For First-line Supervisors

In large companies the numbers of first-line supervisors are also large. Such numbers require the development of in-house facilities and leaders. The seed courses may be provided from the outside, along with training of those who are to be the in-house leaders. Thereafter the in-house leaders take over.

At this level a substantial amount of training will relate to the company's broad approach to quality: quality policies, goals, planning, organization, systems, and procedures. In many companies the training (or management-development) department includes specialists who are qualified to conduct in-house training in such matters. Similarly, when training requires interplay among trainees (as in project teams for quality improvement), there is need for leadership with skills in group dynamics. Such leadership is commonly available on an in-house basis in the form of trainers or "facilitators" from the training department.

Another substantial area of training will be at the tool or technique level. These techniques are quite simple. Leaders for training in such techniques can be developed on an in-house basis, either from the quality department or from the training department.

For Specialists

The term *specialists* here refers to professional categories such as designers and process engineers. Training courses for these categories are built around general use techniques, such as basic statistical methodology, plus techniques specifically applicable to the specialty (e.g., reliability quantification for designers, or process-capability quantification for process engineers).

In some large companies, qualified trainers are available in the form of internal consultants from corporate service departments such as corporate quality assurance. Such departments have been an important source of training materials and training expertise for in-house use.

In those companies where in-house sources are not available, it is necessary to use outside sources at the outset. Potential trainers can be chosen and sent to outside courses. Alternatively outside trainers are brought in to conduct the seed courses. (Some training materials are specially designed to simplify use by in-house trainers.)

In small companies it is seldom economic to develop in-house training at this level. Hence outside sources are used, for example, training at outside courses or use of consultants.

For the Work Force

The chief form of work-force training has been that for the QC circles. The training consists of the study of tools for problem solving, followed by the application of those tools to the solution of quality-related problems.

One widely used approach has been to bring in consultants who specialize in such QC-circle training. These consultants conduct the seed courses for leaders, facilitators, and even for the pioneering QC-circle members. During the growth of the demand for QC-circle training (during the early 1980s), there emerged courses for training leaders directly from the training materials.

Training for Trainers

The approach to the training of trainers has included

1. The use of consultants
2. The use of outside training courses
3. Training directly from specially designed training materials

There are additional ways:

1. *"Leader train leader."* During each course the leader identifies those trainees who might be good candidates to become leaders for future courses.

2. *Learn from the trainees.* Any idea that the learning is all in one direction is naive. The trainees have extensive experience in the realities of the subject matter. They bring up cases for discussion. They raise pertinent questions. They challenge the course materials and the assertions of the trainer. All these constitute inputs for improving the content of the training materials and the know-how of the leader. In this way, a training course may be launched with the awareness that it will be debugged during the first several classes.

Examinations: Certification

To date companies have avoided the use of examinations and certification with respect to courses for managers. It is in fact difficult to write examination questions on managerial subject matter, that is, to secure objectivity in questions or answers. In addition, managers have exhibited considerable cultural resistance to being examined. They prefer to be judged by results on the job.

At nonmanagerial levels (specialists, first-line supervisors, the work force), much of the course content consists of techniques and tools. These do permit objectivity in questions and answers. In addition there is less cultural resistance. Hence some companies do conduct examinations for purposes such as

1. Evaluating the trainees' grasp of the subject matter.
2. Providing a form of recognition to those who are successful in the examination.

WHY TRAINING FAILS

Training in managing for quality can fail for a variety of rather conventional reasons: inadequacies in facilities, training materials, leaders, and budgets. Such inadequacies are usually obvious enough to generate alarm signals to those directing the program.

The more subtle reasons for failure are also the most serious, since they may generate only subtle alarm signals or no signals at all.

Lack of Prior Participation by Line Managers

The line managers should participate in the planning of the training program. Failing this, there is a real risk that the training will become technique-oriented rather than results-oriented, that is, the emphasis will be on the tools rather than on operating results. Such emphasis then carries over into the evaluation of progress, so that progress is measured by such things as how many persons have been trained, how many control charts are in use, or how many pledge cards have been signed.

Too Narrow a Base

The decades since World War II have generated a series of waves of interest and publicity relative to various quality-related tools such as statistical methods, quality awareness, quality cost analysis, and QC circles. Each of these tools has potential merit for companies. However none is broad enough to serve as the basis for taking a company into quality leadership.

The major safeguard against having too narrow a base is to broaden the planning base. The planning should not be left solely to tool-oriented specialists. All too often their proposals are centered on their specialty.

Failure to Change Behavior

Training in managing for quality should be centered on creating a change in behavior. Examples include carrying out an improvement project, replanning some existing plan, or evaluating process capability for some ongoing operation. The purpose of the training should be to assist the participants in making the change in behavior.

Without such provision for change of behavior, the likelihood is that the training will not "take": it will not be put to use, and it will soon be forgotten.

A Role for Upper Managers

Upper managers have a role to play in heading off failures of training programs. That role consists of laying down the guidelines discussed earlier in the section Policy Guidelines. Relative to heading off failures in training, these guidelines include

1. Upper management should establish a broad-based task force to plan the company's approach to training for quality.

2. Quality-related training should require trainees to apply the new knowledge to their own jobs.

TOOLS AND METHODOLOGY

The remaining pages of this chapter are largely devoted to lists of tools and techniques that are a part of the curriculum for training in quality. Some of these tools are statistical in nature. Others are managerial in nature. For the most part, upper managers do not become involved with the details of such lists. However, upper managers should be alert to recognize any underemphasis of either of these categories of tools.

The risk of underemphasis is real. During the 1980s there emerged a strong resurgence of emphasis on statistical methodology, with resulting underemphasis on managerial tools. Upper managers *should not allow such imbalance to continue.* Both types of tools are necessary. Neither is sufficient.

The lists that follow are based on the selection of principal tools. Such lists can never be complete. Most tools exist in multiple forms and variations. New variations are constantly being invented. Most of the terminology has yet to be standardized.

MANAGERIAL TOOLS

The quality-oriented managerial tools are quite numerous; many are of ancient origin. Some are general-use tools that are applicable to all three of the Juran Trilogy processes. Other tools are mainly related to one of those processes. In the interest of brevity, some tools will merely be listed by their usual descriptive name. However, the preceding chapters discuss applications of certain of these tools.

General Use

The more widely used tools include

1. The big-Q concept
2. The factual approach: use of facts (rather than opinions) as a basis for decision making
3. Questionnaire design
4. Interviewing technique
5. Participation: the process of securing inputs from those who will be affected by an intended action
6. Brainstorming: a technique for securing ideas during a meeting of multiple participants
7. Force-field analysis: a process for identifying driving forces and restraining forces as an aid in problem solving
8. Storyboarding: a method of problem analysis featuring incremental accumulation of input information
9. Nominal group technique: a process for reaching a consensus among multiple participants
10. Early warning: a process for discovering, before the fact, the likely effects of intended actions
11. Responsibility matrix: lists the needed decisions and actions, and identifies who does what
12. Training
13. Motivation

Planning-oriented

Some of these tools are discussed at length in chapter 4, "Quality Planning." They include

1. The quality-planning road map
2. The triple-role analysis
3. Flow diagrams; standard symbols
4. Quality-planning spreadsheets
5. Market research
6. Simulation of use
7. The product-development-phase system; the Spiral; concept to customer
8. Joint planning
9. Process capability
10. The Santayana review; lessons learned
11. Data banks
12. Standardization
13. Glossary

Additional planning-oriented tools include

1. Analysis for criticality, competitiveness, salability, value
2. Life-cycle costing
3. Quality warranties
4. Design review
5. Failure-mode and effect analysis; fault-tree analysis
6. Reliability analysis: modeling, quantification, prediction, apportionment, demonstration, Weibull analysis
7. Quality warranties

Control-oriented

Some of these tools are explained in detail in chapter 5, "Quality Control." They include

1. The feedback loop
2. Self-control; controllability

3. Control subjects; goals

4. Control stations

5. Measurement: units of measure, sensors, inspection, checking

6. Sensory evaluation: use of human beings as sensors

7. Human-error analysis; errorproofing

8. Nonhuman control: automated control, computerized control

9. Self-inspection

10. Quality audits, surveillance

11. Quality reports

12. Corrective action; troubleshooting

Examples of still other control-oriented tools include

1. Traceability

2. Seriousness classification of errors

3. Quality rating; certification

4. Preventive maintenance

Improvement-oriented

Quality improvement makes extensive use of the tools of analysis, both statistical and managerial. Other tools are strongly improvement-oriented, and include

1. The project-by-project concept

2. The universal sequence of events for quality improvement; the diagnostic journey; the remedial journey

3. Cost-of-poor-quality estimate

4. Return-on-investment estimate

5. Organizational infrastructure for quality improvement; quality council

6. Project nomination, screening, and selection

7. Project-mission statements

8. The project-team concept; training in team building

9. Rules of the road for dealing with cultural resistance

The Japanese "Seven Management Tools for QC"

In 1972 a committee of the Japanese Union of Scientists and Engineers (JUSE) was established for "developing QC tools." The committee made its recommendations in 1977. Their proposals then underwent field tests and further discussion. A special report (JUSE 1986) describes the resulting "Seven Management Tools for QC." They consist of the following:

1. *The affinity diagram.* This is a method of converting vague concepts into specifics through the use of language and diagrams. In a sense it is a generalization of the "black-box" design process, so as to make it applicable to any broad concept.

2. *The relations diagram.* This is a graphic method of depicting the numerous cause-and-effect relationships within a complex problem. It maps out the various cause-and-effect linkages. It also identifies the interrelationships; that is, an effect within one linkage becomes a cause within another linkage. In addition it identifies the major causes.

3. *The tree diagram.* This generalizes a well-known tool widely used in such forms as fault-tree analysis. It starts with an end result to be attained or avoided. It then identifies the potential contributors to that result. Each contributor may itself be a subresult that has subcontributors. The diagram may extend to multiple levels of analysis.

4. *The matrix diagram.* This generalizes the widely used matrix featuring horizontal rows, vertical columns, and their intersections. The quality-planning spreadsheets are familiar examples.

5. *The matrix data analysis.* This method generalizes the data arrays (horizontal and vertical) so widely used to facilitate evaluating composite relationships.

6. *The PDPC (process decision program chart).* This is similar to the familiar flow diagram but modified to include *unpredictable* outcomes and thereby to assist in anticipating future events. (The conventional flow diagram deals only with predictable events.)

7. *The arrow diagram.* This tool is quite similar to the Gantt chart so extensively used for scheduling, along with the critical-path technique, or PERT (program-evaluation-and-review technique).

STATISTICAL TOOLS

The modern origins of quality-oriented statistical tools are traceable to work carried out within the Bell System during the 1920s. At that time the principal focus was on

1. Sampling inspection tables
2. The Shewhart control chart
3. The evaluation of the quality of manufactured product

Industrial interest grew during the 1940s and 1950s under the stimulus of numerous courses sponsored by the War Production Board during World War II. The emerging quality specialists then evolved new tools as well as variations of earlier methodology.

The "Seven QC Tools"

A parallel development emerged in Japan, resulting in the widespread training of supervisors and QC-circle members in the "Seven QC Tools." The publicity given to the Japanese QC circles then led to wide use of these same tools as the basis for training courses for QC circles in the United States. These seven tools consist of

1. *The check sheet.* This is any blank form used to tally up quality data.

2. *The histogram.* This is a frequency distribution in unsmoothed form.

3. *The cause-and-effect diagram.* This is Professor Ishikawa's "fish-bone diagram" for listing theories of causes.

4. *Pareto analysis.* This is the author's generalization of the phenomenon of the "vital few and useful many." (See pages 90–93 for the background of this tool.)

5. *The control chart.* This is W. A. Shewhart's chart for continuing test of statistical significance. (See Figure 5–6 and the associated explanation.)

6. *The scatter diagram.* This is a graphic representation of the interrelation between variables.

7. *Graphs.* These are pictorial representations in various forms: bar charts, pie charts, time series graphs, etc.

	Quality Evaluation, Estimation	Quality Prediction	Diagnosis	Quality Planning	Quality Control	Quality Improvement
Sampling tables	X				X	
Lot plot	X		X	X	X	
Box plots	X				X	
Probability paper	X		X			
Process capability analysis		X	X	X	X	X
Tests of hypothesis	X		X			
Confidence limits	X	X	X			
Statistical significance	X		X			
PRE-Control				X	X	
Statistical tolerancing				X		X
Design of experiments			X	X		X
Analysis of variance			X	X		X
Orthogonal arrays			X	X		X
Regression analysis			X	X		X
Evolutionary operations			X	X		X
Response surface methodology			X	X		X
Reliability quantification		X	X	X		
Reliability prediction		X		X		
Reliability apportionment				X		
Weibull analysis		X	X	X		
Maintainability analysis		X	X	X		
Process dissection			X			X
Stratification analysis			X			X
Stream-to-stream analysis			X			X
Time-to-time analysis			X			X
Actuarial analysis		X	X			X
Concentration analysis			X			X

FIGURE 10–4   Statistical tools and areas of application

Statistical Tools: Other

In addition to these "classic" statistical tools, there are numerous others that have come into use. Figure 10–4 lists some of the more widely used and indicates the principal areas of use.

HIGH POINTS OF CHAPTER 10

The most fundamental question is whether to break with tradition and extend training in managing for quality to the entire management hierarchy.

Upper managers should be the first to acquire the new training.

A critical decision for upper managers is, Who should determine the curriculum?

For many companies, it is a mistake to adopt a prefabricated "religion" designed by this or that advocate.

The training plans developed by broad-based task forces have been decidedly superior to those developed through other options.

The basic purpose of training should be to secure a change in behavior: to carry out an improvement project; to replan some existing plan; to evaluate process capability for some ongoing operation.

The line managers should participate in the planning of the training program.

TASKS FOR UPPER MANAGERS

Upper management should take steps to extend training in managing for quality to the entire management team: all functions and all levels.

Training in managing for quality should be mandated by upper management.

Upper management should establish a broad-based task force to plan the company's approach to training in managing for quality.

Upper management should mandate that quality-related training require trainees to apply the new knowledge to their own jobs.

When reviewing proposals for quality-oriented training, upper managers should assure that the planned sources of instructors meet the criteria for teaching skills as well as for the needed expertise in the subject matter.

Upper managers can and should establish the criteria to be followed in designing the curriculum.

Upper managers should assure that emphasis on statistical tools does not result in underemphasis on managerial tools.

Epilogue

UPPER MANAGEMENT AND
THE ACTION PLAN

The guiding principle should be, *Make No Small Plans!*

The United States economy faces a quality crisis, so the response must be a revolution in quality. Such a revolution requires that bold, *"stretch"* goals be established by upper management.

Revolutionary quality goals cannot be met merely by more intense application of the traditional ways of managing for quality. In fact, many subordinates will conclude that the goals are not attainable. Their conclusion is valid unless there are some sharp breaks from the traditional ways.

Companies that have carried out successful revolutions have done so by taking some giant steps, usually in the following order:

1. First, they undertook project-by-project improvement at a revolutionary pace. Those improvements provided impressive gains in product performance and in waste reduction, while arming the managers with experience and expertise in the improvement process.

2. Second, they undertook to improve the quality-planning process in order to shut down that hatchery that was creating all those chronic quality problems.

3. Finally, they established strategic quality management by opening up the business plan to include planning for quality, and thereby made the revolution permanent.

Collectively, it adds up to a lengthy, complex revolution that does not come free. It requires up-front resources, notably in managerial time and in training. However, the return on investment is gratifying, both in financial terms and in the exhilaration that comes from leading a winning team.

So, *make no small plans!*

QUALITY MANAGERS AND INPUTS FOR PROPOSALS

Some companies look to quality managers (and other functional specialists) to provide essential inputs to the needed action plans. Such quality managers should likewise think in terms of "no small plans." Such an approach requires at the outset a wholehearted acceptance of the concept of big Q, which is itself a major break with tradition.

In preparing proposals for the approval of upper management, it is important to provide for participation by other interested organizations. Such participation broadens the input base and also depersonalizes the proposal.

A useful strategy for acquiring inputs is to request nominations from the interested managers. Such inputs can be stimulated by raising pertinent questions with the managers—questions such as the following:

What are the company's three most important unsolved quality problems as you see them?

What kind of action plan is needed to solve these problems?

Which areas are most in need of such action: corporate, divisional, interdivisional, interdepartmental, departmental?

What are some major obstacles in the way of improving our quality?

Such questions can be raised in specially organized brainstorming sessions. Alternatively the quality manager "makes the rounds," that is, sits down with each key manager, one at a time, to secure the inputs. Such inputs help to shape the action plan in ways that respond to the realities faced by the affected managers.

These same inputs can help to identify the most likely test sites and to anticipate the nature of the cultural resistance. The very fact of securing inputs from those who will be affected confers a share of ownership and simplifies the ultimate job of selling the action plan.

Any proposal for an action plan requires a choice of strategy. In this connection it is useful to look back briefly at the Preface. There, the following purposes were enumerated:

1. Provide companies with the strategies needed to attain and hold quality leadership.

2. Define the roles of upper managers in leading their companies to that goal.

3. Set out the means to be used by upper managers to supply that leadership.

The foregoing purposes lead to the following questions:

What role does quality play in the success of my company?

How can I evaluate my company's status with respect to quality?

In what directions should I be leading my company?

How can I bring managing for quality into the company's business planning?

What should I be doing different from what I have been doing?

The draft proposal should provide for meeting such purposes and answering such questions.

INPUTS FOR TRAINING PROGRAMS

The extent of training will be keyed to the breadth of the action plan. In addition, the training will be done in phases that are keyed to the timetable of the action plan.

Numerous options for the design of the training plan are set out in chapter 10. This book is designed to serve as an aid in in-house training. Adapting its recommendations to specific company needs should in any case include a selection of the pertinent "high points" (these are summarized at the end of each chapter).

If the company opts for a degree of self-sufficiency, there will be need to

1. Develop qualified trainers or facilitators

2. Prepare local case materials as supplements

3. Assign problems that relate to company operations

4. Adapt the key principles and tasks to local needs

5. Adapt the interactive exercises to local situations (these exercises are in the supplemental materials that accompany this book)

In this connection it is useful to examine the pertinent offerings of the Juran Institute. These include

1. The videocassette series Juran on Quality Improvement.

2. The videocassette series Juran on Quality Planning.

3. The facilitator training courses (a) Facilitating Juran on Quality Planning and (b) Facilitating Juran on Quality Improvement. These are used to develop and certify facilitators for training in quality planning, and in quality improvement, respectively.

4. The videocassette *Juran on Quality Leadership*.

Glossary

Note that many of these terms have multiple meanings. The definitions given below reflect the meanings as applied in the text of this book.

Anatomy of processes   The structural linkage of the multiple operations (tasks, steps, unit processes, and others) which collectively produce the product.

Assembly tree   A process form in which inputs from numerous suppliers converge into subassemblies and assemblies.

Autonomous department   A process form which receives various inputs and converts them into finished goods and services, all within a single self-contained department.

Autopsy   Analysis of products to determine the causes of deficiencies—literally, to see with one's own eyes.

Big Q   A term used to designate a broad concept of quality in which "customers" includes all who are impacted; "product" includes goods and services; "processes" includes business and support processes. For contrast, see *Little Q.*

Brainstorming   A process for securing ideas during a meeting of multiple participants.

Breakthrough   See *Quality improvement.*

Business process   In general, an office process, as distinguished from a factory process. (There is substantial overlap.)

Carryover   The utilization of existing product (or process) design features as elements of new products (or processes).

Cause-and-effect diagram   Prof. Ishikawa's "fish-bone diagram" for listing theories of causes.

Champion   See *Sponsor.*

Charter   See *Project team charter.*

Check list An aid to human memory—a reminder of what to do and not to do. A form of "lessons learned."

Chronic waste The loss due to continuing quality deficiencies which are inherent in the system.

Cloning The application of remedies, derived from a completed quality-improvement project, to similar problems elsewhere in the company.

Company Any organized entity which produces products (goods or services) whether for sale or not, whether for profit or not.

Competitive analysis Analysis of product and process features and performance against those of competing products and processes.

Concept to customer A term used by the Ford Motor Company to designate the progression of events for creating a new model and putting it on the market.

Conformance A state of agreement between actual quality and the quality goal.

Conscious errors Nonconformance to quality goals resulting from actions knowingly taken.

Consumer An individual who buys for self-use.

Control chart W. A. Shewhart's chart for continuing test of statistical significance.

Control station A quality-oriented activity center for carrying out one or more steps of the feedback loop.

Control subject Any product or process feature for which there is a quality goal. The center around which the feedback loop is built.

Controllability The extent to which a process meets the criteria for self-control, enabling workers to detect and correct nonconformances.

COPQ Cost of poor quality.

Corrective action A change which restores a state of conformance with quality goals.

Cost of poor quality Those costs which would disappear if all products and processes were perfect—no deficiencies.

Cost of quality A term difficult to define because it fails to distinguish the cost of providing product features from the cost of poor quality.

Countdown A list of deeds to be done, in a predetermined sequence.

Craftsman A category of worker qualified by training and experience to carry out a recognized work specialty.

Critical processes Processes which present serious dangers to human life, health, and the environment, or which risk the loss of very large sums of money.

Criticality analysis The process of identifying product features which may be critical for various reasons, for example: essential to human safety, legislated mandates, essential to salability.

Cultural needs Needs for job security, self-respect, respect of others, continuity of habit patterns, and still other elements of what are broadly called cultural values.

Cultural pattern A body of beliefs, habits, practices, and so on which the human population has evolved to deal with perceived problems.

Cultural resistance A form of resistance to change based on opposition to the possible social consequences.

Customer Anyone who is impacted by the product or process. Customers may be external or internal.

Customer needs Those desires of customers which can be met by the product features of goods and services.

Customer satisfaction See *Product satisfaction.*

Data bank A compilation of numerous inputs specially organized to facilitate retrieval. A form of "lessons learned."

Deficiency See *Product deficiency.*

Department Any organization unit which is intermediate between a division (that is, a profit center) and the nonsupervisory work force.

Deployment The process of submitting broad quality goals to subordinate levels to secure identification of the deeds and resources needed to meet those broad goals.

Design review A participative process for securing early warning of the impact of a proposed design on subsequent functions.

Detection A concept of managing for quality based on inspection and test to detect and remove defects prior to shipment to customers.

Diagnosis The activity of discovering the cause(s) of quality deficiencies.

Diagnostic journey Those activities of the quality-improvement process which start with the outward symptoms of a quality problem and end with determination of the cause(s).

Dry run A test of a process, under operating conditions.

Early warning Advance notification of upcoming problems, derived (usually) from customers' participation in suppliers' planning. "If you plan it this way, here is the problem I will face."

External customers Those who are impacted by the product but are not members of the company which produces the product.

Facilitator A person specially trained to assist project teams in carrying out their projects.

Feedback Communication of data on quality performance to sources which can take appropriate action.

Feedback loop A systematic series of steps for maintaining conformance to quality goals by feeding performance data back to corrective actuators.

Fire fighting The activity of getting rid of sporadic quality troubles and restoring the status quo.

Fitness for use A short definition of quality, intended to include product features as well as freedom from deficiencies.

Flow diagram A graphic means for depicting the steps in a process.

Foolproofing (also errorproofing) Building safeguards into the technology of a process to reduce inadvertent human error.

Glossary A list of terms and their definitions.

Goal An aimed-at target—an achievement toward which effort is expended.

Goods Physical things: pencils, color television sets.

Guild An organization of craftsmen whose purposes include protecting the quality produced by the members.

Immune system A characteristic of organizations which, like biological immune systems, tends to reject the introduction of new concepts.

Improvement The organized creation of beneficial change; the attainment of unprecedented levels of performance. A synonym is "breakthrough."

Inadvertent errors Human errors which have their origin in unintentional inattention.

Internal customers Those who are impacted by the product, and are also members of the company which produces the product.

Joint planning A concept under which quality planning is done by a team made up of customers and suppliers.

Juran Trilogy® The three managerial processes used in managing for quality: quality planning, quality control, and quality improvement.

Key interface The principal channel of interaction between customer and supplier.

Lessons learned A catchall phrase describing what has been learned from experience.

Life behind the quality dikes A phrase used to describe how life in industrial societies requires high quality to maintain continuity of services and to protect against disasters.

Little Q A term used to designate a narrow scope of quality, limited to clients, factory goods, and factory processes. For contrast, see *Big Q*.

Macroprocess   An operational system involving numerous tasks, usually conducted in multiple functional departments.

Matrix organization   A form of team structure superimposed on a functional hierarchy.

Merchants   Those who buy for resale.

Microprocess   An operational system involving few tasks, usually carried out within a single functional department.

Monopoly   The exclusive right to make certain decisions or to take certain actions.

Operation   A task of limited scope.

Operations   (1) The general activity of carrying out planned processes; (2) organizations which carry out planned processes.

Optimum   A planned result which meets the needs of customer and supplier alike, and minimizes their combined costs.

Pareto principle   The phenomenon that, in any population which contributes to a common effect, a relative few of the contributors account for the bulk of the effect.

Participation   The process of securing inputs from those who will be impacted by an intended action.

Perceived needs   Customers' needs based on their perceptions.

Pilot test   A test of process capability based on a scaling up, intermediate between the planning phase and full-scale operations.

Policy   A guide to managerial action.

President's quality audit   A form of audit conducted by a team of upper managers under the chairmanship of the president.

Process   A systematic series of actions directed to the achievement of a goal.

Process anatomy   See *Anatomy of processes.*

Process capability   The inherent ability of a process to perform under operating conditions.

Process control   The systematic evaluation of performance of a process, and taking corrective action in the event of nonconformance.

Process design   The activity of defining the specific means to be used by the operating forces for meeting the product goals.

Process development   A generic term which includes the activities of product design review, choice of process, process design, provision of facilities, provision of software (methods, procedures, cautions), among others.

Process performance   The actual result attained from conducting processing operations.

Processing   The activity of conducting operations—running the process and producing the product.

Procession   A process form in which the product progresses sequentially through multiple departments, each performing some operation which contributes to the final result.

Processor   See *Processor team.*

Processor team   Any organization unit (of one or more persons) which carries out a prescribed process.

Product   The output of any process.

Product deficiency   A product failure which results in product dissatisfaction.

Product design   The activity of defining the product features required to meet customer needs.

Product development   The activity of determining the product features which respond to customer needs.

Product dissatisfaction   The effect on customers of product failures or deficiencies.

Product feature   A property which is possessed by a product and which is intended to meet certain customers' needs.

Product goal   A quantified expression of the aimed-at values (product tolerances, reliability, and so on) required to respond to customer needs.

Product satisfaction   The result achieved when product features respond to customer needs.

Project   A problem scheduled for solution—a specific mission to be carried out.

Project mission   The intended end result of a project.

Project team   A group of persons assigned to carry out a quality-improvement project.

Project team charter   The list of activities to be carried out by each project team.

Professional   A person specially qualified by education, training, and experience to carry out essential quality-related functions. The most numerous categories are quality engineers and reliability engineers.

Proliferation   The growth, in numbers, of customer needs, product features, process features, and so forth, resulting from the growth of technological activity in volume and complexity.

Public   The members of society in general—an external customer.

QC circle   A volunteer group of work-force members who have undergone training for the purpose of solving work-related problems.

Quality   The word has two major meanings: (1) those product features which respond to customer needs and (2) freedom from deficiencies. A broad term to cover both meanings is "fitness for use."

Quality assurance An independent evaluation of quality-related performance, conducted primarily for the information of those not directly involved in conduct of operations but who have a need to know.

Quality audit An independent review of quality performance.

Quality control A managerial process which consists of the following steps: (1) evaluate actual quality performance, (2) compare actual performance to quality goals, and (3) take action on the difference.

Quality costs See *Cost of quality.*

Quality council A committee of upper managers having the responsibility to establish, coordinate, and oversee managing for quality.

Quality engineering An engineering speciality focused largely on quality planning and analysis for goods and services.

Quality goal An aimed-at quality target.

Quality improvement The organized creation of beneficial change; improvement of performance to an unprecedented level.

Quality instrument panel A report package which summarizes for upper managers the performance with respect to quality.

Quality management The totality of ways for achieving quality. Quality management includes all three processes of the quality trilogy: quality planning, quality control, quality improvement.

Quality planning The activity of (1) determining customer needs and (2) developing the products and processes required to meet those needs.

Quality-planning road map A universal series of input-output steps which collectively constitute quality planning.

Real needs Those fundamental needs which motivate customer action, for example, a real need of a car purchaser is transportation.

Recognition Public acknowledgment of successes which are related to quality improvement.

Reliability The probability that a product will carry out its intended function under specified conditions and for a specified length of time.

Reliability engineering An engineering specialty focused largely on minimizing field failures through reliability modeling, quantification, data banks, and so on.

Remedial journey Those activities of the quality-improvement process which start with the known cause(s) and end with an effective remedy in place.

Responsibility matrix A table which lists the needed decisions and actions, and identifies who does what.

Retrospective analysis Analysis based on feedback of information from prior operations.

Rewards Those salary increases, bonuses, promotions, and so forth which are more or less keyed to job performance.

Salability analysis Evaluation of product salability usually based on a study of customer behavior, perceptions, and opinions, and on competitive product differences.

Santayana review The process of deriving lessons learned from retrospective analysis—conclusions drawn from data on repetitive cycles of prior activity.

Self-control (for an individual worker) A state in which the worker possesses: (1) the means of knowing what is the quality goal, (2) the means of knowing what is the actual quality performance, and (3) the means of changing performance in the event of nonconformance.

Self-inspection (for an individual worker) A state in which the worker makes the decision of whether the work produced conforms to the quality goal.

Sensor A specialized detecting device designed to recognize the presence and intensity of certain phenomena, and to convert this sensed knowledge into "information."

Service Work performed for someone else. Service also includes work performed for someone else *within* companies, for example: payroll preparation, recruitment of new employees, plant maintenance. Such services are often called support services.

Set up The action of assembling the information, materials, equipment, and so on needed to commence operations and of organizing them into a state of readiness to produce.

Simulation A form of planning which makes use of mathematical models or small-scale models; also, a means of providing operating personnel with experience prior to conduct of operations.

Software The term has multiple meanings: (1) instruction programs for computers and (2) information generally: reports, plans, instructions, advice, commands, and so on.

SPC See *Statistical process control*.

Spiral of Progress in Quality A graph which shows the typical progression of activities for putting a product on the market.

Sponsor A manager who is assigned to maintain broad surveillance over specific quality-improvement projects, and to help the project teams in the event of an impasse.

Sporadic quality problems Problems which have their origin in sudden, unplanned causes.

Spreadsheet   An orderly arrangement of planning information consisting (usually) of (1) horizontal rows to set out the elements undergoing planning and (2) vertical columns to set out the resulting product/process/control responses.

SQC   See *Statistical quality control.*

SQM   See *Strategic quality management.*

Stated needs   Needs as seen from customers' viewpoint, and in their language.

Statistical process control   A term used during the 1980s to describe the concept of using the tools of statistics to assist in controlling the quality of operating processes.

Statistical quality control   A term used during the 1950s and 1960s to describe the concept of using the tools of statistics to assist in controlling quality of operating processes.

Statistical significance   A term used to distinguish real changes from false alarms. A change is statistically significant if the odds are heavily against it having been caused by random variations.

Strategic quality management (SQM)   A systematic approach for setting and meeting quality goals throughout the company.

Suboptimization   Pursuit of local goals to the detriment of the overall good.

Supplier   Anyone who provides inputs to a process.

Symptom   The outward evidence of a quality deficiency.

Taylor system   A system of management based on separating planning from execution.

Technique error   A species of human error which is traceable to lack of knowledge of some essential "knack."

Translation   The process of converting the statement of customers' needs from customers' language into suppliers' language.

Trilogy   See *Juran Trilogy.*

Triple role   The roles of customer, processor, and supplier as carried out by every processor team.

TRIPROL™   See *Triple role.*

TRIPROL™diagram   An input-output diagram which depicts the triple role of customer, processor, and supplier.

Troubleshooting   See *Fire fighting.*

Ultimate user   The final destination of the product.

Unit of measure   A defined amount of some quality feature which permits evaluation of that feature in numbers.

Upper managers (also upper management)   The term always includes the corporate officers. In large companies "upper managers" includes the division general managers and their staffs. In very large organizations some individual facilities may also be very large, for example, an office; a factory. In any such case the local manager and his staff are upper managers to those employed at the facility.

Useful many Under the Pareto principle, a large majority of the population which nevertheless accounts for only a small part of the total effect.

User A customer who carries out positive actions with respect to the product, for example, further processing or ultimate use.

Vital few Under the Pareto principle, a small minority of the population which nevertheless accounts for most of the total effect.

Work force All employees except the managerial hierarchy and the "professional" specialists. (The dividing line is not precise, and there are borderline cases.)

Work station An activity center for carrying out the prescribed operations of running the processes and producing the product features.

References

CHAPTER 1

Garvin, David A. 1983. "Quality on the Line." *Harvard Business Review,* September-October, pp. 64–75.

Juran, J. M. 1967. "The QC Circle Phenomenon." *Industrial Quality Control,* January, pp. 329–336.

——. 1973. "The Taylor System and Quality Control." A series of articles in *Quality Progress,* May through December (listed under "Management Interface").

——. 1977. "Quality and Its Assurance: An Overview." Second NATO Symposium on Quality and Its Assurance, London.

——. 1979. "Japanese and Western Quality: A Contrast." *Quality,* January and February.

——. 1981. "Product Quality: A Prescription for the West." *The Management Review,* June and July. First presented at the 25th Conference of the European Organization for Quality Control, Paris.

CHAPTER 3

Bethlehem Review. 1982, no. 3. Reproduced in *The Juran Report,* no. 1, pp. 4–5. Juran Institute, Inc., 1983.

Engle, David, and Ball, David. 1986. "Improving Customer Service for Special Orders." *Proceedings of Annual Conference on Quality Improvement,* IMPRO 85. Juran Institute, Inc.

IMPRO. *Proceedings of the Annual Conference on Quality Improvement.* Published annually by Juran Institute, Inc.

Juran, J. M. 1979. "Japanese and Western Quality: A Contrast." *Quality* (a Hitchcock publication), January and February. Originally presented at the International Conference on Quality Control, Tokyo, 1978.

——. 1985. *A Prescription for the West: Four Years Later.* European

Organization for Quality Control, 29th Annual Conference, 1985. Reprinted in *The Juran Report,* no. 5, Summer. Juran Institute, Inc.

McGrath, James H. 1986. "Successful Institutionalized Improvement in Manufacturing Areas." *Proceedings of the Third Annual Conference on Quality Improvement,* IMPRO 85. Juran Institute, Inc., Wilton, Conn.

CHAPTER 4

Branco, George J., and Willoughby, Robert S. 1987. "Extending Quality Improvement to Suppliers." *Proceedings of the Fourth Annual Conference on Quality Improvement,* IMPRO 86. Juran Institute, Inc., Wilton, Conn.

Business Week, "How Ford Hit the Bull's-Eye with Taurus." June 30, 1986, pp. 69–70.

Fosse, Chris J. 1987. "Quality Assurance Through Strategic Product Development." *Proceedings of the Fifth Annual Conference on Quality Improvement,* IMPRO 87, p. 4B-5-12. Juran Institute, Inc., Wilton, Conn.

Gulliver, Frank R. (British Petroleum). 1987. "Post-Project Appraisals Pay." *Harvard Business Review,* March/April, pp. 128–131.

Iwahashi, Masaru. 1986. "Research Program on the New Product X Through Seven Management Tools for QC." Reports of Statistical Application Research, vol. 33, no. 2 (June), pp. 43–52. Japanese Union of Scientists and Engineers, Tokyo, Japan.

Juran, J. M. 1975. "The Non-Pareto Principle; Mea Culpa," *Quality Progress,* May, pp. 8–9. The story of how Juran came to misname the Pareto principle.

———. 1988. *Juran on Planning for Quality.* New York: The Free Press.

Kegarise, Ronald J., and Miller, George D. 1985. "An Alcoa-Kodak Joint Team." *Proceedings of the Third Annual Conference on Quality Improvement,* IMPRO 85, pp. 29–34. Juran Institute, Inc., Wilton, Conn.

Muroi, Akira. 1987. "Customer's Needs: How to Identify and How to Use Resultant Information." *Proceedings of International Conference on Quality Control,* ICQC 87, pp. 13–18. Japanese Union of Scientists and Engineers, Tokyo, Japan.

Olsson, John Ryding. 1986. "The Market-Leader Method: User-Oriented Development." *EOQC Proceedings,* Stockholm.

Veraldi, L. C. (Ford Motor Company). 1985. M.I.T. conference paper, Chicago, Ill., August 22. EOQC Conference 1986, pp. 62–63.

CHAPTER 5

Juran, J. M. 1988a. *Juran on Planning for Quality*. New York: The Free Press.

——, editor in chief. 1988b. *Juran's Quality Control Handbook*, 4th ed. New York: McGraw-Hill.

CHAPTER 6

Branco, George J., and Willoughby, Robert S. 1987. "Extending Quality Improvement to Suppliers." *Proceedings of the Fourth Annual Conference on Quality Improvement*, IMPRO 86. Juran Institute, Inc., Wilton, Conn.

Brunetti, Wayne. 1987. "Policy Deployment—A Corporate Roadmap." *Proceedings of the Fourth Annual Conference on Quality Improvement*, IMPRO 86, pp. 20–29. Juran Institute, Inc., Wilton, Conn.

Ikezawa and others. 1987. *Features of Companywide Quality Control in Japan*. Report of 44th QC Symposium. International Conference on Quality Control, ICQC. Japanese Union of Scientists and Engineers, Tokyo, Japan.

Ishikawa, Kaoru. 1987. "The Quality Control Audit." *Quality Progress*, January, pp. 39–41.

Juran, J. M. 1964. *Managerial Breakthrough*. New York: McGraw-Hill.

——, editor in chief. 1988a. *Juran's Quality Control Handbook*, 4th ed. New York: McGraw-Hill.

——. 1988b. *Juran on Planning for Quality*. New York: The Free Press.

Kegarise, Ronald J., and Miller, George D. 1986. "An Alcoa-Kodak Joint Team." *Proceedings of the Third Annual Conference on Quality Improvement*, IMPRO 85, pp. 29–34. Juran Institute, Inc., Wilton, Conn.

Kondo, Yoshio. 1988. In *Juran's Quality Control Handbook*, 4th ed. J. M. Juran, editor-in-chief. New York: McGraw-Hill. Kondo provides a detailed discussion of quality audits by Japanese top managements, including the president's audit. See chapter 35F, "Quality in Japan," under Internal QC Audit by Top Management.

McGrath, James H. 1986. "Successful Institutionalized Improvement in Manufacturing Areas." *Proceedings of the Third Annual Conference on Quality Improvement*, IMPRO 85. Juran Institute, Inc., Wilton, Conn.

Onnias, Arturo, 1986. "The Quality Blue Book." *Proceedings of the Third Annual Conference on Quality Improvement*, IMPRO 85, pp. 127–131. Juran Institute, Inc., Wilton, Conn.

Pisano, Daniel J., Jr. 1987. "Replanning the Product Development Process." *Proceedings of the Fourth Annual Conference on Quality Improvement,* IMPRO 86, pp. 260–264. Juran Institute, Inc., Wilton, Conn.

Shimoyamada, Kaoru. 1987. "The President's Audit: QC Audits at Komatsu," *Quality Progress,* January, pp. 44–49.

Wolf, John D. 1985. "Quality Improvement: The Continuing Operational Phase." *Proceedings of the Second Annual Conference on Quality Improvement,* IMPRO 84. Juran Institute, Inc., Wilton, Conn.

CHAPTER 7

Nickell, Warren L., and McNeil, J. Sylvia. 1987. "Process Management in a Marketing Environment." *Proceedings of the Fourth Annual Conference on Quality Improvement,* IMPRO 86, pp. 71–78. Juran Institute, Inc., Wilton, Conn.

Parker, Kenneth T. 1984. "Departmental Activity Analysis: Management and Employees Working Together." *Proceedings,* Annual Conference, International Association of Quality Circles, pp. 202–207.

CHAPTER 8

Ishikawa, Kaoru. 1972. *Guide to Quality Control.* Asian Productivity Organization. Details of the tools taught to Japanese foremen and QC circles, by the leading Japanese authority. Also available from UNIPUB.

Juran, J. M. 1987. "QC Circles in the West." *Quality Progress,* September, pp. 60–61.

——. 1988. *Juran on Planning for Quality.* New York: The Free Press.

CHAPTER 9

IMPRO. *Proceedings of the Annual Conference on Quality Improvement.* Published annually by Juran Institute, Inc.

Juran, J. M. 1964. *Managerial Breakthrough.* Chapter 9, "Resistance to Change: Cultural Patterns." New York: McGraw-Hill.

Mead, Margaret, ed. 1951. *Cultural Patterns and Technical Change.* UNESCO, Paris; also published by Mentor Books, New American Library of World Literature, Inc., New York, 1955.

Scanlon, Robert J. 1986. "Corporate Recognition for Quality Improvement." *Proceedings of the Fourth Annual Conference on Quality Improvement,* IMPRO, pp. 201–204. Juran Institute, Inc., Wilton, Conn.

CHAPTER 10

Ishikawa, Kaoru. 1972. *Guide to Quality Control.* Asian Productivity Organization. Details of the tools taught to Japanese foremen and QC circles, by the leading Japanese authority. Also available from UNIPUB.

Juran, J. M., and Gryna, F. M. 1980. *Quality Planning and Analysis,* 2d ed. New York: McGraw-Hill.

Juran on Quality Improvement (videocassette series). 1981. Juran Institute, Inc., Wilton, Conn.

Nayatani, Yoshinobu. 1986. "Seven Management Tools for QC." *Reports of Statistical Application Research, Japanese Union of Scientists and Engineers,* vol. 33, no. 2 (June). Tokyo, Japan.

Nickell, Warren L. 1985. "Quality Improvement in Marketing." *Proceedings of the Second Annual Conference on Quality Improvement,* IMPRO 84. Juran Institute, Inc., Wilton, Conn.

Sullivan, L. P. 1986. "Quality Function Deployment." *Quality Progress,* June, pp. 39–50.

Index

Prototype construction and testing, 134
Public, 93

QC circles, 10, 58, 59, 256, 283–288, 292,
  293, 308, 340–341
Quality
  definitions of, 15–18
  early strategies for managing, 2–3
  measures of, 18–19
  obstacles to unified approach to, 14–15
Quality audits, 203–205, 208, 314
Quality control, 21–26, 145–175
  control pyramid, 148–150, 263–264
  control stations, 159–160, 267
  corrective action, 168–169, 273–274
  course content for training, 335–336
  decision making, 163–168
  defined, 145–146, 194, 262
  feedback loop, 146–148
  goals, 151–153
  for macroprocesses, 228–230
  measurement of quality, 153–158
  for microprocesses, 249–252
  performance evaluation, 160–163
  planning for, 151
  responsibilities for, 251–252
  statistical methods, role of, 169–171
  upper management and, 150–151, 171–
    175, 194–196
  work force and, 195, 262–280
Quality control manuals, 172–173
Quality costs, 50–51
Quality council, 43–47, 185, 209, 210
Quality department, growth of, 5–6
Quality engineering, 5
Quality goals, 72–73, 151–153, 207, 272–
  273
  bases for setting, 188–189
  deployment of, 189–192
  nominations of, 188
  subject matter of, 187–188, 196
Quality improvement, 21–26, 28–80, 187–
  188
  basic concepts of, 34–41
  course content for training, 336–337
  defined, 28
  delegation, illusion of, 75–77
  for macroprocesses, 230–231
  mandated, 306–308
  for microprocesses, 252–257
  mobilizing for, 42–43
  motivation for, 77–78
  origins of, 33–34
  performance on, 198–199
  progress review, 70–71
  project mission statements, 55–56
  project nomination, 47–52
  project selection, 52–55

project team: see Project team
quality council, 43–47
quality leadership and, 30–31
rates of, 31–33
rewards for, 68–70
timetable of, 71
upper management roles in, 72–75, 79–
  80
work force and, 281–288
Quality-improvement council, 185
Quality-improvement managers, 66
Quality-improvement teams, 215
Quality instrument panels, 229–230
Quality leadership, 30–31
Quality management; see also Quality control; Quality improvement; Quality
  planning
  definition of, 82
  for macroprocesses, 225, 226
  for microprocesses, 239–240
Quality manager, 205, 210
  inputs for proposals and, 352–353
Quality planning, 20–26, 81–144, 351
  anatomy of processes, 129–130
  course content for training, 335
  critical processes, 131
  customers, classification of, 90–93
  customers, identification of, 89–90
  customers' needs, discovery of: see Cus-
    tomers' needs
  definitions and relationships, 82–83
  division of subject, 81
  experienced amateurs and, 83–84
  information organization, 94
  lessons learned, 134–136
  for macroprocesses, 225–228
  for microprocesses, 240–249
  multiple levels of, 85–86
  process capability, 124–127
  process design, 127–128, 131–133
  process development, 123–124
  product design, 112–121
  product development, 108–112
  product goals, 121–122
  quality professionals and, 84–85
  road map, 87–88, 134–135, 227, 258
  Santayana review, 136–140
  structured, 308–311
  transfer to operations, 133–134
  upper management role, 93–94, 103–
    104, 107, 127, 141–144
  work force and, 288–294
Quality professionals, 84–85
Quantification of process capability, 124–
  125

Real needs, 96
Real-time measurement, lack of, 275

Lightning Source UK Ltd.
Milton Keynes UK
UKOW041351170613

9 780743 255776